Instructor's Manual
and Test Bank

to accompany

Theories of
Personality

Fifth Edition

Jess Feist
McNeese State University

Gregory J. Feist
College of William and Mary

Prepared by
Jess Feist
McNeese State University

Boston   Burr Ridge, IL   Dubuque, IA   Madison, WI   New York   San Francisco   St. Louis
Bangkok   Bogotá   Caracas   Kuala Lumpur   Lisbon   London   Madrid   Mexico City
Milan   Montreal   New Delhi   Santiago   Seoul   Singapore   Sydney   Taipei   Toronto

McGraw-Hill Higher Education
A Division of The McGraw-Hill Companies

Instructor's Manual and Test Bank to accompany
THEORIES OF PERSONALITY, FIFTH EDITION
JESS FEIST AND GREGORY J. FEIST

Published by McGraw-Hill Higher Education, an imprint of The McGraw-Hill Companies, Inc.,
1221 Avenue of the Americas, New York, NY 10020. Copyright © The McGraw-Hill Companies,
Inc., 2002, 1998. All rights reserved.

This book is printed on acid-free paper.

2 3 4 5 6 7 8 9 0 QPD QPD 0 3 2 1

ISBN 0-07-231681-0

www.mhhe.com

CONTENTS

PREFACE

This manual is intended as an aid to instructors using Feist and Feist's *Theories of Personality* (5th ed.). It contains two major sections, each divided into 18 chapters that correspond to the chapters in the text.

The first section includes **learning objectives**, designed to provide you with an overview of the important points in each chapter. Next, a **lecture outline** is designed to help you organize your lecture notes and quickly grasp the major concepts of each chapter. If you have some general understanding of the chapter's subject matter, you may be able to lecture directly from the outline. Although the lecture outline is no substitute for your own individual interpretation of each personality theorist, we believe that it will make your task easier. Finally, we have provided **teaching suggestions,** many of which we have used in our own courses on theories of personality. The teaching suggestions include a variety of activities that can be used both in and out of class. Where we have suggested videocassettes or personality inventories, we have also provided addresses and/or telephone numbers of vendors from whom these materials can be obtained.

The second section consists of a **test bank**, which includes essay and multiple choice questions. Each chapter contains about three **essay questions** with a detailed outline of answers. The **multiple choice questions** have been constructed to provide an ample number and variety of questions for each chapter. In all, there are nearly 1,300 multiple choice items, many new or rewritten from earlier editions. Some questions are factual, while others are designed to measure knowledge of broad concepts and general principles. Items with an asterisk are similar but not identical to items in the student Study Guide. We have included enough items for you to choose those most suitable for your particular needs. And of course, you may alter questions as you see fit.

—Jess Feist

—Gregory J. Feist

CHAPTER 1
INTRODUCTION TO PERSONALITY THEORY

LEARNING OBJECTIVES

After studying Chapter 1, students should be able to:

1.   Express their own definition of personality.

2.   Differentiate theory from (a) philosophy, (b) speculation, (c) hypothesis, and
      (d) taxonomy.

3.   Explain the relationship between theory and observations.

4.   List and explain the criteria of a useful theory.

5.   Explain why falsifiability is a positive characteristic of a theory.

6.   Discuss various components for a concept of humanity.

7.   Define reliability and validity and explain why both concepts are important
      in personality research.

LECTURE OUTLINE

I.   Overview of Personality Theory

From the investigations of Freud during the last decade of the 19th century until
the present time, a number of personality theorists have (1) made controlled
observations of human behavior and (2) speculated on the meaning of those
observations. Differences in the theories of these men and women are due to more
than differences in terminology; they stem from differences among theorists on
basic issues concerning the nature of humanity.

II.   What Is Personality?

The term *personality* comes from the Latin word *persona*, meaning the mask
people wear or the role they play in life, but most psychologists use the term to
refer to much more than the face or facade people show to others. Personality

refers to a pattern of relatively permanent traits, dispositions, or characteristics that give some consistency to human behavior

III. What Is a Theory?

The term *theory* is often used quite loosely and incorrectly to imply something other than a useful scientific concept. Scientists use theories to generate research and organize observations.

A. Theory Defined

A theory is a set of related assumptions that allows scientists to use logical deductive reasoning to formulate testable hypotheses

B. Theory and Its Relatives

People often confuse theory with philosophy, speculation, hypothesis, or taxonomy. Although theory is related to each of these concepts, it is not synonymous with any of them.

1. Philosophy

Philosophy—the love of wisdom—is a broader term than theory, but one branch of philosophy—**epistemology**—relates to the nature of knowledge, and theories are used by scientists in the pursuit of knowledge.

2. Speculation

Theories rely on speculation, but that speculation must be based on the controlled observations of scientists. **Science** is the branch of study concerned with observation and classification of data and with the verification of general laws. Theories are practical tools used by scientists to guide research.

3. Hypothesis

A theory is more general than a hypothesis and may generate a multitude of hypotheses, or educated guesses.

4.   Taxonomy

A taxonomy is a classification system, and classification is necessary to science. Taxonomies, however, do not generate hypotheses—a necessary criterion of a useful theory.

C.   Why Different Theories?

Psychologists and other scientists have developed a variety of personality theories because they have differed in their personal background, their philosophical orientation, and the data they chose to observe. In addition, theories permit individual interpretation of the same observations, and each theorist has had his or her own way of looking at things.

D.   Theorists' Personalities and Their Theories of Personality

Because personality theories evolve from a theorist's personality, psychologists interested in the **psychology of science** have begun to study the personal traits of leading personality theorists and their possible impact on their scientific theories and research.

E.   What Makes a Theory Useful?

Scientists use several criteria to evaluate the usefulness of a theory. A useful theory (1) generates research, (2) is falsifiable, (3) organizes data, (4) guides action, (5) is internally consistent, and (6) is parsimonious.

1.   Generates Research

One of the most important functions of a theory is to generate research. A useful theory will stimulate both descriptive research and hypothesis testing. Descriptive research provides a framework for an evolving theory whereas hypothesis testing expands our knowledge of a scientific discipline.

2.   Is Falsifiable

A useful theory should generate research that can either confirm or disconfirm its major tenets; that is, a useful theory must be both **verifiable** and **falsifiable.** A verifiable theory can be supported by research whereas a falsifiable theory is one that can be disconfirmed by research results that are contrary to its basic tenets.

3. Organizes Data

A useful theory of personality must also be able to organize much of what is currently known about personality into some intelligible framework and to integrate new information into its structure; that is, the theory should be able to organize and explain observations gleaned from research.

4. Guides Action

Theories are practical tools in that they provide the practitioner with a road map for making day-to-day decisions.

5. Is Internally Consistent

A useful theory is internally consistent and includes **operational definitions**, which define concepts in terms of specific operations to be carried out by the observer.

6. Is Parsimonious

When two theories are equal on the first five criteria, then the simpler, more parsimonious one is preferred.

IV. Dimensions for a Concept of Humanity

Personality theorists have had different conceptions of human nature, and the authors list six dimensions for comparing these conceptions. These dimensions include **determinism versus free choice, pessimism versus optimism, causality versus teleology, conscious versus unconscious** determinants of behavior, **biological versus social influences** on personality, and **uniqueness versus similarities** among people.

V.   Research in Personality Theory

Personality theories, like other theories, are based on systematic research that allows for the prediction of events. In researching human behavior, personality theorists often use various measuring procedures, which must be both reliable and valid. **Reliability** refers to a measuring instrument's consistency and includes test-retest reliability and internal consistency. **Validity** refers to the accuracy or truthfulness of the test and includes predictive validity and construct validity.

TEACHING SUGGESTIONS

1.   To encourage students to discover their own implicit theory of personality, you can assign a course project calling for students to write a 6- to 10-page essay on their own personality theory. A second part of this assignment would be to have each student design a study that, if tested, would confirm or falsify major tenets of the theory.

2.   Personality theorists have developed a variety of theories because they have had different ways of looking at personality. You may assign students to read a biography of a personality theorist and write a report on possible ways that the early life of that theorist helped shape his or her later personality theory.

3.   Ask students to access *Beyond Biography* on the McGraw-Hill Web site and discuss the positive and negative traits of some of the leading personality theorists.

CHAPTER 2
FREUD: PSYCHOANALYSIS

LEARNING OBJECTIVES

After studying Chapter 2, students should be able to:

1. Describe how Freud's childhood experiences may have influenced his theory of personality.

2. Argue pro or con whether Freud was scientific in his writings.

3. Describe the three provinces of the mind and explain how they relate to the three levels of mental life.

4. Explain Freud's concept of the sexual and aggressive instincts.

5. List the Freudian defense mechanisms and give examples of each.

6. Summarize the psychosexual stages of development and their possible effects of personality development.

7. Explain why Freud's early therapeutic technique relates to contemporary reports of recovered memories.

8. Trace the development of the Oedipus complex for boys and girls.

9. Describe Freud's concept of dreams.

LECTURE OUTLINE

I. **Overview of Freud's Psychoanalytic Theory**

Freud's **psychoanalysis** is the best known of all personality theories because it (1) postulated the primacy of sex and aggression—two universally popular themes; (2) attracted a group of followers who were dedicated to spreading psychoanalytic doctrine; and (3) advanced the notion of unconscious motives, which permit varying explanations for the same observations.

II.   Biography of Sigmund Freud

Although he was born in the Czech Republic in 1856 and died in London in 1939, Sigmund Freud spent nearly 80 years of his life in Vienna. A physician who never intended to practice general medicine, Freud was intensely curious about human nature, and in his practice of psychiatry he was perhaps more interested in learning about the unconscious motives of his patients than in curing neuroses. Early in his professional career, Freud believed that hysteria was a result of being seduced during childhood by a sexually mature person, often a parent or other relative. However, in 1897, he abandoned his *seduction theory* and replaced it with his notion of the *Oedipus complex*. Some recent scholars have contended that Freud's decision to abandon the seduction theory in favor of the Oedipus complex was a major error and influenced a generation of psychotherapists to interpret patients' reports of early sexual abuse as merely childhood fantasies.

III.   Levels of Mental Life

Freud saw mental functioning as operating on three levels: the unconscious, the preconscious, and the conscious.

A.   Unconscious

The unconscious consists of drives and instincts that are beyond awareness but that motivate many of our behaviors. Unconscious drives can become conscious only in disguised or distorted form, such as dream images, slips of the tongue, or neurotic symptoms. Unconscious processes originate from two sources: (1) **repression**, or the blocking out of anxiety-filled experiences and (2) **phylogenetic endowment**, or inherited experiences that lie beyond an individual's personal experience.

B.   Preconscious

The preconscious contains images that are not in awareness but that can become conscious either quite easily or with some level of difficulty.

C.   Conscious

Consciousness is the only level of mental life directly available to us, but it plays a relatively minor role in Freudian theory. Conscious ideas stem from either the perception of external stimuli (**perceptual conscious** system) or from unconscious and preconscious images after they have evaded censorship.

IV. Provinces of the Mind

Freud conceptualized three regions of the mind: the id, the ego, and the superego.

A.   The Id

The id, which is completely unconscious, serves the **pleasure principle** and seeks constant and immediate satisfaction of instinctual needs. As the region of the mind that contains the basic instincts, the id operates through the **primary process**.

B.   The Ego

The ego, or **secondary process**, is governed by the **reality principle**; that is, it is responsible for reconciling the unrealistic demands of both the id and the superego with the demands of the real world.

C.   The Superego

The superego, which serves the **idealistic principle,** has two subsystems: the conscience and the ego-ideal. The **conscience** results from punishment for improper behavior whereas the **ego-ideal** stems from rewards for socially acceptable behavior.

V.   Dynamics of Personality

The term *dynamics of personality* refers to those forces that motivate people. The concept includes both instincts and anxiety.

A.   Instincts

Freud grouped all human drives or urges under two primary instincts: *sex* (Eros or the life instinct) and *aggression* (the destructive or death instinct).

1. The Sexual Instinct

The *aim* of the sexual instinct is pleasure, which can be gained through the **erogenous zones**, especially the mouth, anus, and genitals. The *object* of the sexual instinct is any person or thing that brings sexual pleasure. Both the aim and the object are flexible, so that many sexually motivated behaviors may seem to be unrelated to sex. For example, narcissism, love, sadism, and masochism all possess large components of the sexual drive even though they may appear to be nonsexual. All infants possess **primary narcissism,** or self-centeredness, but the **secondary narcissism** of adolescence and adulthood is not universal. **Sadism,** which is the reception of sexual pleasure from inflicting pain on another, and **masochism,** which is the reception of sexual pleasure from painful experiences, satisfy both sexual and aggressive drives.

2. The Destructive Instinct

The destructive instinct aims to return a person to an inorganic state, but it is ordinarily directed against other people and is called **aggression.**

B. Anxiety

Only the ego feels anxiety, but the id, superego, and outside world can each be a source of anxiety. **Neurotic anxiety** is apprehension about an unknown danger and stems from the ego's relation with the id; **moral anxiety** is similar to guilt and results from the ego's relation with the superego; and **realistic anxiety,** which is similar to fear, is produced by the ego's relation with the real world.

VI. Defense Mechanisms

Defense mechanisms operate unconsciously to protect the ego against the pain of anxiety.

A. Repression

Repression involves forcing unwanted, anxiety-loaded experiences into the unconscious. It is the most basic of all defense mechanisms because it is an active process in each of the others. Many repressed experiences remain unconscious for a lifetime, but others become conscious in a disguised form.

B.   Undoing and Isolation

Undoing is the ego's attempt to do away with unpleasant experiences and their consequences, usually by means of ceremonial repetitious actions. Isolation is marked by obsessive thoughts. It is the ego's attempt to isolate an experience by surrounding it with a blacked-out region of insensibility.

C.   Reaction Formation

A reaction formation is marked by the repression of one impulse and the ostentatious expression of its exact opposite.

D.   Displacement

Displacement is the redirecting of unacceptable urges and feelings onto people and objects in order to disguise or conceal their true nature.

E.   Fixation

Fixations develop when psychic energy is blocked at one stage of development, making psychological change difficult.

F.   Regression

Regressions take place when a person reverts to earlier, more infantile modes of behavior.

G.   Projection

Projection is seeing in others those unacceptable feelings or behaviors that actually reside in one's own unconscious. When carried to extremes, projection can become **paranoia**, which is characterized by delusions of persecution.

H.   Introjection

Introjection involves the incorporation of positive qualities of another person in order to reduce feelings of inadequacy.

I.   Sublimation

Whereas other defense mechanisms are of dubious social value, sublimations contribute to the welfare of society. They involve elevating the aim of the sexual instinct to a higher level and are manifested in social and cultural accomplishments.

VII. Stages of Development

Freud saw psychosexual development as proceeding from birth to maturity through four overlapping stages: the infantile stage, the latency stage, the genital stage, and the psychologically mature stage.

A.   Infantile Period

The infantile stage encompasses the first 4 to 5 years of life and is divided into three subphases.

1.   Oral Phase

During the oral phase, an infant is primarily motivated to receive pleasure through the mouth. *Weaning* is the principal source of frustration during this stage.

2.   Anal Phase

At about the second year of life, a child goes through an anal phase when *toilet training* is the chief frustration. If parents use punitive training methods, a child may develop the **anal triad** of orderliness, stinginess, and obstinacy, all of which mark the **anal character**.

3.   Phallic Phase

Boys and girls begin to have differing psychosexual development during the phallic phase, which occurs around 3 or 4 years of age. For both genders, *suppression of masturbation* is the principle source of frustration. At this time, young children experience the **Oedipus complex** in which they have sexual feelings for one parent and hostile feelings for the other. The male **castration complex**, which takes the form of **castration anxiety**, or fear of losing the penis, breaks up the male Oedipus complex and results in a well-formed male superego. For girls, however, the castration complex, in the form of **penis envy**, precedes the female Oedipus complex, a situation that leads to only a gradual and incomplete shattering of the female Oedipus complex and a weaker, more flexible female superego.

B.   Latency Period

Freud believed that psychosexual development goes through a latency stage—from about age 5 until puberty—in which the sexual instinct is partially suppressed.

C.   Genital Period

The genital period begins with puberty, when adolescents experience a reawakening of the genital aim of Eros, and it continues throughout adulthood.

D.   Maturity

Freud hinted at a stage of psychological maturity in which the ego would be in control of the id and superego and in which consciousness would play a more important role in behavior.

VIII. Applications of Psychoanalytic Theory

Freud built his theory on observations from history, art, and literature, but his primary source of data came from his clinical experiences with neurotic patients whose dreams and slips of the tongue he analyzed as part of his psychotherapy. His psychoanalytic theory has been applied to psychotherapy, dream interpretation, and Freudian slips.

A.   Freud's Early Therapeutic Technique

During his early years as a therapist, Freud used a very aggressive technique whereby he strongly suggested to patients that they had been sexually seduced as children. He later abandoned this technique, along with his belief that most patients had been seduced during childhood. The current frequency with which therapy patients accuse their parents or other adults of criminal sexual acts has prompted some investigators to look at the validity of these claims.

B.   Freud's Later Therapeutic Technique

Beginning in the late 1890s, Freud adopted a much more passive type of psychotherapy, one that relied heavily on free association, dream interpretation, and transference. The goal of Freud's later psychotherapy was to uncover repressed memories, and the therapist uses dream analysis and free association to do so. With **free association**, patients are required to say whatever comes to mind, no matter how irrelevant or distasteful. Successful therapy rests on the patient's **transference** of childhood sexual or aggressive feelings onto the therapist and away from symptom formation. Patients' **resistance** to change is seen as progress because it indicates that therapy has advanced beyond superficial conversation.

C.   Dream Analysis

In interpreting dreams, Freud differentiated the **manifest content** (conscious description) from the **latent content** (the unconscious meaning of the dream that lies hidden from the dreamer). Nearly all dreams are wish-fulfillments, although the wish is usually unconscious and can be known only through dream interpretation. Dreams that are not wish-fulfillments follow the principle of **repetition compulsion** and often occur after people have had a traumatic experience. To interpret dreams, Freud used both dream symbols and the dreamer's associations to the dream content.

D.   Freudian Slips

Freud believed that **parapraxes**—that is, slips of the tongue or pen, misreadings, incorrect hearings, misplacing of objects, and temporary forgetting of names or intentions—are not chance accidents but reveal a person's unconscious intentions.

IX.   Related Research

Although Freudian theory has generated much related research, it rates low on **falsifiability** because most research findings can be explained by other theories.

Throughout the years, however, many researchers have investigated hypotheses inspired by psychoanalytic theory.

A.   Defense Mechanisms

George Valliant has added to the list of Freudian defense mechanisms and has found evidence that some of them are *neurotic* (reaction formation idealization, and undoing), some are *immature and maladaptive* (projection, isolation, denial, displacement, and dissociation), and some are *mature and adaptive* (sublimation, suppression, humor, and altruism). Valliant found that neurotic defense mechanisms are successful over the short term; immature defenses are unsuccessful and have the highest degree of distortion; whereas mature and adaptive defenses are successful over the long term, maximize gratification, and have the least amount of distortion

B.   Oral Fixation

Some recent research has found that aggression is higher in people who bite their finger nails than it is in non-nail biters, especially in women. Other research found that people who are orally fixated tend to see their parents more negatively than do people who are less orally fixated.

X.   Critique of Freud

Freud regarded himself as a scientist, but many present-day critics consider his methods to be outdated, unscientific, and permeated with sexual bias. On the six criteria of a useful theory, we rated psychoanalysis high on its ability to generate research, very low on its falsifiability, and average on organizing knowledge, guiding action, and being parsimonious. Because it lacks operational definitions, we rated psychoanalysis low on internal consistency.

XI.   Concept of Humanity

Freud's view of humanity was deterministic and pessimistic. He also emphasized causality over teleology, unconscious determinants over conscious processes, and biology over culture, but he took a middle position on the dimension of uniqueness versus similarities among people.

TEACHING SUGGESTIONS

1. Freud's theories have influenced Western civilization for nearly a century, but during the past 40 years, they have been subject to severe criticism. Students may debate Freud's relevancy for the 21st century. Students wishing to take an anti-Freudian position may read Richard Webster's *Why Freud Was Wrong: Sin, Science, and Psychoanalysis* (1995) or Louis Breger's *Freud: Darkness in the Midst of Vision* (2000). Proponents of Freudian theory may wish to look at Peter Gay's *Freud: A Life for Our Time* (1988). Other sources include *Time* magazine's November 29, 1993, cover story on Freud and *Scientific American's* December 1996, report on Why Freud isn't dead.

2. Another interesting topic of debate is the accuracy of repressed memories. Materials for such a debate include Leon Jaroff's "Lies of the Mind" (1993), Janice Haaken's "Viewpoint: The Debate Over Recovered Memory of Sexual Abuse" (1995), and Elizabeth Loftus's "The Repressed Memory Controversy" (1994).

3. An interesting video of the life of Freud is *Sigmund Freud: Analysis of a Mind*, a 50-minute A & E biography available from

    New Video Group

    126 Fifth Avenue

    New York, NY 10011

REFERENCES

Breger, L. (2000). *Freud: Darkness in the midst of vision*. New York: Wiley.

Gay, P. (1988). *Freud: A life for our time*. New York: Norton.

Gray, P. (1993, November 29) The assault on Freud. *Time, 142*, 46–51.

Haaken, J. (1995). Viewpoint: The debate over recovered memory of sexual abuse: A feminist-psychoanalytic perspective. *Psychiatry, 58,* 189–198.

Horgan, J. (1996, December). Why Freud isn't dead. *Scientific American, 275*, 106–11.

Jaroff, L. (1993, November 29). Lies of the mind. *Time, 142*, 52–59.

Loftus, E. F. (1994). The repressed memory controversy. *American Psychologist, 49,* 443–445.

Webster, R. (1995). *Why Freud was wrong: Sin, science, and psychoanalysis*. New York: Basic Books.

CHAPTER 3
ADLER: INDIVIDUAL PSYCHOLOGY

LEARNING OBJECTIVES

After studying Chapter 3, students should be able to:

1. Distinguish between striving for superiority and striving for success.

2. Describe the role of subjective perceptions in Adler's theory of personality.

3. Discuss Adler's concept of fictionalism.

4. Explain how seemingly contradictory behaviors may reflect a single goal of striving for superiority.

5. Explain organ dialect and give examples of how it is expressed in a person's behavior.

6. Define social interest and give examples of what it is and what it is not.

7. Discuss Alder's concept of creative power and be prepared to debate the validity of this concept.

8. Define causality and teleology and discuss Adler's teleological approach.

9. List and describe three types of Adlerian safeguarding tendencies.

10. Discuss Adler's ideas on birth order.

11. Discuss research on Adler's hypotheses concerning early recollections.

LECTURE OUTLINE

I. **Overview of Adler's Individual Psychology**

An original member of Freud's psychoanalytic group, Alfred Adler broke from Freud and advocated a theory of personality and an approach to psychotherapy that were nearly diametrically opposed to those of Freud. Whereas Freud's view of humanity was deterministic, pessimistic, and rooted in biology, Adler's view was idealistic, optimistic, and rooted in social experiences.

II.   Biography of Alfred Adler

Alfred Adler was born in 1870 in a town near Vienna, a second son of middle-class Jewish parents. As a young child he was weak and sickly, a condition that contrasted sharply with his healthy older brother, Sigmund. Adler developed a strong rivalry with Sigmund—a rivalry that was similar to his later relationship with Freud. Like Freud, Adler was a physician, and in 1902, he became a charter member of Freud's organization. However, personal and professional differences between the two men led to Adler's departure from the Vienna Psychoanalytic Society in 1911. Adler soon founded his own group, the Society for Individual Psychology. Unlike Freud, who was a gifted writer, Adler was merely a mediocre writer. His strengths were his energetic oral presentations and his insightful ability to understand family dynamics. During the last few years of his life, Adler lived in the United States and earned a reputation as a gifted public speaker. He died in 1937 in Scotland while on a lecture tour.

III.   Introduction to Adlerian Theory

Although Adler's individual psychology is both complex and comprehensive, its main tenets can be organized into six main topics: (1) striving for success or superiority, (2) subjective perceptions, (3) unity and self-consistency of personality, (4) social interest, (5) style of life, and (6) creative power.

IV.   Striving for Success or Superiority

The sole dynamic force behind all our actions, according to Adler, is the striving for success or superiority.

A.   The Final Goal

The final goal of success or perfection toward which all people strive unifies personality and makes all behavior meaningful. People are not always conscious of their final goal, even though they may be aware of their immediate subgoals.

B.   The Striving Force as Compensation

Because people are born with small, inferior bodies, they *feel* inferior and attempt to overcome these feelings through their natural tendency to move toward completion. The striving force can take one of two courses: personal gain (superiority) or community benefit (success).

C.   Striving for Personal Superiority

Psychologically unhealthy individuals strive for personal superiority with little concern for other people. Although they may appear to be interested in others, their basic motivation is personal benefit.

D.   Striving for Success

In contrast, psychologically healthy people strive for the success of all humanity, but they do so without losing their personal identity.

V.   Subjective Perceptions

People's subjective view of the world—not reality—shapes their behavior.

A.   Fictionalism

Fictions are people's beliefs and expectations of the future. Adler held that fictions guide behavior, because people act *as if* these fictions are true. Adler emphasized **teleology** over **causality**; that is, he favored explanations of behavior in terms of future goals rather than past causes.

B.   Organ Inferiorities

Adler believed that all humans are "blessed" with organ inferiorities and that these small, inferior organs stimulate subjective feelings of inferiority and move people toward perfection or completion.

VI.   Unity and Self-Consistency of Personality

Adler believed that all of our behaviors are directed toward a single purpose and that the entire personality functions in a self-consistent manner.

A.   Organ Dialect

People sometimes use a physical disorder to express style of life, a condition Adler called organ dialect.

B.   Conscious and Unconscious

Conscious and unconscious processes are unified and operate to achieve a single goal. The part of our goal that is not clearly understood is unconscious; to the extent that we comprehend our goal, it is conscious.

VII. Social Interest

Human behavior has value to the extent that it is motivated by social interest, or a feeling of oneness with all of humanity.

A.   Origins of Social Interest

Although social interest exists as potentiality in all people, it must be fostered in a social environment. Adler believed that both mothers and fathers have crucial roles in furthering the social interest of their children and that the parent–child relationship can be strong that it negates the effects of heredity.

B.   Importance of Social Interest

Without social interest, societies could not exist, because individuals could not protect themselves from danger. Thus, an infant's helplessness predisposes it toward a nurturing person. According to Adler, social interest is "the sole criterion of human values," and the "barometer of normality." The worthiness of all one's actions must be viewed by these standards.

VIII. Style of Life

The manner of a person's striving is called style of life. It is a product of the interaction of heredity, environment, goal of success, social interest, and creative power. Style of life is relatively well set by 4 or 5 years of age, but Adler believed

that healthy individuals are marked by flexible behavior and that they have some
limited ability to change their style of life.

IX. Creative Power

Adler believed that heredity and environment provide the building materials for our
style of life, but he insisted that ultimately style of life is shaped by our creative
power; that is, it is shaped by our ability to freely choose which building materials
to use and how to use them. In other words, Adler contended that people have
considerable ability to freely choose their actions and their personality.

X. Abnormal Development

Creative power is not limited to healthy people; unhealthy individuals also create
their own personalities. Thus, each of us is free to choose either a useful or a useless
style of life.

A.   General Description

The most important factor in abnormal development is *underdeveloped social
interest*. In addition, people with a useless style of life tend to (1) set their goals too
high, (2) live in their own private world, and (3) have a rigid and dogmatic style
of life.

B.   External Factors in Maladjustment

Adler listed three factors that relate to abnormal development.

1.   Exaggerated Physical Deficiencies

Severe physical defects do not by themselves cause abnormal development,
but they may contribute to it by generating subjective and exaggerated feelings
of inferiority.

2.   Pampered Style of Life

Children who see themselves as being pampered develop low levels of social interest and continue to have an overriding drive to establish a permanent parasitic relationship with their mother or a mother substitute.

3.   Neglected Style of Life

Children who feel neglected often use these feelings as building material for a useless style of life—one characterized by distrust of other people.

C.   Safeguarding Tendencies

Both normal and neurotic people create symptoms as a means of protecting their fragile self-esteem. These safeguarding tendencies maintain a neurotic style of life and protect a person from public disgrace.

1.   Excuses

The most common safeguarding tendency is excuses, which frequently take the form of "Yes, but" or "If only." By making excuses for their shortcomings, people can preserve their inflated sense of personal worth.

2.   Aggression

People often safeguard a weak self-esteem by behaving aggressively toward themselves or others. Safeguarding through aggression may take the form of **depreciating** others' accomplishments, **accusing** others of being responsible for one's own failures, and **accusing one's self** as a means of inflicting suffering on others.

3.   Withdrawal

People with a neurotic style of life often try to escape from life's problems by running away from them; that is, they withdraw or safeguard themselves by maintaining distance. People can withdraw psychologically by **moving backward, standing still, hesitating,** or **constructing obstacles**.

D.   Masculine Protest

Both men and women sometimes overemphasize the desirability of being manly, a condition Adler called the masculine protest. The frequently found inferior status of women is not based on physiology but on historical developments and social learning.

XI.   Applications of Individual Psychology

Adler applied the principles of individual psychology to family constellation (birth order), early recollections, dreams, and psychotherapy.

A.   Family Constellation

Adler believed that people's perception of how they fit into their family is related to their style of life. He claimed that firstborns are likely to have strong feelings of power and superiority, to be overprotective, and to have more than their share of anxiety. Secondborns (like Adler himself) are likely to have strong social interest, provided they do not get trapped trying to overcome their older sibling. Youngest children are likely to be pampered and to lack independence, whereas only children may have even less social interest and tend to expect others to take care of them.

B.   Early Recollections

A more reliable method of determining style of life is to ask people for their earliest recollections (ERs). Adler believed that ERs are not chance memories but templates on which people project their current style of life. These recollections need not be accurate accounts of early events; they have psychological importance because they reflect our current view of the world.

C.   Dreams

Adler believed that dreams can provide clues to solving future problems. However, dreams are disguised to deceive the dreamer and therefore are most accurately interpreted by another person.

D. Psychotherapy

The goal of Adlerian therapy is to create a relationship between therapist and patient that fosters the patient's social interest, courage, and self-esteem. To ensure that the patient's social interest will eventually generalize to other relationships, the therapist adopts both a maternal and a paternal role.

XII. Related Research

Although birth order, or family constellation, has been widely studied by psychologists and other social scientists, a research area more pertinent to Adlerian theory is early recollections, a topic that is beginning to receive increased attention by researchers.

A. Early Recollections and Personal Traits

Research shows that early recollections are related to a number of personal traits, such as birth order, depression, college major, alcoholism, criminal behavior, and eating disorder. Nichols and Feist (1994) showed that optimists and pessimists had quite different early recollections. In general, they found that optimists were more likely to include other people in their ERs, see themselves as active, have clear and vivid ERs, have more sustained interpersonal interactions in their ERs, recall events in which they gained success, and have more pleasant ERs. Other research (Buchanan, Kern, & Bell-Dumas, 1991) suggested that made-up early recollections may be as meaningful as actual ones.

B. Early Recollections and Psychotherapy Outcomes

Research has also shown that early recollections are related to success in counseling and psychotherapy. For example, Savill and Eckstein (1987) found that patients receiving therapy changed their ERs from pre- to post-treatment. In addition, Statton and Wilborn (1991) demonstrated that change as a result of counseling may be capable of producing changes in early recollections.

XIII. Critique of Adler

Individual psychology rates high on its ability to generate research, organize data, and guide the practitioner. It receives a moderate rating on parsimony, but the authors rated it low on internal consistency because it lacks operational definitions and low on falsification because many of its related research findings can be explained by other theories.

XIV Concept of Humanity

Adler saw people as forward moving, social animals who are motivated by goals they set (both consciously and unconsciously) for the future. People are ultimately responsible for their own unique style of life. Thus, Adler's theory rates high on free-choice, social influences, and uniqueness; very high on optimism and teleology; and average on unconscious influences.

TEACHING SUGGESTIONS

1.   The concepts of birth order and family constellation are popular with students. You may call on volunteers to list their birth order along with the gender and age-spread of siblings. Students unfamiliar with the volunteer will be interested in guessing core personality traits of members of the volunteer's family. Some of the guesses will probably hit the mark and others will be off the mark. Count the "hits" and "misses" and determine whether the guesses are better than chance or more valid than astrological predictions.

2.   A more productive procedure is that of early recollections. Again, ask for student volunteers to relate their three or four earliest recollections. These accounts can be either oral or written. After one person's recollections are presented to the class, you and your students may find a theme that runs throughout that person's other

early recollections. If Adler's notion is valid, then each of these early memories should relate to the person's current style of life.

REFERENCES

Buchanan, L. P., Kern, R., & Bell-Dumas, J. (1991). Comparison of content in created versus actual early recollections. *Individual Psychology, 47,* 348–355.

Nichols, C. C., & Feist, J. (1994). Explanatory style as a predictor of earliest recollections. *Individual Psychology, 50,* 31–39.

Savill, G. E., & Eckstein, D. G. (1987). Changes in early recollections as a function of mental status. *Individual Psychology, 43,* 3–17.

Statton, J. E., & Wilborn, B. (1991). Adlerian counseling and the early recollections of children. *Individual Psychology, 47,* 338–347.

CHAPTER 4
JUNG: ANALYTICAL PSYCHOLOGY

LEARNING OBJECTIVES

After studying Chapter 4, students should be able to:

1. Describe how Jung's own life experiences may have influenced his concept of human personality.

2. Describe the Jungian levels of the psyche.

3. List and describe eight major archetypes.

4. Discuss Jung's typology with the major attitudes and functions.

5. Identify and describe Jung's stages of personality development.

6. Describe Jung's concept of self-realization.

7. Explain Jung's idea of word association.

8. Discuss Jung's concept of dreams and how they relate to the unconscious.

9. Summarize research of Jungian types and both physical attraction and academic performance.

LECTURE OUTLINE

I. Overview of Jung's Analytical Psychology

Carl Jung believed that people are extremely complex beings who are partially motivated by forces beyond their personal experience—that is, the repeated experiences of their ancestors that make up the *collective unconscious*. Humans possess a variety of opposing qualities, such as introversion and extraversion, masculinity and femininity, and rational and irrational drives.

II. Biography of Carl Jung

Carl Jung was born in Switzerland in 1875, the oldest surviving child of an idealistic Protestant minister and his practical but clairvoyant wife. Jung's early experience with parents who were quite opposite of each other probably influenced his own theory of personality. Jung decided to become a physician after dreaming of making scientific discoveries. Soon after receiving his medical degree, he became acquainted with Freud's writings and eventually with Freud himself. Not long after he traveled with Freud to the United States, Jung became disenchanted with Freud's pansexual theories, broke with the International Psychoanalytic Association, and began his own approach to theory and therapy, which he called **analytical psychology**. From a critical midlife crisis during which he nearly lost contact with reality, Jung emerged to become one of the leading thinkers of the 20th century. He died in 1961 at age 85.

III. Levels of the Psyche

Jung saw the human psyche as being divided into a conscious and an unconscious level, with the latter subdivided into a personal and a collective unconscious.

A. Conscious

Images sensed by the ego are said to be conscious. The **ego** thus represents the conscious side of personality, and in the psychologically mature individual, the ego is secondary to the *self*.

B. Personal Unconscious

The unconscious refers to those psychic images not sensed by the ego. Some unconscious processes flow from our personal experience and are repressed, forgotten, or subliminally perceived. These experiences make up the personal unconscious, a concept analogous to Freud's notion of an unconscious. Contents of the personal unconscious are called **complexes**, which are emotionally toned groups of related ideas.

C. Collective Unconscious

Ideas that are beyond our personal experiences and that originate from the repeated experiences of our ancestors become part of our collective unconscious. Collective unconscious images are not inherited ideas, but rather they refer to our innate tendency to react in a particular way whenever our personal experiences stimulate an inherited predisposition toward action.

D.   Archetypes

Contents of the collective unconscious are called archetypes. Jung believed that archetypes originate through the repeated experiences of our ancestors and that they are expressed in certain types of dreams, fantasies, delusions, and hallucinations. Several archetypes acquire their own personality, and Jung identified these by name.

1.   Persona

The persona is the side of our personality that we show to others. People who confuse their persona with their self remain unaware of their individuality and are blocked from becoming self-realized.

2.   Shadow

The shadow is the dark side of our personality. To reach full psychological maturity, or self-realization, people must first realize or accept their shadow, and this acceptance is their first test of courage.

3.   Anima

A second hurdle in achieving maturity is for men to accept their anima, or feminine side. Men who fail to become acquainted with their anima run the risk of projecting their feminine traits on to the women in their life and thus never quite know these women.

4.   Animus

The second test of courage for women is to embrace their animus, or masculine disposition. Women who reject their masculine side tend to attribute their masculine dispositions to the men in their lives.

5. Great Mother

The great mother is the archetype both of nourishment and destruction. It is found in fairy tales, legends, and myths as a witch, a fairy godmother, Mother Nature, or rebirth.

6. Wise Old Man

The wise old man is the archetype of wisdom and meaning, but his wisdom is shallow and superficial, such as the wizard in the *Wizard of Oz*.

7. Hero

The hero archetype is the image we have of a conqueror who vanquishes evil, but who has a single fatal flaw. Achilles and his vulnerable heel is an example of the Hero archetype.

8. Self

The most comprehensive archetype is the self; that is, the image we have of fulfillment, completion, or perfection. The ultimate in psychological maturity is **self-realization,** which is symbolized by the **mandala,** or perfect geometric figure.

IV. Dynamics of Personality

Jung saw the dynamics of personality as depending on complex energy systems.

A. Causality and Teleology

Jung accepted a middle position between the philosophical issues of causality and teleology. A causal position holds that present events originate from earlier experiences, whereas a teleological stance suggests that present events are motivated by goals and aspirations for the future.

B. Progression and Regression

To achieve self-realization, people must adapt to both their external and internal worlds. Progression involves adaptation to the outside world and the forward flow of psychic energy, whereas regression refers to adaptation to the inner world and the backward flow of psychic energy.

V. Psychological Types

Eight basic psychological types emerge from the union of two attitudes and four functions.

A. Attitudes

Attitudes (which include introversion and extraversion) are predispositions to act or react in a characteristic manner.

1. Introversion

Introversion is the turning of psychic energy inward and an orientation toward subjectivity. In Jungian psychology, introversion does not mean shy or withdrawn, but rather it refers to people with subjective perceptions tuned to their inner world.

2. Extraversion

A turning outward of psychic energy, with an orientation toward the objective world, is called extraversion. Extraverts are influenced more by the real world than by their subjective perception of that world. Introverts and extraverts often mistrust and misunderstand one another, but each orientation has strengths and weaknesses, and psychologically healthy people have a balance of these two attitudes.

B. Functions

Four possible functions can combine with introversion and extraversion to form eight general personality **types**. The four functions are thinking, feeling, sensing, and intuiting.

1. Thinking

Thinking enables us to recognize the meaning of stimuli. *Extraverted thinking people* rely on concrete thoughts that are usually similar to those of other extraverted thinking people, whereas *introverted thinking people* give their own interpretation to external stimuli.

2. Feeling

Jung used the term feeling to mean placing a *value* on something. *Extraverted feeling people* make evaluations that agree with widely accepted standards of judgment, whereas *introverted feeling people* base their judgments on subjective perceptions.

3. Sensation

Sensation is the perceptions of sensory stimuli. *Extraverted sensing people* perceive external sensory stimuli (sights, sounds, etc.) in much the same way that others do, whereas *introverted sensing people* have their own individualized view of these stimuli.

4. Intuition

Intuition is the perception of elementary data that are beyond our awareness. *Extraverted intuitive people* are guided by their hunches, and they may make practical decisions without awareness of sensory data. *Introverted intuitive people* also perceive stimuli on an unconscious level, but they color those stimuli according to their own subjective attitudes. Jung referred to thinking and feeling as **rational functions** and to sensation and intuition as **irrational functions**.

VI. Development of Personality

Jung was unique among personality theorists with his emphasis on the second half of life. He saw middle and old age as times when people may acquire the ability to attain self-realization.

A. Stages of Development

Jung divided development into four broad stages.

1.   Childhood

Childhood has three substages: (1) the *anarchic*, when an infant has little awareness of self; (2) the *monarchic*, when the young child begins to form an ego and to develop verbal communication; and (3) the *dualistic*, when children begin to identify themselves as separate individuals.

2.   Youth

Youth, the period from puberty until middle life, is a time for extraverted development and for being in touch with the real world of schooling, occupation, courtship, marriage, and family.

3.   Middle Life

If people have courageously solved the problems of childhood and youth, they will probably have a successful middle life—that period from about 35 or 40 until old age. Jung believed that people should adopt a more introverted attitude during this time and prepare themselves for old age.

4.   Old Age

Jung saw old age not as a time for despair but as an opportunity for psychological rebirth, self-realization, and preparation for death.

B.   Self-Realization

Self-realization, or **individuation,** involves a psychological rebirth and an integration of various parts of the psyche into a unified or whole individual. Self-realization represents the highest level of human development and is probably an even more difficult process to attain than self-actualization, as described by Maslow (see Chapter 17).

VII. Jung's Methods of Investigation

Jung used the word association test, dream analysis, and active imagination during the process of psychotherapy, and all these methods contributed to his theory of personality.

A.   Word Association Test

Jung used the word association test early in his career to uncover complexes embedded in the personal unconscious. The technique requires a patient to utter the first word that comes to mind after the examiner reads a stimulus word.

B.   Dream Analysis

According to Jung, dreams have both a cause and a purpose and thus can be useful in explaining past events and in making decisions about the future. *Big dreams* and *typical dreams*, both of which come from the collective unconscious, have meanings that lie beyond the experiences of a single individual.

C.   Active Imagination

Jung also used active imagination to arrive at collective images. This technique requires the patient to concentrate on a single image until that image begins to appear in a different form. Eventually, the patient should see figures that represent archetypes and other collective unconscious images.

D.   Psychotherapy

The goal of Jungian therapy is to help neurotic patients become healthy and to move healthy people in the direction of self-realization. Jung was eclectic in his choice of therapeutic techniques and treated old people differently than young people.

VIII. Related Research

Most research related to Jungian theory has revolved around the notion of psychological types and has used the Myers-Briggs Type Indicator, an instrument that uses slightly different terminology than Jung's.

A.   Types and Attraction

Some research suggests that extraverts and introverts have different preferences in their choice of partners. For example, Hester (1996) found that extraverts, in contrast to introverts, prefer partners with high self-confidence and that intuitive types are more attracted to creative people. Other research has found that people with similar types tend to stay together longer than do people of opposite types.

B.   Types and Academic Performance and Success

Research by Schurr and colleagues (1997) indicated that college freshmen who were most likely to eventually graduate were those who scored high on Judging and Sensing. That is, students who are mostly likely to graduate are those who are most tolerant of routine and who are conscientious and structured.

IX.   Critique of Jung

Although Jung considered himself a scientist, many of his writings have more of a philosophical than a psychological flavor. As a scientific theory, the authors give it a moderate rating on its ability to generate research but a very low rating on its ability to withstand falsification. Jungian theory is about average on its ability to organize knowledge but low on its ability to guide action. The authors also rated it low on internal consistency and parsimony.

X.   Concept of Humanity

Jung saw people as extremely complex beings who are a product of both conscious and unconscious personal experiences. More importantly, people are also motivated by inherited remnants that spring from the collective experiences of their early ancestors. Because Jungian theory is a psychology of opposites, it receives a moderate rating on the issues of free will, optimism/pessimism, and causality/teleology. It rates very high on unconscious influences and low on uniqueness and social influences.

TEACHING SUGGESTIONS

1.   The Myers-Briggs Type Indicator (MBTI) is a popular personality inventory that yields scores on four bipolar factors: Extraversion vs. Introversion, Sensing vs.

Intuition, Thinking vs. Feeling, and Judging vs. Perceptive. Your students may enjoy taking and scoring the MBTI. They can fill out their own profile and receive an interpretation of the results. If the MBTI is not available at your counseling or testing center, it can be purchased through

Consulting Psychologists Press

3803 E. Bayshore Road

Palo Alto, CA 94303

(414) 969-8901

FAX (415) 969-8608

2. A few years before his death, Carl Jung was interviewed on film by Richard Evans of the University of Houston. (Evans has filmed interviews with several personality theorists as well as other famous psychologists.) The original Jung/Evans dialogue lasted about 3 hours, but in 1967, Evans edited the interview into a 36-minute film, which is available from

Audio-Visual Services

University Division of Media and Learning Resources

The Pennsylvania State University

University Park, PA 16802

(814) 865-6314 or 1-800-826-0132

REFERENCES

Hester, C. (1996). The relationship of personality, gender, and age to Adjective Check List profiles of the ideal romantic partner. *Journal of Psychological Type, 36,* 28–35.

Schurr, K. T., Ruble, V., Palomba, C., Pickerill, B., & Moore, D. (1997). Relationships between the MBTI and selected aspects of Tinto's model for college attrition. *Journal of Psychological Type, 40,* 31–42.

CHAPTER 5
KLEIN:OBJECT RELATIONS THEORY

LEARNING OBJECTIVES

After studying Chapter 5, students should be able to:

1. Define object relations theory and compare it to Freudian theory.

2. Discuss the psychological life of the infant as seen from Klein's viewpoint.

3. Explain Klein's concepts of the paranoid-schizoid and depressive positions.

4. List and discuss Klein's psychic defense mechanisms.

5. Compare and contrast Klein's concept of the Oedipus complex to that of Freud.

6. Discuss Mahler's ideas on psychological birth.

7. Explain Kernberg's view of object relations.

8. Discuss Kohut's views of object relations.

9. Explain Bowlby's attachment theory.

LECTURE OUTLINE

I. **Overview of Object Relations Theory**

Unlike Adler and Jung, who ultimately rejected Freud's theories, Melanie Klein tried to validate and extend Freud's ideas within the framework of psychoanalysis. Klein and other object relations theorists have generally sought to extend Freud's developmental stages downward to the first few months after birth. Most of these theorists have examined the importance of the mother–child relationship.

II. **Biography of Melanie Klein**

Melanie Klein was born in Vienna in 1892, the youngest and least favored of four children of a struggling physician and his second wife. Her closest childhood friend was an idolized older brother. When this brother died, Melanie was devastated. While still in mourning for her beloved brother, she married Arthur Klein, an engineer and a close friend of her brother. Her marriage, which eventually ended in divorce, produced three children, a daughter and two sons. Klein's daughter, Melitta, became a psychoanalyst and was one of her mother's most bitter critics. Klein had neither a Ph.D. nor an M.D. degree, but she became an analyst by being psychoanalyzed and studying psychoanalysis. As a psychoanalyst, she specialized in analyzing children, including her own. In 1927, she moved to London where she practiced until her death in 1960. She never reconciled with her daughter Melitta, who refused to attend her mother's funeral.

III. Introduction to Object Relations Theory

Object relations theory differs from Freudian theory in at least three ways: (1) it places more emphasis on interpersonal relationships, (2) it stresses the infant's relationship with the mother rather than the father, and (3) it suggests that people are motivated primarily for human contact rather than for sexual pleasure. The term **object** in object relations theory refers to any person or part of a person that infants introject onto their psychic structure and then later project onto other people. Thus, an object is something like Freud's notion of a superego, which children introject. That is, children take into their psychic structure the morals and ideals that they see in their parents.

IV. Psychic Life of the Infant

Klein believed that infants begin life with an inherited predisposition to reduce the anxiety that they experience as a consequence of the clash between the life instinct and the death instinct.

A.   Fantasies

Klein assumed that very young infants possess an active fantasy life, albeit on an unconscious level. Their most basic fantasies are images of the "good" breast and the "bad" breast. Later, these and other unconscious fantasies are shaped by both reality and by inherited predispositions.

B.   **Objects**

Klein agreed with Freud that drives have an object, but she was more likely to emphasize the child's relationship with these objects (parents' face, hands, breast, penis, etc.), which she saw as having a life of their own within the child's fantasy world.

V.   **Positions**

In their attempts to reduce the conflict produced by good and bad images, infants organize their experience into positions, or ways of dealing with both internal and external objects. Although these positions have names that suggest pathology, Klein used them to refer to normal as well as abnormal development.

A.   **Paranoid-Schizoid Position**

The struggles that infants experience with the good breast and the bad breast lead to two separate and opposing feelings: a desire to harbor the breast and a desire to bite or destroy it. To tolerate these two feelings, the ego splits itself by retaining parts of its life and death instincts while projecting other parts onto the breast. It then has a relationship with the *ideal breast* and the *persecutory breast*. To control this situation, the infant adopts the paranoid-schizoid position, which is a tendency to see the world as having the same destructive and omnipotent qualities that the infant possesses.

B.   **Depressive Position**

By depressive position, Klein meant the anxiety that infants experience around 6 months of age over losing their mother and yet, at the same time, wanting to destroy her. The depressive position is resolved when infants fantasize that they have made up for their previous transgressions against their mother and also realize that their mother will not abandon them.

VI. Psychic Defense Mechanisms

According to Klein, children adopt various psychic defense mechanisms to protect their ego against anxiety aroused by their own destructive fantasies.

A. Introjection

Klein defined introjection as the fantasy of taking into one's own body the images that one has of an external object, especially the mother's breast. Infants usually introject good objects as a protection against anxiety, but they also introject bad objects in order to gain control of them.

B. Projection

The fantasy that one's own feelings and impulses reside within another person is called projection. Again, children project both good and bad images, especially onto their parents.

C. Splitting

Infants tolerate good and bad aspects of themselves and of external objects by splitting, or mentally keeping apart, incompatible images. If not carried to extreme, splitting can be beneficial to people because it allows them to like themselves while still recognizing some unlikable qualities.

D. Projective Identification

The psychic defense mechanism in which infants split off unacceptable parts of themselves, project them onto another object, and finally introject them in an altered form is called projective identification. Unlike projection, which exists mostly in fantasy, projective identification takes place in the real world.

VII. Internalizations

After introjecting external objects, infants organize them into a psychologically meaningful framework, a process Klein called internalization.

A.   Ego

Internalizations are aided by the early ego's ability to feel anxiety, to deploy defense mechanisms, and to form object relations in both fantasy and reality. However, a unified ego emerges only after first splitting itself into the two parts: those that deal with the life instinct and those that relate to the death instinct.

B.   Superego

Klein believed that the superego emerged much earlier than Freud had held. To her, the superego preceded rather than followed the Oedipus complex. Klein also saw the superego as being quite harsh and cruel.

C.   Oedipus Complex

Again, Klein's conception of the Oedipus complex differed from Freud's. First, she believed that the Oedipus complex begins during the first few months of life, then reaches its zenith during the **genital stage**, at about age 3 or 4, or the same time that Freud had suggested it began. Second, Klein held that much of the Oedipus complex is based on children's fear that their parents will seek revenge against them for their fantasy of emptying the parent's body. Third, Klein believed that, for healthy development, children should retain positive feelings for both parents during the Oedipal years.

1.   Male Oedipal Development

According to Klein, the little boy adopts a "feminine" position very early in life and has no fear of being castrated as punishment for his sexual feelings for his mother. Later, he projects his destructive drive onto his father, whom he fears will bite or castrate him. The male Oedipus complex is resolved when the boy establishes good relations with both parents.

2.   Female Oedipal Development

The little girl also adopts a "feminine" position toward both parents quite early in life. She has a positive feeling both for her mother's breast and for her father's penis, which she believes will feed her with babies. Sometimes the girl develops hostility toward her mother, whom she fears will retaliate against her and rob her of her babies, but, in most cases, the female Oedipus complex is resolved without any jealousy toward the mother.

VIII. Later Views on Object Relations

A number of other theorists have expanded and altered Klein's theory of object relations. Notable among them are Margaret Mahler, Heinz Kohut, Otto Kernberg, and John Bowlby.

A.   Margaret Mahler's View

Mahler, a native of Hungary who practiced psychoanalysis in both Vienna and New York, developed her theory of object relations from careful observations of infants as they bonded with their mothers during their first 3 years of life. In their progress toward achieving a sense of identity, children pass through a series of three major developmental stages. First is **normal autism**, which covers the first 3 or 4 weeks of life. During this time, infants satisfy their needs within the all-powerful protective orbit of their mother's care and without an awareness of any other person. Second is **normal symbiosis**, when infants behave as if they and their mother were an omnipotent, symbiotic unit. Third is **separation-individuation**, which spans the time from about 4 months until about 3 years. During this time, children become psychologically separated from their mothers and achieve *individuation*, or a sense of personal identity.

B.   Heinz Kohut's View

Like Kernberg, Kohut was a native of Vienna, but he spent most of his professional life in the United States. More than any of the other object relations theorists, he emphasized the development of the *self*. In caring for infants' physical and psychological needs, adults treat them as if they had a sense of self. The parents' behaviors and attitudes then help children form a sense of self that gives unity and consistency to their experiences.

C.   Otto Kernberg's View

Kernberg, a native of Vienna, has spent most of his professional career in the United States. Like Freud, his theories of infantile development have been built mostly on his clinical experiences with older patients. Kernberg believed that the key to understanding personality is the mother–child relationship. Children who experience a healthy relationship with their mother develop an integrated ego, a punitive superego, a stable self-concept, and satisfying interpersonal relations. In contrast, children who have poor relations with their mother will have difficulty integrating their ego and may suffer from some form of psychopathology during adulthood.

D.   John Bowlby's Attachment Theory

John Bowlby, a physician and native of England, received training in child psychiatry from Melanie Klein. Like other object relations theorists, Bowlby believed that early childhood attachments to parents have a considerable influence on later personality development. By studying human and other primate infants, Bowlby observed three stages of **separation anxiety**. First, an infant will *protest*; second, it shows *apathy and despair,* and finally, the human infant will become *emotionally detached* from other people, including the primary caregiver. Children who experience this third stage lack warmth and emotion in their later relationships. Bowlby influenced Mary Ainsworth, a psychologist who has developed techniques for measuring attachment style.

IX. Psychotherapy

The goal of Kleinian psychotherapy was to reduce depressive anxieties and persecutory fears and to lessen the harshness of internalized objects. To do this, Klein encouraged patients to re-experience early fantasies, while she pointed out the differences between reality and fantasy as well as between conscious and unconscious wishes. The understanding that patients gained from this procedure allowed them to feel less persecuted by internalized objects and to project previously frightening internal objects onto objects in the external world.

X.   Related Research

Object relations theories stress the importance of early bonding, and recent research in this area has focused on attachment theory and interpersonal relationships of both children and adults.

A.   Attachment Theory and Children's Object Relationships

Kirsh and Cassidy (1997) found that children with secure attachment, compared with children with insecure attachment, have both better attention and better memory. Other research (Fury, Carlson, & Sroufe, 1997) suggests that securely attached young children grow up to become adolescents who feel comfortable in friendship groups that allowed new members to easily become part of those groups. Still other studies (Fury et al., 1997) have shown that 8- and 9-year-old children who were securely attached during infancy produced family drawings that demonstrated interpersonal security.

B.   Attachment Theory and Adult Relationships

Research with adults suggests that those with secure attachments experience more trust, closeness, and positive emotions than do adults with other attachment styles. Other research with college students has found that those with secure relationships had less hostility and were more independent than students with avoidant or ambivalent relationships.

XI.   Critique of Object Relations Theory

Object relations theory shares with Freudian theory an inability to be either falsified or verified through empirical research; that is, findings consistent with the theory can also be explained by some other model. Nevertheless, some clinicians regard the theory as being a useful guide to action and as possessing substantial internal consistency. However, the theory must be rated low on parsimony and on its ability to organize knowledge and to generate research.

XII. Concept of Humanity

Object relations theorists see personality as being a product of the early mother–child relationship, and thus they stress determinism over free choice. The powerful influence of early childhood also gives these theories a low rating on uniqueness and high ratings on causality, unconscious forces, and social influences. Klein and other object relations theorists rate average on optimism versus pessimism.

TEACHING SUGGESTIONS

1. Students with young children or who are well acquainted with young children will find Bowlby's attachment theory interesting. They can discuss their experiences with infants who exhibit some level of separation. In most cases, infants will have reached only the first stage of separation. That is, when separated from their primary caregiver, infants will show protest. The instructor can ask students to take notes on an infant's behavior when initially separated from its mother or other primary caregiver. According to Bowlby, the infant will cry, resist soothing by other people, and make attempts at looking for the caregiver. Students can compare notes with one another as well as check the accuracy of Bowlby's hypothesis.

REFERENCES

Fury, G., Carlson, E. Al, & Sroufe, L. A. (1997). Children's representations of
attachment relationships in family drawings. *Child Development, 68,* 1154–1164.

Kirsh, S. J., & Cassidy, J. (1997). Preschoolers' attention to and memory for
attachment-relevant information. *Child Development, 68,* 1143–1153.

CHAPTER 6
HORNEY: PSYCHOANALYTIC SOCIAL THEORY

LEARNING OBJECTIVES

After studying Chapter 6, students should be able to:

1. Compare and contrast Horney's theory with that of Freud.

2. Discuss Horney's concepts of basic hostility and basic anxiety.

3. List and discuss Horney's categories of neurotic needs.

4. Describe Horney's three neurotic trends.

5. Explain Horney's concept of intrapsychic conflicts.

6. Discuss the modes of expression for self-hatred.

7. Discuss Horney's concept of feminine psychology.

8. Discuss research on morbid dependency and explain how it relates to Horney's view of moving toward other people.

9. Discuss research on hypercompetitiveness and explain how it relates to Horney's concept of moving against other people.

10. Explain how Horney's picture of the neurotic personality relates to normal personality.

LECTURE OUTLINE

I.   Overview of Horney's Psychoanalytic Social Theory

Karen Horney built her psychoanalytic social theory on the assumption that social and cultural conditions, especially during childhood, are primary influences on later personality. Although Horney's books are concerned mostly with neurotic personalities, many of her observations also apply to normal individuals. Like Klein, Horney's early ideas were influenced by Freud. However, she objected to Freud's basically masculine theory, which looked first at male development and then applied those observations to women.

II.   Biography of Karen Horney

Karen Horney was born in Germany in 1885, the youngest of two children born to a stern, devoutly religious older sea captain and his young wife. Horney was one of the first women in Germany admitted to medical school, where she specialized in psychiatry. She also became acquainted with Freudian theory and was analyzed by Karl Abraham, one of Freud's close associates. In her mid-40s, Horney left Germany to settle in the United States, first in Chicago and then in New York. She soon abandoned orthodox psychoanalysis in favor of a more socially oriented theory, one that also had a more positive view of feminine development. Horney died in 1952 at age 65.

III.   Introduction to Psychoanalytic Social Theory

Although Horney's writings deal mostly with neuroses and neurotic personalities, her theories suggest much that is appropriate to normal development. She agreed with Freud that early childhood traumas are important, but she placed far more emphasis on social factors.

A.   Horney and Freud Compared

Horney criticized Freudian theory on at least three accounts: (1) its rigidity toward new ideas, (2) its skewed view of feminine psychology, and (3) its overemphasis on biology and the pleasure principle.

B.   The Impact of Culture

Horney insisted that modern culture is too competitive and that competition leads to hostility and feelings of isolation. These conditions lead to exaggerated needs for affection and cause people to overvalue love. Both normal and neurotic personalities experience intrapsychic conflicts through their desperate attempts to find love.

C.   The Importance of Childhood Experiences

Neurotic conflict stems largely from childhood traumas, most of which are traced to lack of genuine love. Children who do not receive genuine affection feel threatened and adopt rigid behavioral patterns in an attempt to gain love.

IV.   Basic Hostility and Basic Anxiety

All children need feelings of safety and security, but these can be gained only through the love of their parents. Unfortunately, parents often neglect, dominate, reject, or overindulge their child, conditions that lead to the child's feelings of basic hostility toward their parents. However, children often repress their feelings of basic hostility, which leads to feelings of deep insecurity and a pervasive sense of apprehension called basic anxiety. People can protect themselves from basic anxiety by a number of protective devices, including (1) affection; (2) submissiveness; (3) power, prestige, or possession; and (4) withdrawal. Normal people have the flexibility to use any or all of these approaches, but neurotics are compelled to rely rigidly on only one.

V.   Compulsive Drives

Neurotics are frequently trapped in a vicious circle in which their compulsive need to reduce basic anxiety leads to a variety of self-defeating behaviors; these behaviors then produce more basic anxiety, and the cycle continues.

A.   Neurotic Needs

In her early theory, Horney identified 10 categories of neurotic needs that mark neurotics in their attempt to reduce basic anxiety. These included the neurotic need (1) for affection and approval, (2) for a powerful partner (3) to restrict one's life within narrow borders, (4) for power, (5) to exploit others, (6) for social recognition or prestige, (7) for personal admiration, (8) for ambition and personal

achievement, (9) for self-sufficiency and independence, and (10) for perfection
and unassailability.

B.   Neurotic Trends

Later, Horney grouped these 10 neurotic needs into three basic neurotic trends,
which apply to both normal and neurotic individuals in their attempt to solve
basic conflict.

1.   Moving Toward People

People often strive to protect themselves against basic anxiety and feelings of
helplessness by moving toward people. This strategy results in undue *compliance* to
others' wishes.

2.   Moving Against People

Aggressive people assume that everyone is hostile, and, therefore, they adopt the
strategy of moving against people, exploiting them for their own benefit.

3.   Moving Away From People

People who feel *detached* from others adopt the neurotic trend of moving away
from people, insisting on privacy, independence, and self-sufficiency.

VI.   Intrapsychic Conflicts

Besides these culturally induced needs and trends, people experience inner tensions,
or intrapsychic conflicts. These intrapsychic conflicts become part of people's
belief systems and take on a life of their own, separate from the interpersonal
conflicts that created them.

A.   The Idealized Self-Image

People who do not receive love and affection during childhood are impeded in their
natural tendency toward self-realization and are blocked in their attempt to acquire
a stable sense of identity. Feeling alienated from self, they create an idealized self-
image, or an extravagantly positive picture of themselves that exists only in their
mind. Horney recognized three aspects of the idealized self-image.

1.   The Neurotic Search for Glory

As neurotic people begin to believe that their idealized self-image is real, they try to incorporate it into all aspects of their lives. This leads to the neurotic search for glory, or a comprehensive drive toward actualizing the ideal self. The neurotic search for glory includes the need for perfection (the **tyranny of the should**), neurotic ambition, and the drive toward a vindictive triumph.

2.   Neurotic Claims

Neurotic people believe that their idealized fantasy world is real and that the rest of the world is skewed. Consequently, they believe that they are entitled to special privileges, and they make neurotic claims on other people that are consistent with their idealized view of themselves.

3.   Neurotic Pride

A third aspect of the idealized self-image is neurotic pride, or a false pride based not on reality but on a distorted and idealized view of self.

B.   Self-Hatred

Neurotic individuals dislike themselves because reality always falls short of their idealized view of self. Therefore, they learn self-hatred, which can be expressed as (1) relentless demands on the self, (2) merciless self-accusation, (3) self-contempt, (4) self-frustration, (5) self-torment or self-torture, and (6) self-destructive actions and impulses.

VII. Feminine Psychology

Horney believed that psychological differences between men and women are not due to anatomy but to culture and social expectations. Her view of the Oedipus complex differed markedly from Freud's in that she again insisted that any sexual attraction or hostility of child to parent would be the result of learning and not biology.

VIII. Psychotherapy

The goal of Horney's psychotherapy was to help patients grow toward self-realization, give up their idealized self-image, relinquish their neurotic search for glory, and change self-hatred to self-acceptance. Horney believed that, fortunately, patients wish to get better, even though they may find comfort in their present misery. Horney also believed that successful therapy is built on self-analysis and self-understanding.

IX. Related Research

Horney's theory has been one of the least productive of all personality theories in generating research. However, her concepts of moving toward and moving against other people have stimulated some research.

A.   Morbid Dependency

Horney's notion of morbid dependency (moving toward others) and its contemporary offspring—codependency—have produced research indicating that people with neurotic needs to move toward others will go to great extremes to win the approval of other people. For example, research (Lyon & Greenberg, 1991) with college women who had an alcoholic parent found that these women were much more likely to donate time to a self-centered man than to a kind and gentle one.

B.   Hypercompetitiveness

Horney's concept of moving against people relates to the notion of hypercompetitiveness. Early research found that hypercompetitiveness was positively related to low self-esteem, neuroticism, and narcissism. Later research (Ryckman, Hammer, Kaczor, & Gold, 1996) on a healthy type of competitiveness—called personal developmental competitiveness—suggests that this style of competition is related to social concern. Still other research (Burckle, Ryckman, & Gold, 1999 found that highly competitive college women were more likely than other college women to suffer from disordered eating, such as anorexia and bulimia.

X.   Critique of Horney

Although Horney's theory has not generated much research, it has provided an interesting way of looking at humanity. The strength of her theory was her vivid portrayal of the neurotic personality, As scientific theory, however, it rates very low in generating research, and low on its ability to be falsified, organize knowledge, and serve as a guide to action. The theory receives a moderate rating on internal consistency and parsimony.

XI.   Concept of Humanity

Horney's concept of humanity was based mostly on her clinical experiences with neurotic patients, but it can easily be extended to normal people. In summary, Horney's view of humanity is rated high on free choice, optimism, unconscious influences, and social factors; average on causality versus teleology; and low on uniqueness.

TEACHING SUGGESTIONS

1.   Horney's concept of morbid dependency and the current notion of codependency can spark a lively discussion among college students, some of whom may feel strongly that codependency does not exist. Ask students to give examples of codependency and then ask them for possible explanations of such relationships. How would social learning theory explain a codependent relationship? How would Adler interpret this relationship?

2.   The study by Lyon and Greenberg (1991) poses an intriguing question. Why would college women with an alcoholic parent offer more help to an exploitative person

than to a nurturing person? Before students are exposed to Horney's theory, the instructor may wish to summarize this study and ask students for their explanations for Lyon and Greenberg's findings. The instructor should discuss this study *before* the students read the chapter. This discussion should ignite interest in Horney's theory and motivate students to learn more about this fascinating theory.

REFERENCES

Burckle, M. A., Ryckman, R. M., & Gold, J. A. (1999). Forms of competitive attitude and achievement orientation in relation to disordered eating. *Sex Roles, 40,* 853–870.

Lyon, D., & Greenberg, J. (1991). Evidence of codependency in women with an alcoholic parent: Helping out Mr. Wrong. *Journal of Personality and Social Psychology, 61,* 435–439.

Ryckman, R. M., Hammer, M., Kaczor, L. M. & Gold, J. A. (1996). Construction of a Personal Development Competitive Attitude scale. *Journal of Personality Assessment, 66,* 374–375.

CHAPTER 7
FROMM: HUMANISTIC PSYCHOANALYSIS

LEARNING OBJECTIVES

After studying Chapter 7, students should be able to:

1. Compare and contrast the theories of Fromm with those of Horney and Freud.

2. Discuss Fromm's basic assumptions about personality, including the three existential dichotomies.

3. Describe the existential (human) needs identified by Fromm.

4. Discuss Fromm's mechanisms of escape from freedom.

5. Define positive freedom and explain what Fromm meant by the term.

6. Describe Fromm's character orientations.

7. Discuss Fromm's three severe personality disorders.

8. Describe Fromm's research methods.

LECTURE OUTLINE

I. **Overview of Fromm's Humanistic Psychoanalysis**

   Erich Fromm's humanistic psychoanalysis looks at people from many perspectives, including psychology, history, and anthropology. Although Fromm was influenced by both Freud and Horney, his theory is much broader than Horney's and much more socially oriented than Freud's.

II. **Biography of Erich Fromm**

   Erich Fromm was born in Germany, in 1900, the only child of orthodox Jewish parents. His humanistic philosophy grew out of an early reading of the biblical prophets and an association with several Talmudic scholars. A thoughtful young man, Fromm was also influenced by the writings of Freud and Marx, as well as by socialist ideology. After receiving his Ph.D., Fromm studied psychoanalysis and was analyzed by Hanns Sachs, a student of Freud. Fromm's first wife was Frieda Fromm-

Reichmann, but the marriage eventually ended in divorce. In 1934, Fromm moved to the United States and began a psychoanalytic practice in New York, where he also resumed his friendship with Karen Horney, whom he had known in Germany. Much of his later years were spent in Mexico and Switzerland, where he continued to write books that gained him a worldwide reputation beyond psychology and psychoanalysis. He died in Switzerland in 1980.

III.   Fromm's Basic Assumptions

Fromm assumed that human personality can only be understood in the light of history. He believed that humans have been torn away from their prehistoric union with nature and left with no powerful instincts to adapt to a changing world. On the other hand, they have acquired the ability to reason, which means they can think about their isolated condition. Fromm called this situation the **human dilemma**.

IV.   Human Needs

According to Fromm, our human dilemma cannot be solved by satisfying our animal needs. It can only be addressed by fulfilling our uniquely human needs, which would move us toward a reunification with the natural world. Fromm also referred to these distinctively human needs as **existential needs.**

A.   Relatedness

Fromm called our desire for union with another person relatedness. We can relate to others through (1) submission, (2) power, and (3) love. However, **love**, or the ability to unite with another while retaining one's own individuality and integrity, is the only relatedness need that can solve our basic human dilemma.

B.   Transcendence

Being thrown into the world without their consent, humans have the urge to rise above their passive and accidental existence—to transcend their nature—by destroying or creating people or things. Humans can destroy through **malignant**

aggression, or killing for reasons other than survival, but they can also create and care about their creations.

C.   Rootedness

By rootedness, Fromm meant the need to establish roots and to feel at home again in the world. Like the other existential needs, rootedness can take either a productive or a nonproductive mode. With the productive strategy, we grow beyond the security of our mother and establish ties with the outside world. With the nonproductive strategy, we become fixated and afraid to move beyond the security and safety of our mother or a mother substitute.

D.   Sense of Identity

The fourth human need is for a sense of identity, or our awareness of ourselves as a separate person. The drive for a sense of identity is expressed nonproductively as conformity to a group and productively as individuality.

E.   Frame of Orientation

By frame of orientation, Fromm meant a road map or consistent philosophy by which we find our way through the world. This need is expressed nonproductively as a striving for irrational goals and productively as movement toward rational goals.

V.   The Burden of Freedom

As the only animal possessing self-awareness, humans are the freaks of the universe. Historically, as people gained more political freedom, they began to experience more isolation from others and from the world and to feel free from the security of a permanent place in the world. As a result, freedom becomes a burden, and people experience **basic anxiety**, or a feeling of being alone in the world.

A.   Mechanisms of Escape

To reduce the frightening sense of isolation and aloneness, people may adopt one of three mechanisms of escape.

1.   Authoritarianism

The tendency to give up one's independence and to unite with a powerful partner—authoritarianism—can take the form of either masochism or sadism. Masochism stems from feelings of powerlessness and can be disguised as love or loyalty. Sadism involves attempts to achieve unity by exploiting or hurting others.

2.   Destructiveness

Feelings of isolation can also produce destructiveness, an escape mechanism that is aimed at doing away with other people or things.

3.   Conformity

A third mechanism of escape is conformity, or surrendering of one's individuality in order to meet the wishes of others.

B.   Positive Freedom

Positive freedom is the spontaneous activity of the whole, integrated personality, which is achieved when a person becomes reunified with others and with the world. It is the successful solution to the human dilemma of being part of the natural world and yet separate from it.

VI.   Character Orientations

People relate to the world by acquiring and using things (assimilation) and by relating to self and others (socialization), and they can do so either nonproductively or productively.

A.   Nonproductive Orientations

Strategies that fail to move people closer to positive freedom and self-realization are nonproductive.

1.   Receptive

People who rely on the receptive orientation believe that the source of all good lies outside themselves and that the only way they can relate to the world is to receive things, including love, knowledge, and material objects. Positive qualities include loyalty and trust; negative ones are passivity and submissiveness.

2.   Exploitative

People with an exploitative orientation also believe that the source of good lies outside themselves, but they aggressively take what they want rather than passively receiving it. Positive qualities of exploitative people include pride and self-confidence; negative ones are arrogance and conceit.

3.   Hoarding

Hoarding characters try to save what they have already obtained, including their opinions, feelings, and material possessions. Positive qualities include loyalty, negative ones are obsessiveness and possessiveness.

4.   Marketing

People with a marketing orientation see themselves as commodities and value themselves against the criteria of their ability to sell themselves. They have fewer positive qualities than other orientations because they are essentially empty. However, they can be open-minded and adaptable.

B.   The Productive Orientation

Psychologically healthy people work toward positive freedom through productive *work*, *love*, and *reasoning*. Productive love necessitates a passionate love of all life and is called **biophilia**.

VII. Personality Disorders

Unhealthy people are characterized by their inability to work, think, and, especially, to love productively. Fromm recognized three major personality disorders: necrophilia, malignant narcissism, and incestuous symbiosis.

A.   Necrophilia

In Fromm's framework, necrophilia is the love of death and the hatred of all humanity. Necrophilious people do not simply behave in a destructive manner; their destructiveness is a reflection of a basic character.

B.   Malignant Narcissism

Malignant narcissism is so powerful that it convinces people that everything belonging to them is of great value and anything belonging to others is worthless. Narcissistic people often suffer from **moral hypochondrias**, or preoccupation with excessive guilt.

C.   Incestuous Symbiosis

Incestuous symbiosis is an extreme dependence on one's mother or mother surrogate to the extent that one's personality is blended with that of the host person. Fromm believed that a few people, such as Hitler, possessed all three of these disorders, a condition called the *syndrome of decay*.

VIII. Psychotherapy

The goal of Fromm's psychotherapy was the satisfaction of the basic human needs of relatedness, transcendence, rootedness, a sense of identity, and a frame of orientation. The therapist accomplishes this through shared communication in which the therapist is simply a human being rather than a scientist.

IX.   Fromm's Methods of Investigation

Fromm's personality theory rests on data he gathered from a variety of sources, including psychotherapy, cultural anthropology, and psychohistory.

A.   Social Character in a Mexican Village

Fromm and his associates spent several years investigating social character in a isolated farming village in Mexico and found evidence of all the character orientations except the marketing one. In general, this anthropological study's findings were consistent with Fromm's theoretical views on social character.

B.   A Psychohistorical Study of Hitler

Fromm applied psychohistorical techniques to the study of several historical people, including Adolf Hitler, whom Fromm regarded as the most conspicuous example of someone with the syndrome of decay. In his account, Fromm describes Hitler's necrophilia, malignant narcissism, and incestuous symbiosis.

X.   Related Research

Fromm did not express his ideas for the purpose of generating research, and his theory is among the least productive in terms of empirical study. However, there has been research interest in the marketing character. Saunders and Munro (2000) have developed the Saunders Consumer Orientation Index (SCOI) to assess the marketing character and have found that college students and other adults who score high on the SCOI—that is, people with a marketing orientation—tend to be more angry, depressed, and anxious than people low on the marketing orientation.

XI.   Critique of Fromm

Fromm evolved a theory that provide insightful ways of looking at humanity, and the strength of that theory is Fromm's lucid writing on a broad range of human issues. As a scientific theory, however, the theory receives low ratings. It rates very low on its ability to generate research and to open itself to falsification; it rates low on usefulness to the practitioner, internal consistency, and parsimony. Because it is quite broad in scope, Fromm's theory rates high on organizing existing knowledge.

XII. Concept of Humanity

Fromm's concept of humanity came from a rich variety of sources, including history, anthropology, economics, and clinical work. Because humans have the ability to reason but have few strong instincts, they are "freaks of nature." To achieve self-actualization, they must satisfy their human, or existential, needs through productive love and work. In summary, we rated Fromm's theory as average on free choice, optimism, unconscious influences, and uniqueness; low on causality; and very high on social influences.

TEACHING SUGGESTIONS

1. Fromm was one of many well-known psychologists interviewed by Richard Evans, and that interview is still available on videotape. The film is in two parts, each about 50 minutes long. They can be rented or purchased from

    > Audio-Visual Services
    > University Division of Media and Learning Resources
    > The Pennsylvania State University
    > University Park, PA 16802
    > Phone (814) 865-6314 or 1-800-826-0132

2. Fromm's concept of the syndrome of decay included three personality disorders: (1) necrophilia, or love of death; (2) malignant narcissism, or extreme self-interest; and (3) incestuous symbiosis, or a passionate devotion to one's mother or a mother substitute. Fromm identified Adolf Hitler as the most conspicuous example of a person with the syndrome of decay. If Fromm's conception is valid, we would see the syndrome of decay traits in contemporary personalities. Ask students to search for recent examples of well-known people with the syndrome of decay, including serial killers or heads of state who manifest the love of death. Your students should pay special attention to malignant narcissism and incestuous symbiosis.

REFERENCES

Saunders, S., & Munro, D. (2000). The construction and validation of a consumer orientation questionnaire (SCOI) designed to measure Fromm's (1955) "marketing character" in Australia. *Social Behavior and Personality, 28*, 219–240.

CHAPTER 8
SULLIVAN: INTERPERSONAL THEORY

LEARNING OBJECTIVES

After studying Chapter 8, students should be able to:

1. Describe specific ways in which Sullivan's early experiences, especially during preadolescence, may have influenced his theory of personality.

2. Compare and contrast tensions of needs and tensions of anxiety.

3. Give examples of how the malevolent dynamism might affect a young child.

4. Distinguish between Sullivan's concepts of intimacy and lust.

5. List and describe the basic personifications of Sullivan's theory.

6. Name and define the levels of cognition described by Sullivan.

7. List the Sullivanian epochs and describe their principal characteristics.

8. Explain the process of psychotherapy from the perspective of interpersonal theory.

9. Discuss recent research on intimate relationships both within and outside of the psychotherapy encounter.

LECTURE OUTLINE

I. Overview of Sullivan's Interpersonal Theory

Although Sullivan had a lonely and isolated childhood, he evolved a theory of personality that emphasized the importance of interpersonal relations. He insisted that personality is shaped almost entirely by one's relationships with other people. Sullivan's principal contribution to personality theory was his conception of developmental stages, which he saw as having strong interpersonal influences.

II. Biography of Harry Stack Sullivan

Harry Stack Sullivan, the first American to develop a comprehensive personality theory, was born in a small farming community in upstate New York in 1892. A socially immature and isolated child, Sullivan nevertheless formed one close interpersonal relationship with a boy five years older than him. In his interpersonal theory, Sullivan believed that such a relationship has the power to transform an immature preadolescent into a psychologically healthy individual. Sullivan had only one somewhat undistinguished year of college work before he entered medical school, and after receiving a medical degree, his career showed little promise of success. Six years after becoming a physician, and with no training in psychiatry, he gained a position at St. Elizabeth's Hospital in Washington, D.C., as a psychiatrist. There, his ability to work with schizophrenic patients won him a reputation as a therapeutic wizard. However, despite achieving much respect from an influential group of associates, Sullivan had few close interpersonal relations with any of his peers. He died alone in Paris in 1949, at age 56.

III. Tensions

Sullivan conceptualized personality as an energy system, with energy existing either as tension (potentiality for action) or as energy transformations (the actions themselves). He further divided tensions into needs and anxiety.

A.   Needs

Needs can relate either to the general well-being of a person or to specific zones, such as the mouth or genitals. General needs can be either physiological, such as food or oxygen, or interpersonal, such as **tenderness** and intimacy.

B.   Anxiety

Unlike needs—which are conjunctive and call for specific action to reduce them—anxiety is disjunctive and calls for no consistent actions for its relief. All infants learn to be anxious through the **empathic** relationship that they have with their mothering one. Sullivan compared anxiety to a blow on the head and contended that it was the chief disruptive force in interpersonal relations. A complete absence of anxiety and other tensions is called **euphoria**.

IV.   Dynamisms

Sullivan used the term dynamism to refer to a typical pattern of behavior. Dynamisms may relate either to specific zones of the body or to tensions.

A.   Malevolence

The disjunctive dynamism of evil and hatred is called malevolence, defined by Sullivan as a feeling of living among one's enemies. Those children who become malevolent have difficulty giving and receiving tenderness or being intimate with other people.

B.   Intimacy

The conjunctive dynamism marked by a close personal relationship between two people of equal status is called intimacy. Whereas malevolence blocks healthy personality development, intimacy facilitates development and decreases both anxiety and loneliness.

C.   Lust

In contrast to both malevolence and intimacy, lust is an isolating dynamism, because it is a self-centered need. Whereas intimacy presupposes tenderness or love, lust is based solely on sexual gratification and requires no other person for its satisfaction.

D.   Self-System

The most inclusive of all dynamisms is the self-system, or that pattern of behaviors that protects people against anxiety and maintains their interpersonal security. Like intimacy, the self-system is a conjunctive dynamism, but because its primary job is to protect the self from anxiety, it tends to stifle personality change. Experiences that are inconsistent with people's self-system threaten their security and necessitate their use of **security operations**, which consist of behaviors designed to reduce interpersonal tensions. One such security operation is **dissociation**, which includes all those experiences that a person blocks from awareness. Another is **selective inattention**, which involves blocking only certain experiences from awareness.

V.   Personifications

Sullivan believed that people acquire certain images of self and others throughout the developmental stages, and he referred to these subjective perceptions as personifications.

A.   Bad-Mother, Good-Mother

The bad-mother personification grows out of infants' experiences with a nipple that does not satisfy their hunger needs. All infants experience the bad-mother personification, even though their real mothers may be loving and nurturing. Later, infants acquire a good-mother personification as they become mature enough to recognize the tender and cooperative behavior of their mothering one. Still later, these two personifications combine to form a complex and contrasting image of the real mother.

B.   Me Personifications

During infancy, children acquire three me personifications: (1) the **bad-me**, which grows from experiences of punishment and disapproval, (2) the **good-me**, which results from experiences with reward and approval, and (3) the **not-me**, which allows a person to dissociate or selectively inattend experiences related to anxiety.

C.   Eidetic Personifications

One of Sullivan's most interesting observations was that people often create imaginary traits that they project onto others. Included in these eidetic personifications are the **imaginary playmates** that preschool-aged children often have. These imaginary friends enable children to have a safe, secure relationship and to practice interpersonal relations with no threat of negative consequences.

VI.   Levels of Cognition

Sullivan recognized three levels of cognition, or ways of perceiving things:

prototaxic, parataxic, and syntaxic.

A.   Prototaxic Level

Experiences that are impossible to put into words or to communicate to others are

called prototaxic. Newborn infants experience images mostly on a prototaxic level,

but adults, too, frequently have preverbal experiences that are momentary and

incapable of being communicated.

B.   Parataxic Level

Experiences that are prelogical and nearly impossible to accurately communicate to

others are called parataxic. Included in these are erroneous assumptions about cause

and effect, which Sullivan termed **parataxic distortions**.

C.   Syntaxic Level

Experiences that can be accurately communicated to others are called syntaxic.

Children become capable of syntaxic language at about 12 to 18 months of age

when words begin to have the same meaning for them that they do for others.

VII. Stages of Development

Sullivan saw interpersonal development as taking place over seven stages, from

infancy to mature adulthood. Personality change can take place at any time, but it

is most likely to occur during transitions between stages.

A.   Infancy

Sullivan's definition of infancy includes the period from birth until the emergence

of syntaxic language. During infancy, a child's relationship with the mothering one

includes two opposing forces, tenderness and anxiety. Because anxiety is a tension

in opposition to needs and because it is expressed in the same way as hunger needs

(i.e., by crying), mothers sometimes feed an anxious baby, which leads to tension

increasing to the point of terror. Such terror is reduced by the built-in protections of **apathy** and **somnolent detachment** that allow the baby to go to sleep. During infancy, children use **autistic language**, which takes place on a prototaxic or parataxic level.

B.   Childhood

The childhood stage lasts from the beginning of syntaxic language until the need for playmates of equal status. The child's primary interpersonal relationship continues to be with the mother, who is now differentiated from other persons who nurture the child. Another important relationship during childhood is with imaginary playmates.

C.   Juvenile Era

The juvenile era begins with the need for peers of equal status and continues until the child develops a need for an intimate relationship with a chum, or a single best friend. During the juvenile stage, children should learn how to *compete, compromise,* and *cooperate.* These three abilities, as well as an orientation toward living, help a child develop intimacy, the chief dynamism of the next developmental stage.

D.   Preadolescence

Perhaps the most crucial of Sullivan's stages is preadolescence. This is because mistakes made earlier can be rectified during preadolescence, whereas errors made during preadolescence are nearly impossible to overcome in later life. Preadolescence spans the time from the need for a single best friend until the eruption of lust, or from about age 8 or 9 until puberty. Preadolescents typically form close relationships with friends of the same gender, although cross-gender chumships are also possible. Children who do not learn intimacy during preadolescence have added difficulties relating to potential sexual partners during later stages.

E.   Early Adolescence

With puberty comes the lust dynamism and the beginning of early adolescence. Development during this stage is marked by a coexistence of intimacy with a single friend of the same gender and sexual interest in many persons of the opposite gender. However, if children have no preexisting capacity for intimacy, they may confuse lust with love and develop sexual relationships that are devoid of true intimacy. Sullivan believed that people who emerge from early adolescence in command of both their intimacy and lust dynamisms will have few serious interpersonal difficulties in later life.

F.   Late Adolescence

Chronologically, late adolescence may start at any time after about age 16, but psychologically, it begins when a person is able to feel both intimacy and lust toward the same person. Late adolescence is characterized by a stable pattern of sexual activity and the growth of the syntaxic mode as young people learn how to live in the adult world.

G.   Adulthood

Late adolescence flows into adulthood, a time when a person establishes a stable relationship with a significant other person. However, not everyone reaches emotional adulthood.

VIII. Psychological Disorders

Sullivan believed that disordered behavior can only be understood with reference to a person's interpersonal world. Most of Sullivan's early therapeutic experiences were with schizophrenic patients with whom he had very good success in treating.

IX.   Psychotherapy

Sullivan pioneered the notion of the therapist as a *participant observer* who establishes an interpersonal relationship with the patient. This dyadic relationship between a patient and a participating therapist serves as a model, helping the patient learn to improve relationships with significant others. Sullivanian therapists attempt to help patients develop foresight, discover difficulties in interpersonal relations, and restore their ability to participate in consensually validated experiences.

X.   Related Research

In the years immediately following Sullivan's death, psychologists conducted little empirical research that flowed directly from his theory. However, more recently, a number of researchers have studied the impact of two-person relationships, which relate directly to Sullivan's notion of the therapist as a participant observer in an interpersonal relationship.

A.   Therapist-Patient Relationships

William Henry, Hans Strupp, and their associates at Vanderbilt have used the Structural Analysis of Social Behavior to study the dynamics between a therapist's personality and behavior and a patient's reactions and outcomes. An early study (Henry, Schacht, & Strupp, 1990) reported that patients developed relatively stable behaviors that were consistent with the way their therapists treated them. More recently, a team of researchers (Hilliard, Henry, & Strupp, 2000) found that the early developmental histories of both the therapists and the patients contributed to therapeutic outcome. Indeed, therapists' personal histories had a more powerful effect than their training on patient outcome.

B.   Intimate Relationships with Friends

Some researchers (Yaughn & Nowicki, 1999) have examined Sullivan's notion that healthy interpersonal relationships are complementary, meaning that each person satisfies the healthy needs of the other person. These investigators found partial support for this hypothesis; that is, they found that college women, but not men, reported complementary interpersonal styles with their close friends. They also found that women were more likely than men to engage in a wide variety of activities with their intimate friends.

C.   Imaginary Friends

Researchers have also studied Sullivan's notion of imaginary playmates and have found that children who have identifiable eidetic playmates are more socialized, less aggressive, more intelligent, more creative, and have a better sense of humor than children who do not report having an imaginary playmate (Bouldin & Pratt, 1999; Fern, 1991; Seiffge-Krenke, 1993, 1997).

XI.   Critique of Sullivan

Despite Sullivan's insights into the importance of interpersonal relations, his theory of personality and his approach to psychotherapy have become less popular in recent years. In summary, his theory rates very low on falsifiability and low in its ability to generate research and to present a parsimonious picture of personality. We rate it about average in its capacity to organize knowledge, to guide action, and to be self-consistent.

XII.   Concept of Humanity

Sullivan saw human personality as being shaped largely from interpersonal relations. Thus, his theory places great emphasis on social influences and very little on biological ones. In addition, Sullivanian theory rates high on unconscious determinants of behavior, low on uniqueness, and about average on free choice, optimism, and causality.

TEACHING SUGGESTIONS

1. Sullivan's notion of an imaginary playmate during the preschool years will be
   fascinating to many of your students who will be able to recall their own imaginary
   friend or to recount such a playmate of their own child or of a sibling. After reading
   some of the research on the positive aspects of having had an imaginary friend,
   your students may be more open to discussing their own experiences. Some may be
   able to recall demanding that parents set an extra place at the dining table or
   leaving room in the family car for an imaginary friend. You may wish to conduct
   an informal study of the characteristics of adults who have had an identifiable
   imaginary friend during childhood. Are such people more likely to be men or
   women? What is their birth order? Are they more or less creative than other
   students? You and your students may wish to investigate other questions
   as well.

2. Before discussing Sullivan's theory, you might ask your students if they believe that
   a personality theorist must be psychologically healthy and free from serious
   personal problems in order to construct a useful theory of personality. The
   relatively minor childhood idiosyncrasies of Freud, Jung, Horney, Klein, and Fromm
   do not negate the value of their adult personality theories. Sullivan, however,
   probably had a more difficult childhood than any of these theorists, and his adult
   interpersonal relations were not very satisfying. (See *Beyond Biography* on the
   McGraw-Hill Web site for more information on Sullivan's conflicted sexual
   orientation.) Can a psychiatrist with such an unhappy life be the author of a
   scientific theory? Must scientists and artists be relatively free from
   psychopathology to create useful products? Your students may debate such
   questions as a prelude to studying the life and interpersonal theory of Harry
   Stack Sullivan.

REFERENCES

Bouldin, P., & Pratt, C. (1999). Characteristics of preschool and school-age children with imaginary companions. *Journal of Genetic Psychology, 166*, 397–410.

Fern, T. L. (1991). Identifying the gifted child humorists. *Roeper Review, 14*, 30–34.

Henry, W. P., Schacht, T. E., & Strupp, H. H. (1990). Patient and therapist introject, interpersonal process, and differential psychotherapy outcome. *Journal of Consulting and Clinical Psychology, 58*, 768–774.

Hilliard, R. B., Henry, W. P., & Strupp, H. H. (2000). An interpersonal model of psychotherapy: Linking patient and therapist developmental history, therapeutic process, and types of outcome. *Journal of Consulting and Clinical Psychology, 68*, 125–133.

Seiffge-Krenke, I. (1993). Close friendship and imaginary companions in adolescence. In B. Laursen (Ed.), *Close friendships in adolescence. New directions for child development* (pp. 73-87). San Francisco: Jossey-Bass.

Seiffge-Krenke, I. (1997). Imaginary companions in adolescence: Sign of deficient or positive development? *Journal of Adolescence, 20*, 137–154.

Yaughn, E., & Nowicki, S., Jr. (1999). Close relationships and complementary interpersonal styles among men and women. *Journal of Social Psychology, 139*, 73–78.

CHAPTER 9
ERIKSON: POST-FREUDIAN THEORY

LEARNING OBJECTIVES

After studying Chapter 9, students should be able to:

1. Describe Erikson's ideas on ego psychology and compare Erikson's notion of ego with that of Freud.

2. Compare and contrast Erikson's and Freud's stages of psychological development.

3. List Erikson's stages of psychological development, their crises, their basic strengths, and their core pathologies.

4. Explain Erikson's epigenetic principle.

5. Discuss Erikson's use of psychohistory as a research method.

6. Describe play construction and its role in Erikson's research on gender differences.

7. Describe Erikson's anthropological studies.

8. Describe recent research on Erikson's concepts of identity and generativity.

LECTURE OUTLINE

I. **Overview of Erikson's Post-Freudian Theory**

    Erikson postulated eight stages of psychosocial development through which people progress. Although he differed from Freud in his emphasis on the ego and on social influences, his theory is an extension rather than a repudiation of Freud's psychoanalysis.

II. **Biography of Erik Erikson**

    Erik Erikson was born in Germany in 1902, the son of a Jewish mother and an unknown father. Possibly because he never knew his biological father, Erikson experienced several "identity crises" throughout his life. As a schoolboy, he was accepted neither as a Jew (the religion of his mother and step-father) nor as a Gentile. At age 18 he left home to pursue the life of a wandering artist and to search for self-identity. He gave up that life to teach young children in Vienna, where he met Anna Freud, who introduced him to psychoanalysis. When he moved to the United States and accepted a position at the Harvard Medical School, Erikson had no academic degree but had graduated from the Vienna Psychoanalytic Institute. In addition to Harvard, Erikson taught at Yale, the University of California at Berkeley, and several other institutions. He died in 1994, a month short of his 92nd birthday.

III. The Ego in Post-Freudian Psychology

One of Erikson's chief contributions to personality theory was his emphasis on ego rather than id functions. According to Erikson, the ego is the center of personality and is responsible for a unified sense of self. It consists of three interrelated facets: the *body ego*, the *ego ideal*, and *ego identity*. Major changes in ego can take place at any stage, but they are most likely to occur during adolescence.

A. Society's Influence

The ego develops within a given society and is influenced by child-rearing practices and other cultural customs. Historically, all cultures and nations have developed a **pseudospecies**, or a fictional notion that they are superior to other cultures.

B. Epigenetic Principle

The ego develops according to the epigenetic principle; that is, it grows according to a genetically established rate and in a fixed sequence. Part of each developmental stage exists before that stage reaches its zenith, and part continues to grow during the ascendancy to later stages.

IV. Stages of Psychosocial Development

Each of the eight stages of development is marked by a conflict between a **syntonic** (harmonious) element and a **dystonic** (disruptive) element, which produces a **basic strength** or ego quality. Also, from adolescence on, each stage is characterized by an identity crisis or turning point, which may produce either adaptive or maladaptive adjustment.

A.   Infancy

Erikson's view of infancy (the first year of life) is similar to Freud's concept of the oral stage, except that Erikson expanded the notion of incorporation beyond the mouth to include sense organs such as the eyes and ears.

1.   Oral-Sensory Mode

The psychosexual mode of infancy is oral-sensory, which is characterized by both receiving and accepting.

2.   Basic Trust Versus Basic Mistrust

The psychosocial crisis of infancy is basic trust versus basic mistrust. For future psychological growth, the infant must learn both to trust (the syntonic element) and to mistrust (the dystonic element).

3.   Hope: The Basic Strength of Infancy

From the crisis between basic trust and basic mistrust emerges hope, the basic strength of infancy. Infants who do not develop hope retreat from the world, and this *withdrawal* is the **core pathology** of infancy.

B.   Early Childhood

The second to third year of life is early childhood, a period that compares to Freud's anal stage but also includes mastery of other body functions such as walking, urinating, and holding.

1.   Anal-Urethral-Muscular Mode

The psychosexual mode of early childhood is anal-urethral-muscular, and children of this age behave both *impulsively* and *compulsively*.

2.   Autonomy Versus Shame and Doubt

The psychosocial crisis of early childhood is autonomy versus shame and doubt. Again, both the syntonic and dystonic elements are essential for proper psychosocial growth.

3.   Will: The Basic Strength of Early Childhood

The psychosocial crisis between autonomy on the one hand and shame and doubt on the other produces will, the basic strength of early childhood. Early willfulness is the beginning of free will, which reaches its zenith during adulthood. Early childhood's core pathology is **compulsion**.

C.   Play Age

From about the third to the fifth year, children experience the play age, a period that parallels Freud's phallic phase. Unlike Freud, however, Erikson saw the Oedipus complex as an early model of lifelong playfulness and a drama played out in children's minds as they attempt to understand the basic facts of life.

1.   Genital-Locomotor Mode

The primary psychosexual mode of the play age is genital-locomotor, meaning that children have both an interest in genital activity and an increasing ability to move around.

2.   Initiative Versus Guilt

The psychosocial crisis of the play age is initiative versus guilt, and the proper balance between the two produces purpose, the basic strength of the play age.

3.   Purpose: The Basic Strength of the Play Age

The conflict between initiative and guilt helps children to act with purpose and to set goals. But if children have too little purpose, they develop **inhibition**, the core pathology of the play age.

D.   School Age

The period from about 6 to 12 or 13 years of age is called the school age, a time of psychosexual latency and of psychosocial growth beyond the family.

1.   Latency

Because sexual development is latent during the school age, children can use their energies to learn the customs of their culture, including both formal and informal education.

2.   Industry Versus Inferiority

The psychosocial crisis of this age is industry vs. inferiority. Children need to learn to work hard, but they also must develop some sense of inferiority.

3.   Competence: The Basic Strength of the School Age

From the conflict of industry and inferiority emerges competence, the basic strength of the school age. Lack of industry leads to **inertia**, the core pathology of this stage.

E.   Adolescence

Adolescence begins with puberty and is marked by a person's struggle to find **ego identity**. It is a time of psychosexual growth, but it is also a period of psychosocial latency, when little social growth is expected.

1.   Puberty

The psychosexual mode of adolescence is puberty, or genital maturation. Puberty itself presents few sexual problems, but it signals a search for personal identity.

2.   Identity Versus Identity Confusion

The psychosocial crisis of adolescence is identity versus identity confusion. Psychologically healthy individuals emerge from adolescence with a sense of who they are and what they believe; however, some identity confusion is normal, even for psychologically mature teenagers.

3.   Fidelity: The Basic Strength of Adolescence

The conflict between identity and identity confusion produces fidelity, or faith in some ideological view of the future. Lack of belief in one's own selfhood results in **role repudiation**, the core pathology of adolescence. Role repudiation, an inability to bring together one's various self-images, can take the form of either *diffidence* or *defiance*.

F.   Young Adulthood

Young adulthood, from about age 18 to 30, begins with the acquisition of intimacy and ends with the development of generativity, or the training of the next generation.

1.   Genitality

The psychosexual mode of young adulthood is genitality, which is expressed as mutual trust between partners in a stable sexual relationship.

2.   Intimacy Versus Isolation

The psychosocial crisis of young adulthood is intimacy versus isolation. Intimacy is the ability to fuse one's identity with that of another without fear of losing it, whereas isolation is the fear of losing one's identity in an intimate relationship.

3.   Love: The Basic Strength of Young Adulthood

The crisis between intimacy and isolation results in the capacity to love, or mature devotion that overcomes basic differences between two people. The core pathology of young adulthood is **exclusivity**, or inability to love another person.

G.   Adulthood

The period from about age 31 to 60 is adulthood, a time when people make significant contributions to society.

1.   Procreativity

The psychosexual mode of adulthood is procreativity, or the caring for one's children, the children of others, and the material products of one's society.

2.   Generativity Versus Stagnation

The psychosocial crisis of adulthood is generativity versus stagnation, and the successful resolution of this crisis results in **care.**

3.   Care: The Basic Strength of Adulthood

Erikson defined care as taking care of the persons and products that one has learned to care for. The core pathology of adulthood is **rejectivity,** or the rejection of certain individuals or groups that one is unwilling to take care of.

H.   Old Age

The final stage of development is old age, from about age 60 until death. This time can be productive both for individuals and for their society.

1.   Generalized Sensuality

The psychosexual mode of old age is generalized sensuality, or taking pleasure in a variety of sensations and an appreciation of the traditional lifestyle of the opposite sex.

2.   Integrity Versus Despair

The psychosocial crisis of old age is the struggle between integrity (the maintenance of ego-identity) and despair (the surrender of hope).

3.   Wisdom: The Basic Strength of Old Age

The struggle between integrity and despair may produce wisdom (the basic strength of old age), but it may also lead to **disdain,** a core pathology marked by feelings of being finished or helpless.

V.   Erikson's Methods of Investigation

Erikson relied mostly on anthropology, psychohistory, and play construction to explain and describe human personality.

A. Anthropological Studies

Erikson's two most important anthropological studies were of the Sioux of South Dakota and the Yurok of northern California. Both studies demonstrated his notion that culture and history help shape personality.

B. Psychohistory

Erikson combined the methods of psychoanalysis and historical research to study several personalities, most notably Gandhi and Luther. In both cases, the individual experienced an identity crisis that produced a basic strength rather than a core pathology.

C. Play Construction

Erikson's technique of play construction became controversial when he found that 10- to 12-year-old boys used toys to construct elongated objects and to produce themes of rising and falling. In contrast, girls arranged toys in low and peaceful scenes. Erikson concluded that anatomical differences between the sexes play a role in personality development.

VI. Related Research

Erikson's theory has generated a moderately large body of research, especially in the areas of identity and generativity.

A. Identity in Early Adulthood

Ravenna Helson and Jennifer Pals (2000) have studied identity in young women and found that those with anchored identity had a clear and strong sense of well-being and saw themselves as a separate and equal partner in their marriage Also, identity established in early adulthood was associated with stable marriages and high levels of creativity. In addition, Pals (1999) found that women who had solid identity and high creative potential at age 21 were more likely than other women to have had a challenging and creative work experience at age 52.

B.   Generativity in Midlife

People high in generativity should have a lifestyle marked by creating and passing on knowledge, values, and ideals to a younger generation, and should benefit from a pattern of helping younger people. Research by Dan McAdams and colleagues (McAdams, 1999; McAdams, Diamond, de St. Aubin, & Mansfield, 1997; McAdams & de St. Aubin, 1992) found that adults at midlife who contributed to the well-being of young people had a clear sense of who they were and what life had to offer them. Other research from this team found that highly generative adults were likely to have coherent and cohesive life stories and identities. Similarly, Pratt, Norris, Arnold and Filyer (1999) found that generativity is an important component of a mature adulthood.

VII. Critique of Erikson

Although Erikson's work is a logical extension of Freud's psychoanalysis, it offers a new way of looking at human development. As a useful theory, it rates high on internal consistency and on its ability to generate research. We rate the theory about average on its ability to be falsified, to organize knowledge, to guide the practitioner, and to express ideas in a simple yet comprehensive fashion.

VIII. Concept of Humanity

Erikson viewed humans as basically social animals who have limited free choice and who are motivated by past experiences, which may be either conscious or unconscious. In addition, we rate Erikson high on both optimism and uniqueness of individuals.

TEACHING SUGGESTIONS

1.   During the mid-1960, Richard Evans interviewed Erikson on film. Videotapes of their talk are available in two parts, each 50 minutes in length. In Part 1, Erikson

covers his relationship with Freud and discusses the eight stages of development. In Part 2, Erikson elaborates on ego identity and identity crisis and discusses cross-cultural research. These interviews can be rented or purchased from

Audio-Visual Services

University Division of Media and Learning Resources

The Pennsylvania State University

University Park, PA 16802

Phone (814) 865-6314 or 1-800-826-0132

2. Another video of interest to students is called *Erik Erikson: A Life's Work*. This videocassette contains biographical information on Erikson, an interview in which Erikson discusses his basic theory, and a presentation of Erikson's eight stages that highlight the dichotomies at each stage. This video is available from

Insight Media

2162 Broadway

New York, NY 10024-6620

Phone (212) 721-6316 or 1-800-233-9910

3. College students will be curious about their own level of identity and intimacy. Doreen Rosenthal, Ross Gurney, and Susan Moore (1981) developed the Erikson Psychosocial Stage Inventory (EPSI) to measure how completely people have resolved each of their first six psychosocial conflicts. The EPSI has 12 items for each of six subscales: Trust, Autonomy, Initiative, Industry, Identity, and Intimacy. Half the items reflect successful resolution of a crisis and half reflect unsuccessful resolution. Respondents pick one of five choices from "almost always true" (5) to "hardly ever true" (1) on a 5-point Likert rating scale. The EPSI is most appropriate for adolescents and late adolescents, but college students can learn

much about themselves from this inventory. Items for the scale are found in the Appendix of Rosenthal, Gurney, & Moore (1981). A manual is available from the senior author, whose address is in the article.

REFERENCES

Helson, R., & Pals, J. (2000). Creative potential, creative achievement, and personal growth. *Journal of Personality, 68*, 1–27.

McAdams, D. P. (1999). Personal narratives and the life story. In L. A. Pervin & O. P. John (Eds.), *Handbook of personality: Theory and research* (pp. 478–500). New York: Guilford.

McAdams, D. P., & de St. Aubin, E. (1992). A theory of generativity and its assessment through self-report, behavioral acts, and narrative themes in autobiography. *Journal of Personality and Social Psychology, 62*, 1003–1015.

McAdams, D. P, Diamond, A., de St. Aubin, E., & Mansfield, E. D. (1997). Stories of commitment: The psychosocial construction of generative lives. *Journal of Personality and Social Psychology, 72*, 678–694.

Pals, J. (1999). Identity consolidation in early adulthood. *Journal of Personality, 67*, 295–329.

Pratt, M. W, Norris, J. E., Arnold, M. L., & Filyer, R. (1999). Generativity and moral development as predictors of value—socialization narratives for young persons across the adult life span: From lessons learned to stories shared. *Psychology and Aging, 14*, 414–426.

Rosenthal, D. A., Gurney, R. M., & Moore, S. M. (1981). From trust to intimacy: A new inventory for examining Erikson's stages of psychosocial development. *Journal of Youth and Adolescence, 10*, 525–537.

CHAPTER 10
SKINNER: BEHAVIORAL ANALYSIS

LEARNING OBJECTIVES

After studying Chapter 10, students should be able to:

1. Discuss the contributions of E. L. Thorndike and J. B. Watson to Skinner's learning theory.

2. Explain Skinner's philosophy of science.

3. Discuss the effects of positive reinforcement, negative reinforcement, and punishment on behavior.

4. Explain the differences between operant and classical conditioning.

5. Describe the process of shaping behavior.

6. Distinguish between conditioned and generalized reinforcers.

7. Identify and give examples of four different schedules of reinforcement.

8. Discuss ways in which natural selection influences personality.

9. Discuss Skinner's view on inner states and complex behavior.

10. List the methods of social control and self-control, according to Skinner.

11. Explain Skinner's approach to understanding the unhealthy personality.

LECTURE OUTLINE

I. **Overview of Skinner's Behavior Analysis**

Unlike any theory discussed to this point, the **radical behaviorism** of B. F. Skinner avoids speculations about hypothetical constructs and concentrates almost exclusively on observable behavior. Besides being a radical behaviorist, Skinner was also a *determinist* and an *environmentalist*; that is, he rejected the notion of free will, and he emphasized the primacy of environmental influences on behavior.

II.   **Biography of B. F. Skinner**

B. F. Skinner was born into an upper-middle class family in Pennsylvania in 1904.
As a youngster, he was interested in constructing gadgets, playing music, and writing
novels. While in college, Skinner wanted to be a writer, and after graduation he
spent a year trying to achieve this goal. Having no success, he changed his identity
from that of a writer to psychologist. He spent the next eight years at Harvard,
five of which were after he earned his Ph.D. Skinner's first job came at age 32 when
he accepted a teaching and research position at the University of Minnesota.
During his nine years in Minneapolis, he invented a controversial and well-
publicized baby tender and also trained pigeons to guide bombs into enemy ships.
After World War II, Skinner moved to the University of Indiana, but not before he
had written *Walden Two* and realized his earlier ambition of being a writer. In 1948
(the same year *Walden Two* was published), he returned to Harvard where he
remained until his death in 1990. (For more information on Skinner's search for
identity, see *Beyond Biography* on the McGraw-Hill Web site.)

III. **Precursors to Skinner's Scientific Behaviorism**

Modern learning theory received a strong impetus from the work of Edward L.
Thorndike who began working with animals more than a century ago. Thorndike's
law of effect stated that responses followed by a satisfier tend to be learned, a
concept that anticipated Skinner's use of reinforcement to shape behavior.
The second person to influence Skinner was John Watson, who argued that
psychology must deal with the control and prediction of behavior and that
behavior—not introspection, consciousness, or the mind—is the basic data
of scientific psychology.

IV.   Scientific Behaviorism

Skinner believed that human behavior, like any other natural phenomena, is subject to the laws of science, and that psychologists should not attribute inner motivations to it. Although he rejected internal states (thoughts, emotions, desires, etc.) as being outside the realm of science, Skinner did not deny their existence. He simply insisted that they should not be used to explain behavior.

A.   Philosophy of Science

Skinner believed that scientific behaviorism allows for an interpretation of behavior but not an explanation of its causes. Scientists should begin by studying simple phenomena and later evolve generalized principles that permit interpretation.

B.   Characteristics of Science

Skinner believed that science has three main characteristics. First, science is cumulative; second, it is an attitude that values empirical observation, and third, it is a search for order and lawful relationships. Skinner believed that the primary goals of science are to predict, control, and describe. He also believed that scientific behaviorism can accomplish each of these goals because it rests on the assumption that human behavior is determined and lawful.

V.   Conditioning

Skinner recognized two kinds of conditioning: classical and operant.

A.   Classical Conditioning

In classical conditioning (also called respondent or Pavlovian), a neutral (conditioned) stimulus is paired with an unconditioned stimulus a number of times until it is capable of bringing about a previously unconditioned response, now called the conditioned response. An important early example of classical conditioning is the case of Albert B. (Little Albert).

B.   Operant Conditioning

With operant conditioning, reinforcement is used to increase the probability that a given behavior will recur. Thus, in classical conditioning, behavior is *elicited,* whereas in operant conditioning it is *emitted.* Three factors are essential in operant conditioning: (1) the *antecedent,* or environment in which behavior takes place; (2) the *behavior,* or response; and (3) the *consequence* that follows the behavior.

1.   Shaping

Psychologists and others use **successive approximations** to shape complex behavior. With this procedure, gross approximations of the target behavior are initially reinforced, but later only more specific responses are followed by reward. Different histories of reinforcement result in **operant discrimination**, meaning that different people will respond differently to the same environmental contingencies. People may also respond similarly to somewhat different environmental stimuli, a process Skinner called **stimulus generalization**.

2.   Reinforcement

Anything within the environment that strengthens a behavior is a **reinforcer**. Any behavior that increases the probability that the species or the individual will survive tends to be strengthened. **Positive reinforcement** is any stimulus that, when added to a situation, increases the probability that a given behavior will occur. **Negative reinforcement** is the strengthening of behavior by removing an aversive stimulus. Both positive and negative reinforcement strengthen behavior.

3.   Punishment

The presentation of an aversive stimulus or the removal of a positive one is called punishment. The effects of punishment are much less predictable than those of reward, an observation that led Skinner to de-emphasize punishment. Other undesirable effects of punishment include the suppression of behavior, the conditioning of negative feelings toward the punished, and the inappropriate spread of effects. Both punishment and reinforcement can result from either natural consequences or from human imposition.

4.   Conditioned and Generalized Reinforcers

Conditioned reinforcers are those things that are not by nature satisfying (e.g., money), but that can become so because they are associated with a primary reinforcers such as food. Generalized reinforcers are conditioned reinforcers that have become associated with several primary reinforcers. Attention, approval, affection, submission to others, and money are all conditioned generalized reinforcers.

5.   Schedules of Reinforcement

Reinforcement can follow behavior on either a **continuous schedule** or on an **intermittent schedule**. There are four basic intermittent schedules: (1) **fixed-ratio**, on which the organism is reinforced intermittently according to the number of responses it makes; (2) **variable-ratio**, on which the organism is reinforced after an *average* of a predetermined number of responses; (3) **fixed-interval**, on which the organism is reinforced for the first response following a designated period of time; and (4) **variable interval,** on which the organism is reinforced after the lapse of varied periods of time.

6.   Extinction

The tendency of a previously acquired response to become progressively weakened upon nonreinforcement is called extinction. **Operant extinction** takes place when the experimenter systematically withholds reinforcement of previously learned behavior until the probability of that behavior diminishes to zero. The rate of operant extinction depends largely on the schedule of reinforcement under which the behavior was learned.

VI.   The Human Organism

Skinner believed that human behavior is shaped by three forces: (1) natural selection, (2) cultural practices, and (3) the individual's history of reinforcement, which we discussed above.

A.   Natural Selection

As a species, our behavior is shaped by the *contingencies of survival,* that is, those behaviors (e.g., sex and aggression) that were beneficial to the human species tended to survive, whereas those that did not tended to drop out.

B.   Cultural Evolution

Those societies that evolved certain cultural practices (e.g., tool making and verbal behavior) tended to survive. Thus, such cultural practices are reinforcing to the group, though not always to the individual.

C.   Inner States

Skinner did not ignore various inner states, such as self-awareness, drives, emotions, and purposes and intentions, but he rejected explanations of behavior in terms of any nonobservable hypothetical construct.

1.   Self-Awareness

Humans not only have consciousness, but they also are aware of themselves as part of their environment. Private events, such as self-awareness, are part of our inner environment, but they cannot be directly communicated to others.

2.   Drives

To Skinner, drives refer to the effects of deprivation and satiation and thus are related to the probability of certain behaviors. Drives, however, are not the causes of behavior.

3.   Emotions

Skinner believed that emotions can be accounted for by the contingencies of survival and the contingencies of reinforcement. Like drives, they do not cause behavior.

4.   Purpose and Intention

Although purpose and intention exist within a person's inner environment, they cannot be directly seen by others and are therefore beyond scientific study.

D.   Complex Behavior

Although human behavior is subject to the same principles of operant conditioning as simple animal behavior, it is much more complex and difficult to predict and control.

1.   Higher Mental Processes

Higher mental processes (e.g., thinking and reminiscing) are covert behaviors that take place within the skin but not inside a "mind." As behaviors, they are subject to the same contingencies of reinforcement as are overt behaviors.

2.   Creativity

Skinner explained creativity as a consequence of mutations and natural selection. To him, creativity is the result of random or accidental behaviors that happen to be rewarded.

3.   Unconscious Behavior

Humans rarely observe the relationship between their genetic and environmental variables and their own behavior. In this sense, Skinner said, most behavior is unconscious. Many behaviors are automatic or unconscious because not thinking about them has been reinforced.

4.   Dreams

Skinner viewed dreams as covert and symbolic forms of behavior that are subject to the same contingencies of reinforcement as any other behavior.

5.   Social Behavior

The group mind does not exist; only individuals can behave. During the history of the species, humans have formed groups because to do so was reinforcing. However, living within a particular society is not always reinforcing, and people sometimes try to escape both from families and from nations.

E.   Control of Human Behavior

Ultimately, all human behavior is controlled by the environment; will power plays no part.

1.   Social Control

Societies exercise control over their members through laws, rules, and customs that transcend any one person's means of countercontrol. Skinner identified four basic methods of social control: (1) *operant conditioning*, including positive and negative reinforcement and punishment: (2) *describing contingencies*, or using language to inform people of the consequence of their behaviors; (3) *deprivation and satiation*, techniques that increase the likelihood that people will behave in a certain way; and (4) *physical restraint*, including the jailing of criminals.

2.   Self-Control

Although Skinner denied the existence of free will, he did recognize that people manipulate variables within their own environment and thus exercise some measure of self-control. Skinner listed at least seven techniques of self-control: (1) *physical restraint*, (2) *physical aids*, such as tools; (3) *changing environmental stimuli*; (4) *arranging the environment* to allow escape from aversive stimuli; (5) *drugs*; and (6) *doing something else*.

VII.   The Unhealthy Personality

Social and self control sometimes produce counteracting strategies and inappropriate behaviors.

A.   Counteracting Strategies

People can counteract excessive social control by escaping from it, revolting against it, or by using passive resistance.

B.   Inappropriate Behaviors

Inappropriate behaviors follow from self-defeating techniques of counteracting social control or from unsuccessful attempts at self-control. Skinner listed several common patterns of inappropriate behavior, all of which can be reinforcing: (1) taking *drugs*; (2) engaging in *excessively vigorous behavior* as a means of escaping from an aversive stimulus; (3) using *excessively restrained behavior*, which may result in stubbornness or even hysterical paralysis; (4) *blocking out reality*, or paying no attention to aversive stimuli; (5) expressing inappropriate behaviors that are based on *defective self-knowledge*; and (6) using aversive self-stimulation, such as *self-punishment* or masochistic behaviors.

VIII. Psychotherapy

Skinner, of course, was not a psychotherapist, and he even criticized psychotherapy as being one of the major obstacles to a scientific study of human behavior. Nevertheless, others have used operant conditioning principles to shape behavior in a therapeutic setting. Behavior therapists play an active role in the treatment process, using behavior modification techniques and pointing out the positive consequences of some behaviors and the aversive effects of others.

IX.   Related Research

Skinner's theory has generated more research than nearly any other personality theory. In general, much of this research can be divided into two questions: (1) How does conditioning affect personality? and (2) How does personality affect conditioning?

A.   How Conditioning Affects Personality

A multitude of studies have demonstrated that operant conditioning and shaping can change personality (that is, behavior). For example, Stephen Higgins and colleagues (2000) found that a contingency management program was more effective in deterring cocaine use than was a traditional counseling approach.

B.   How Personality Affects Conditioning

Some research suggests that different personalities may react differently to the same environmental stimuli, meaning that the same reinforcement strategies will not have the same effect on all people. Pickering and Gray (1999) and Corr, Pickering, and Gray (1997) found that learning was improved for participants high in anxiety but was diminished for those low in anxiety. Other research has demonstrated that infants as young as 2 or 3 months of age react differently to conditioning tasks, and that extraverted adults seem to learn better from reinforcers, whereas introverts learn more quickly from punishment.

X.   Critique of Skinner

Skinner's ideas have been controversial for nearly 60 years, yet they have been widely adopted by therapists, parents, teachers, and others who wish to change or control human behavior. On the six criteria of a useful theory, we rate Skinner's approach very high on its ability to generate research and to guide action, high on its ability to be falsified, and about average on its ability to organize knowledge. In addition, it rates very high on internal consistency and high on simplicity.

XI.   Concept of Humanity

On the one hand, Skinner had an extremely deterministic view of human nature, but, on the other hand, he remained somewhat optimistic about humanity's ability to improve itself. In addition, Skinner's concept of humanity was a completely causal one that emphasized unconscious behavior and the uniqueness of each person's history of reinforcement within a mostly social environment.

TEACHING SUGGESTIONS

1. Perhaps the most widely known debate in the history of American psychology took place during the mid-1950s and early 1960s between Skinner and Carl Rogers. The two men had fundamental philosophical differences regarding the issue of freedom and control, an issue that remains unresolved. Because the argument over people's ability to exercise some control over their actions is still unsettled, the instructor may wish to conduct either a formal or an informal debate on the issue of environmental control versus individual freedom. Although no solution is likely to come from such a debate, the exercise should be stimulating and informative. It may help some students develop a richer understanding of Skinner's position that ultimately all control of behavior resides outside the individual.

2. Several videotape interviews with Skinner are available to show to your class. One such set was made by Richard Evans, who has also interviewed several other personality theorists. Produced in 1966, the Evans/Skinner dialog is in two 50-minute parts. In Part 1, Skinner talks about Freudian theory and explains important concepts of operant conditioning. In Part 2, Skinner discusses his novel, *Walden Two*, and explains how operant conditioning can apply to society. These interviews are available for rent or purchase from

    Audio-Visual Services

    University Division of Media and Learning Resources

    The Pennsylvania State University

    University Park, PA 16802

    Phone (814) 865-6314 or 1-800-826-0132

Skinner has also sat for interviews on the application of operant conditioning principles to education and counseling. A two-part interview on education and a one-part program on counseling can be rented or purchased from

Psychological & Educational Films

3334 East Coast Hwy, Suite 252

Corona Del Mar, CA 92625

Phone (714) 494-5079

REFERENCES

Corr, T. J., Pickering, A. D., & Gray, J. A. (1997). Personality, punishment and procedural learning: A test of J. A. Gray's anxiety theory. *Journal of Personality, Social Psychology, 73*, 337–344.

Higgins, S. T., Wong, C. J., Badger, G. J., Haug Ogden, D. E., & Dantona, R. L. (2000). Contingent reinforcement increases cocaine abstinence during outpatient treatment and 1 year of follow-up. *Journal of Consulting and Clinical Psychology, 68*, 64–72.

Pickering, A. D., & Gray, J. A. (1999). The neuroscience of personality. In L. A. Pervin and O. P. John (Eds.), *Handbook of personality: Theory and research* (pp. 277–299). New York: Guilford Press.

CHAPTER 11
BANDURA: SOCIAL COGNITIVE THEORY

LEARNING OBJECTIVES

After studying Chapter 11, students should be able to:

1. Describe Bandura's concept of human agency.

2. Define reciprocal determinism.

3. Describe specific examples of how chance encounters and fortuitous events influence behavior.

4. Define self-efficacy and discuss its possible effects on behavior.

5. Describe the sources of self-efficacy and evaluate their relative importance in contributing to self-efficacy.

6. Define proxy agency and explain how it relates to personal agency.

7. Define collective efficacy and give several examples.

8. Describe external and internal factors in self-regulation.

9. Give examples of Bandura's ideas on selective activation and disengagement of internal control.

10. Explain the processes governing observational learning.

11. Discuss Bandura's explanation of how dysfunctional behaviors are acquired.

LECTURE OUTLINE

I. Overview of Bandura's Social Cognitive Theory

Bandura's social cognitive theory assumes an agentic perspective, meaning that humans have some capacity to exercise control over events that shape their lives. Bandura believes that (1) human activity is a function of behavior, person variables, and the environment; (2) people have the capacity for language and self-reflectiveness; (3) people can learn in the absence of a response; (4) humans have the ability to see the connection between their actions and the consequences of their actions; and (5) people are quite flexible and can learn a wide variety of responses.

II. Biography of Albert Bandura

Albert Bandura was born in Canada in 1925, but he has spent his entire professional life in the United States. He completed a Ph.D. in clinical psychology at the University of Iowa in 1951 and since then has worked almost entirely at Stanford University, where he continues to be the most active of all personality theorists in investigating hypotheses generated by his social cognitive theory.

III. Human Agency

Bandura believes that human agency is the essence of humanness; that is, humans are defined by their ability to organize, regulate, and enact behaviors that they believe will produce desirable consequences. Human agency has four core features: (1) *intentionality*, or a proactive commitment to actions that may bring about desired outcomes; (2) *foresight*, or the ability to set goals; (3) *self-reactiveness*, which includes monitoring their progress toward fulfilling their choices; and (4) *self-reflectiveness*, which allows people to think about and evaluate their motives, values, and life goals.

IV. Reciprocal Determinism

Bandura holds that human functioning is molded by the reciprocal interaction of (1) *behavior*; (2) *personal factors*, including cognition; and (3) the *environment*—a model he calls reciprocal determinism. Bandura sees no incompatibility between human agency and determinism. Behavior is influenced by external forces, but people retain the capacity to choose to behave in ways that influence their environment, which then helps shape their future behavior.

A.   Differential Contributions

Bandura does not suggest that the three factors in the reciprocal determinism model make equal contributions to behavior. The relative influence of behavior, environment, and person depends on which factor is strongest at any particular moment.

B.   Chance Encounters and Fortuitous Events

The lives of many people have been fundamentally changed by a chance meeting with another person or by a fortuitous, unexpected event. Chance encounters and fortuitous events enter the reciprocal determinism paradigm at the environment point, after which they influence behavior in much the same way as do planned events.

V.   Self System

Bandura views the self system as a set of cognitive structures that gives some degree of consistency to peoples' behavior. The self system allows people to observe and symbolize their own behavior and to regulate it on the basis of how they see the future. Bandura believes that people are not so flexible as to react to every environmental change, but he also rejects the idea that people are motivated by a small number of traits or personal dispositions. An important part of the self system is self-efficacy.

A.   Self-Efficacy

How people behave in a particular situation depends in part on their self-efficacy. Self-efficacy combines with environmental variables, prior behavior, and other personal variables to predict behavior.

1.   What Is Self-Efficacy?

Self-efficacy refers to people's beliefs about their ability to exercise some control over their own functioning. Efficacy expectations differ from *outcome expectations,* which refer to people's prediction of the likely consequences of their behavior. Self-efficacy differs from self-esteem in that self-efficacy is specific to a given situation, whereas self-esteem is more global.

2.   What Contributes to Self-Efficacy?

Self-efficacy is acquired, enhanced, or decreased by any one or combination of four sources: (1) enactive attainments, or **mastery experiences**, which ordinarily are the most powerful source; (2) **social modeling**, or observing someone else succeed or fail at a task; (3) **social persuasion,** or listening to a trusted person's encouraging words; and (4) **physical and emotional states** such as anxiety, which usually lowers self-efficacy.

3.   Does Self-Efficacy Predict Performance?

High and low self-efficacy combine with responsive and unresponsive environments to produce four possible predictive variables. High efficacy and a responsive environment is the best predictor of successful outcomes; low efficacy and a responsive environment may produce depression as people see that others can do what they cannot; high efficacy and an unresponsive environment may result in people intensifying their efforts, or, if that fails, giving up; and low efficacy and an unresponsive environment often leads to apathy and learned helplessness.

B.   Proxy Agency

Bandura recognizes the influence of proxy agency through which people exercise partial control over everyday living by relying on the efforts of others. Successful living in the 21st century requires people to seek proxies to supply their food, deliver information, provide transportation, and so forth. Without the use of proxies, modern people would be forced to spend most of their time seeking the necessities of survival.

C.   Collective Efficacy

Collective efficacy refers to the level of confidence that people have that their combined efforts will produce social change. Personal efficacy, proxy agency, and collective efficacy complement each another to shape people's lifestyles. At least four factors can lower collective efficacy. First, events in other parts of the world can leave people with a sense of helplessness; second, complex technology can reduce people's collective confidence; third, entrenched bureaucracies discourage change; and fourth, the scope and magnitude of problems such as wars, famine, overpopulation, and crime contribute to a sense of powerlessness.

D.   Self-Regulation

By using reflective thought, humans can manipulate their environments and produce desired consequences of their actions, which gives them some ability to regulate their own behavior. People use both reactive and proactive strategies for self-regulation; that is, they reactively attempt to reduce the gap between accomplishment and goals, and they proactively set newer and higher goals. People have the capacity to manipulate external factors that influence their future behavior, but they also have the ability to regulate internal factors by monitoring their behavior and evaluating it in terms of their personal goals.

1.   External Factors in Self-Regulation

Two external factors contribute to self-regulation. First, *standards of evaluation* provide people with an external standard, such as par in golf or grades in a college course. Second, *external reinforcement* helps regulate the behavior of those people who are not satisfied with internal rewards. External factors in self-regulation include rules learned from others, observation of others, praise, money, food, and so forth.

2.   Internal Factors in Self-Regulation

Bandura recognizes three internal requirements for self-regulation: (1) *self-observation*, (2) *judgmental process,* and (3) *self reaction*. Self-observation suggests that we must monitor our own performance and have some awareness of what we are doing. Judgmental processes imply that we judge our performance according to our goals, our personal standards, standards of reference, our evaluation of our behavior, and our level of belief that success is due to our own efforts. Self-reaction means that we respond positively or negatively to our behavior depending on how it measures up to our personal standards.

3.   Self-Regulation Through Moral Agency

Internalized self-sanctions prevent people from violating personal moral standards either through selective activation or disengagement of internal control. **Selective activation** refers to the notion that self-regulatory influences are not automatic but operate only if activated. It also means that people react differently in different situations depending on their evaluation of the situation. **Disengagement of internal control** suggests that people are capable of separating themselves from the negative consequences of their behavior. People in ambiguous moral situations, who are uncertain that their behavior is consistent with their own social and moral standards of conduct, may separate their conduct from its injurious consequences through disengagement of internal standards. Ambiguous moral behavior can be disengaged or selectively activated through four techniques.

a.   Redefine the Behavior

With redefinition of behavior, people justify otherwise reprehensible actions by cognitively restructuring them, a manipulation that allows people to minimize or escape responsibility. People can use redefinition of behavior to disengage themselves from reprehensible conduct in three ways: (1) *moral justification*, as when otherwise unacceptable behavior is transformed into desirable or even noble behavior; (2) making advantageous, or *palliative comparisons* between their behavior and the even more reprehensible behavior of others; (3) using *euphemistic labels* to change the moral tone of their behavior.

b.   Disregard or Distort the Consequences of Behavior

Second, people can *distort or obscure the relationship between behavior and its injurious consequences*. People can do this by minimizing, disregarding, or distorting the consequences of their behavior.

c.   Dehumanize or Blame the Victims

Third, people can blur responsibility for their actions either by *dehumanizing their victims* or by *attributing blame to them*.

d.   Displace or Diffuse Responsibility

Fourth, people can disengage themselves from personal responsibility by *displacing responsibility onto others* or by *diffusing* it among a number of other people.

VI.   Learning

People learn through observing others and by attending to the consequences of their own actions. Although Bandura believes that reinforcement aids learning, he contends that people can learn in the absence of reinforcement and even in the absence of a response.

A.   Observational Learning

Bandura believes that reinforcement is not always necessary for learning, as when we learn from observing others. Observational learning is more efficient than learning through direct experience.

1.   Modeling

The core of observational learning is modeling, which is more than simple imitation; it involves adding and subtracting from observed behavior. Modeling also calls for generalizing from one observation to another. At least three principles influence modeling: (1) people are most likely to model high-status people; (2) people who lack skill, power, or status are most likely to model; and (3) people tend to model behavior that they see as important to themselves, and they are more likely to model behavior they see as being rewarding to the model.

2.   Processes Governing Observational Learning

Bandura recognized four processes that govern observational learning: (1) *attention*, or noticing what a model does; (2) *representation*, or symbolically representing new response patterns in memory; (3) *behavior production*, or producing the behavior that one observes; and (4) *motivation*, or being motivated to perform the observed behavior.

B.   Enactive Learning

All behavior is followed by some consequence, but whether that consequence reinforces the behavior depends on the person's cognitive evaluation of the situation. Learning is enhanced when people (1) notice the effects of their actions, retain this information, and use it as a guide for future actions; (2) think about the future consequences of their actions; and (3) attend to the present consequences of their actions.

VII.   Dysfunctional Behavior

Dysfunctional behavior is learned through the mutual interaction of the person (including cognitive and neurophysiological processes), the environment (including interpersonal relations), and behavioral factors (especially previous experiences with reinforcement).

A.   Depression

People who develop depressive reactions often (1) underestimate their successes and overestimate their failures, (2) set personal standards too high, or (3) treat themselves badly for their faults.

B.   Phobias

Phobias are learned by (1) direct contact, (2) inappropriate generalization, and (3) observational experiences. Once learned they are maintained by negative reinforcement, as the person is reinforced for avoiding fear-producing situations.

C.   Aggressive Behaviors

When carried to extremes, aggressive behaviors can become dysfunctional. In a study of children observing live and filmed models being aggressive, Bandura and his associates found that aggression tends to foster more aggression.

VIII. Therapy

The goal of social cognitive therapy is self-regulation. Bandura noted three levels of treatment: (1) *induction* of change, (2) *generalization* of change to other appropriate situations, and (3) *maintenance* of newly acquired functional behaviors. Social cognitive therapists sometimes use **systematic desensitization**, a technique aimed at diminishing phobias through relaxation.

VIII. Related Research

Bandura's concept of self-efficacy has generated a great deal of research demonstrating that people's beliefs are related to their ability to enact a wide variety of performances, including smoking cessation and academic performance.

A.   Self-Efficacy and Smoking Cessation

Saul Shiffman and his colleagues (2000) studied the effects of daily fluctuations in self-efficacy on smoking lapses and relapses among ex-smokers who had quit on their own for at least 24 hours. They found that when these participants smoked even a single cigarette, their daily self-efficacy became more variable, leading to future lapses and relapses among ex-smokers. Ex-smokers who believed in their ability to quit smoking were able to maintain high self-efficacy and to avoid lapses and relapse.

B.   Self-Efficacy and Academic Performance

Bandura and a group of Italian researchers (Bandura, Barbaranelli, Caprara, & Pastorelli, 1996) studied level of self-efficacy and its relation to academic performance in middle-school children living near Rome. They found that children who believed that their parents had confidence in their academic ability were likely to have high academic aspirations, high academic self-efficacy, and high self-regulatory efficacy. Moreover, they found that each of these factors related either directly or indirectly to high academic performance.

X.   Critique of Bandura

Bandura's theory is one of the highest rated of any in the text largely because it was constructed through a careful balance of innovative speculation and accurate observations, which were based on rigorous research. In summary, Bandura's theory rates very high on its ability to generate research as well as on internal consistency and parsimony. In addition, it rates high on its ability to be falsified, to organize knowledge, and to guide the practitioner.

XI.   Concept of Humanity

Bandura sees humans as being relatively fluid and flexible. People can store past experiences and then use this information to chart future actions. Although people are goal-directed, they are also influenced by previous experiences. Thus, Bandura rates in the middle on teleology versus causality and on free choice versus determinism. His theory rates high on optimism, conscious influences, and uniqueness, and very high on social determinants of personality.

TEACHING SUGGESTIONS

1.   The concepts of chance encounters and fortuitous events are fascinating ones. Regardless of how carefully people plan their life, a chance encounter or fortuitous event may substantially alter their life's course. Ask for volunteers to talk about ways in which chance changed their life. Married students will be able to describe unplanned and unexpected events that led to their meeting a future spouse or to an unpredictable event that changed a nonromantic relationship into a romantic one.

Similarly, other students will be able to reveal ways in which chance influenced a choice of curriculum or career. After students describe these chance encounters and fortuitous events, ask them to guess how their lives would be different if the encounter or event had not happened. Would a married person have met someone similar to his or her present spouse and have lived a life not unlike the present one? Bandura believes that chance encounters and fortuitous events enter the reciprocal determinism paradigm at the point of environment (E). After that, the unplanned event may become overwhelmed by person (P) and behavior (B), or it may markedly change both P and B, thus completely changing a person's life. Ask students to judge the lasting significance of their chance encounter or fortuitous event.

2.   Albert Bandura was one of the last personality theorists interviewed by Richard Evans. The filmed dialogue is in two parts, each just under 30 minutes long. In Part 1, Bandura discusses social learning, modeling, and aggression. In Part 2, he talks about his classic Bobo Doll experiment and discusses violence in the media. These, videotapes, which reveal Bandura's unique sense of humor, are available from

> Audio-Visual Services
>
> University Division of Media and Learning Resources
>
> The Pennsylvania State University
>
> University Park, PA 16802
>
> Phone (814) 865-6314 or 1-800-826-0132

REFERENCES

Bandura, A., Barbaranelli, C., Caprara, G. V., & Pastorelli, C. (1996). Multifaceted impact
of self-efficacy beliefs on academic functioning. *Child Development, 67,*
1206–1222.

Shiffman, S., Balabanis, M. H., Paty, J. A., Engberg, J., Gwaltney, C. J., Liu, K. S., Gnys,
M., Hickcox, M., & Paton, S. M. (2000). Dynamic effects of self-efficacy on
smoking lapse and relapse. *Healthy Psychology, 19,* 315–323.

CHAPTER 12
ROTTER AND MISCHEL:
COGNITIVE SOCIAL LEARNING THEORY

LEARNING OBJECTIVES

After studying Chapter 12, students should be able to:

1. List Rotter's four variables of prediction and briefly explain each.

2. Discuss Rotter's basic prediction formula and its uses.

3. List and give examples of Rotter's categories of needs.

4. Discuss Rotter's generalized expectancies and their measurement.

5. Explain the difference between internal and external control, and list several misconceptions regarding internal and external control of reinforcement.

6. Explain Rotter's approach to psychotherapy.

7. Discuss Mischel's conditional view of personality.

8. Critique Mischel's notion of the consistency paradox.

9. Discuss Mischel and Shoda's cognitive-affective view of personality.

10. Discuss research on Rotter's locus of control model.

LECTURE OUTLINE

I. **Overview of Cognitive Social Learning Theory**

    Both Julian Rotter and Walter Mischel believe that cognitive factors, more than immediate reinforcements, determine how people will react to environmental forces. Each suggests that our expectations of future events are major determinants of performance. Like Bandura, both Rotter and Mischel built a theory of personality on human studies.

II. **Biography of Julian Rotter**

    Julian Rotter was born in Brooklyn in 1916. As a high-school student, he became familiar with some of the writings of Freud and Adler, but he did not major in psychology while at Brooklyn College. However, when he graduated, he had more credits in psychology than in his major, chemistry. In 1941, he received a Ph.D. in clinical psychology from Indiana University. After World War II, he took a position at Ohio State, where one of his students was Walter Mischel. In 1963, he moved to the University of Connecticut and has remained there since his retirement.

III. Introduction to Rotter's Social Learning Theory

Rotter's **interactionist** position holds that human behavior is based largely on the *interaction* of people with their meaningful environments. Rotter assumes that human personality is learned and can change at any time. However, he also believes that personality has a basic unity, which preserves it from changing as a result of minor or insignificant experiences. In addition, Rotter adopts a goal-directed view of motivation, insisting that we choose courses of action that advance us toward an anticipated goal, a view he refers to as the **empirical law of effect**.

IV. Predicting Specific Behaviors

Human behavior is most accurately predicted by an understanding of four variables: behavior potential, expectancy, reinforcement value, and the psychological situation.

A.   Behavior Potential

Behavior potential is the possibility that a particular response will occur at a given time and place in relation to its likely reinforcement. The behavior potential in any situation is a function of both expectancy and reinforcement value.

B.   Expectancy

People's expectancy in any given situation is their confidence that a particular reinforcement will follow a specific behavior in a specific situation or situations.

Expectancies can be either general or specific, and the overall likelihood of success is a function of both generalized and specific expectancies.

C.   Reinforcement Value

Reinforcement value is a person's preference for any particular reinforcement over other reinforcements if all are equally likely to occur. The total value of a reinforcement is equal to its positive aspects minus its negative value.

Internal reinforcement is the individual's perception of an event, whereas **external reinforcement** refers to society's evaluation of an event.

Reinforcement-reinforcement sequences suggest that the value of an event is a function of one's expectation that a particular reinforcement will lead to future reinforcements.

D.   Psychological Situation

The psychological situation is that part of the external and internal world to which a person is responding. Behavior is a function of the interaction of people with their meaningful environment.

E.   Basic Prediction Formula

Hypothetically, in any specific situation, behavior can be predicted by the basic prediction formula, which states that the potential for a behavior to occur in a particular situation in relation to a given reinforcement is a function of peoples' expectancy that the behavior will be followed by that reinforcement in that situation.

V.   Predicting General Behaviors

The basic prediction formula is too specific to give clues as to how a person will generally behave.

A.   Generalized Expectancies

To make more general predictions of behavior, we must know people's generalized expectancies, or their expectations based on similar past experience that a given behavior will be reinforced. Generalized expectancies include people's needs, or behaviors that move them toward a goal.

B.   Needs

Needs refer to functionally related categories of behaviors. Rotter listed six broad categories of needs, with each need being related to behaviors that lead to the same or similar reinforcements.

1.   Categories of Needs

Rotter listed six broad categories of needs, with each need being related to behaviors that lead to the same or similar reinforcements: (1) **recognition-status** refers to the need to excel, to achieve, and to have others recognize one's worth; (2) **dominance** is the need to control the behavior of others, to be in charge, or to gain power over others; (3) **independence** is the need to be free from the domination of others; (4) **protection-dependency** is the need to have others take care of us and to protect us from harm; (5) **love and affection** are needs to be warmly accepted by others and to be held in friendly regard; and (6) **physical comfort** includes those behaviors aimed at securing food, good health, and physical security.

2.   Need Components

A need complex has three essential components: (1) **need potential**, or the possible occurrences of a set of functionally related behaviors directed toward the satisfaction of similar goals; (2) **freedom of movement,** or a person's overall expectation of being reinforced for performing those behaviors that are directed toward satisfying some general need; and (3) **need value**, or the extent to which people prefer one set of reinforcements to another. Need components are analogous to the more specific concepts of behavior potential, expectancy, and reinforcement value.

C. General Prediction Formula

Hypothetically, the general prediction formula could be used to make more generalized predictions than those allowed by the basic prediction formula. The general prediction formula states that need potential is a function of freedom of movement and need value. Rotter's two most famous scales for measuring generalized expectancies are the Internal-External Control Scale and the Interpersonal Trust Scale.

D. Internal and External Control of Reinforcement

The Internal-External Control Scale (popularly called "locus of control scale") attempts to measure the degree to which people perceive a causal relationship between their own efforts and environmental consequences. People who score high (in the direction of internal control) believe that reinforcement is generally contingent on their own actions or personal traits.

E. Interpersonal Trust Scale

The Interpersonal Trust Scale measures the extent to which one expects the word or promise of another person to be true. People with high interpersonal trust are not gullible; rather, they possess many positive and desirable characteristics.

VI. Maladaptive Behavior

Rotter defined maladaptive behavior as any persistent behavior that fails to move a person closer to a desired goal. It is usually the result of unrealistically high goals in combination with low ability to achieve them. That is, people often behave inappropriately when their need value is higher than their freedom of movement.

VII. Psychotherapy

In general, the goal of Rotter's therapy is to achieve harmony between a client's freedom of movement and need value. The therapist is actively involved in trying to (1) change the importance of the clients' goals and (2) eliminate their unrealistically low expectancies for success.

A.   Changing Goals

Maladaptive behaviors follow from three categories of inappropriate goals: (1) conflict between goals, (2) destructive goals, and (3) unrealistically lofty goals. In the first instance, the therapist attempts to change the need value of one or both goals. In the second case, the therapist points out the negative consequences of the destructive goal. And in the third case, the therapist helps the client reevaluate the goal.

B.   Eliminating Low Expectancies

In helping clients change low expectancies of success, Rotter uses a variety of approaches, including reinforcing positive behaviors, ignoring inappropriate behaviors, giving advice, modeling appropriate behaviors, and pointing out the long-range consequences of both positive and negative behaviors.

VIII. Introduction to Mischel's Cognitive-Affective Personality System

Like Bandura and Rotter, Walter Mischel believes that cognitive factors, such as expectancies, subjective perceptions, values, goals, and personal standards, are important in shaping personality. In his early theory, Mischel seriously questioned the consistency of personality, but more recently, he and Yuichi Shoda have advanced the notion that behavior is also a function of relatively stable personal dispositions and cognitive-affective processes interacting with a particular situation.

IX.   Biography of Walter Mischel

Walter Mischel was born in Vienna in 1930, the second son of upper-middle-class parents. When the Nazis invaded Austria in 1938, his family moved to the United States and eventually settled in Brooklyn. Mischel received an M.A. from City College of New York and a Ph.D. from Ohio State, where he was influenced by both

Julian Rotter and George Kelly. He has held academic positions at Colorado,

Harvard, Stanford, and Columbia, where he remains as an active researcher.

X.   **Background of the Cognitive-Affective Personality System**

Mischel originally believed that human behavior was mostly a function of the

situation, but presently he has recognized the importance of relatively permanent

cognitive-affective units. Nevertheless, Mischel's theory continues to recognize the

apparent inconsistency of some behaviors.

A.   **Consistency Paradox**

The consistency paradox refers to the observation that, although both laypeople

and professionals tend to believe that behavior is quite consistent, research suggests

that it is not. Mischel recognizes that, indeed, some traits are consistent over time,

but he contends that there is little evidence to suggest that they are consistent from

one situation to another.

B   **Person-Situation Interaction**

Mischel believes that behavior is best predicted from an understanding of the

person, the *situation,* and the *interaction* between person and situation. Thus,

behavior is not the result of some global personality trait, but of people's

perceptions of themselves in a particular situation.

XI. **Cognitive-Affective Personality System**

However, Mischel does not believe that inconsistencies in behavior are due solely to

the situation; he recognizes that inconsistent behaviors reflect *stable patterns of*

variation within a person. He and Shoda see these stable variations in behavior in

the following framework: *If A, then X; but if B, then Y.* For example, people may

react with deference toward an authority figure, but in a different situation, they

may react with aggression. This pattern of variability in people's behavior is their

behavioral signature, or their unique and stable pattern of behaving differently in different situations.

A.   Behavior Prediction

Mischel's basic theoretical position for predicting and explaining behavior is as follows: If personality is a stable system that processes information about the situation, then individuals encountering different situations should behave differently as situations vary. Therefore, Mischel believes that, even though people's behavior may reflect some stability over time, it tends to vary as situations vary.

B.   Situation Variables

Situation variables include all those stimuli that people attend to in a given situation. In some cases, situation variables are more powerful than personal variables, but in other cases, the reverse is true.

C.   Cognitive-Affective Units

Cognitive-affective units include all those psychological, social, and physiological aspects of people that permit them to interact with their environment with some stability in their behavior. Mischel identified five such units.

1.   Encoding Strategies

First are encoding strategies, or people's individualized manner of categorizing information they receive from external stimuli.

2.   Competencies and Self-Regulatory Strategies

Second are the competencies and self-regulatory strategies. One of the most important of these competencies is intelligence, which Mischel argues is responsible for the apparent consistency of other traits. In addition, people use self-regulatory strategies to control their own behavior through self-formulated goals and self-produced consequences.

3.   Expectancies and Beliefs

Expectancies and beliefs include people's guesses about the consequences of each of the different behavioral possibilities. Knowledge of people's beliefs about the outcome of any situation is generally a better predictor of behavior than is knowledge of their abilities.

4.   Goals and Values

The fourth cognitive-affective unit includes people's subjective goals and values, which tend to render behavior fairly consistent.

5.   Affective Responses

Mischel's fifth cognitive-affective unit is affective responses, which includes emotions, feelings, and physiological reactions. Affective responses do not exist in isolation; they influence each other and are inseparable form the cognitive processes.

XII. Related Research

The theories of both Rotter and Mischel have sparked an abundance of related research, with Rotter's *locus of control* being one of the most frequently researched areas in psychology and Mischel's notion of *delay of gratification* and his *cognitive-affective personality system* also receiving wide attention.

A.   Locus of Control and Health-Related Behaviors

One adjunct of the locus of control concept is the health locus of control, and research in this area suggests that self-mastery of health and people's belief about their personal control over health-related behaviors predict subsequent health status. This body of research has included such health-related behaviors as smoking (Bunch & Schneider, 1991; Norman, 1995), abusing alcohol (Jih, Sirgo, & Thomure, 1995), and unwise eating (Ludtke & Schneider, 1996). In general, this research indicates that people high on internal locus of control, compared

with those high on external locus of control, are more likely to enact
health-related behaviors.

B.   An Analysis of Reactions to the O. J. Simpson Verdict

Mischel, Shoda, and two of their colleagues (Mendoza-Denton, Ayduk, Shoda, &
Mischel, 1997) used the cognitive-affective personality system to analyze the
verdict in the O. J. Simpson murder trial. They found that European Americans and
African Americans had different ways of looking at the Simpson verdict. Although
their reactions tended to follow along racial lines, participants' race itself was not
as important as their thoughts and feelings in determining their reactions to the
verdict. More specifically, European Americans who agreed with the verdict had
thoughts and emotions very similar to those of African Americans who were elated
by the verdict. Moreover, African Americans who disagreed with the verdict
thought and felt much the same as European Americans who were dismayed by the
not-guilty verdict.

XIII. Critique of Cognitive Social Learning Theory

Cognitive social learning theory combines the rigors of learning theory with the
speculative assumption that people are forward-looking beings. We rate it high
on internal consistency, parsimony, and its ability to organize knowledge and
generate research, and we rate it about average on its ability to guide action and to
be falsified.

XIV. Concept of Humanity

Rotter and Mischel see people as goal-directed, cognitive animals whose
perceptions of events are more crucial than the events themselves. Cognition
enables different people to see the same situation differently and to place different
values on the reinforcers that follow their behavior. Cognitive social learning
theory rates very high on social influences and high on uniqueness of the individual,

free choice, teleology, and conscious processes. On the dimension of optimism versus pessimism, Rotter's view is slightly more optimistic, whereas Mischel's view is about in the middle.

TEACHING SUGGESTIONS

1. Students are usually quite interested in Rotter's notion of locus of control. The entire Internal-External Scale is printed in Rotter's "Generalized expectancies for internal versus external control of reinforcement" (1996). If students fill out and score this scale, they should remember that it measures generalized expectancies and does not apply well to specific situations. They should also realize that extreme scores in either direction are not necessarily desirable. People who score in the direction of internal locus of control (but not too far) should have a general belief that they can exercise some personal control over their life.

2. Is behavior produced by global personality dispositions or by the particular situation in which a person is involved? Most students would probably agree with Mischel that behavior stems from an interaction of the two. However, the relative weight of personal factors and situational factors may be debatable. Students can conduct some out-of-class research by asking their friends and family members what they believe regarding this question. By asking others what a certain person would do in a particular situation, your class can gather data that relates to Mischel's consistency paradox.

REFERENCES

Bunch, J. M., & Schneider, H. G. (1991). Smoking-specific locus of control. *Psychological Reports, 69,* 1075–1081.

Jih, C-S., Sirgo, V. I., & Thomure, J. C. (1995). Alcohol consumption, locus of control, and self-esteem of high school and college students. *Psychological Reports, 76,* 851–857.

Ludtke, H. A., & Schneider, H. G. (1996). Habit-specific locus of control scales for drinking, smoking, and eating. *Psychological Reports, 78,* 363–369.

Mendoza-Denton, R., Ayduk, O. N., Shoda, Y., and Mischel, W. (1997). Cognitive-affective processing system analysis of reactions to the O. J. Simpson criminal trial verdict. *Journal of Social Issues, 53,* 563–581.

Norman, P. (1995). Health locus of control and health behaviour: An investigation into the role of health value and behaviour-specific efficacy beliefs. *Personality and Individual Differences, 18,* 213–218.

Rotter, J. B. (1966). Generalized expectancies for internal versus external control of reinforcement. *Psychological Monographs, 80* (Whole No. 609).

CHAPTER 13
CATTELL AND EYSENCK:
TRAIT AND FACTOR THEORIES

LEARNING OBJECTIVES

After studying Chapter 13, students should be able to:

1.   Explain the basics of factor analytic procedures in measuring personality traits.

2.   Describe Cattell's methods of data collection and investigation.

3.   Distinguish between Cattell's source traits and dynamic traits.

4.   Explain the function of the dynamic calculus.

5.   Discuss Cattell's research on the genetic basis of traits.

6.   Describe Eysenck's approach to the measurement of personality.

7.   Name and describe Eysenck's three general types, or superfactors.

8.   Discuss research on the relationship between personality and disease.

9.   Explain why Cattell and Eysenck have derived a different number of personality factors.

10.   Discuss recent research on creative artists and scientists.

LECTURE OUTLINE

I.   **Overview of Factor Analytic Theory**

Cattell and Eysenck have each used **factor analysis** to identify traits, or relatively permanent dispositions of people. Cattell has identified a large number of personality traits, whereas Eysenck has extracted only three general factors.

II.   **Biography of Raymond B. Cattell**

Raymond B. Cattell was born in England in 1905, the second of three sons of middle-class parents. He graduated from the University of London with a degree in chemistry and physics, but had already developed an interest in psychology. When he received a Ph.D. from the University of London, he could find no jobs in academic psychology. After 12 years working away from an academic setting, he decided to go the United States on a temporary basis. However, he remained there until his death in 1998, a few weeks shy of his 93rd birthday. In the United States, he taught at Columbia University, Clark University, Harvard, and the University of Illinois, where he spent most of his active career. During the last 20 years of his life, he was associated with the Hawaii School of Professional Psychology.

III. Basics of Factor Analysis

Factor analysis is a mathematical procedure for reducing a large number of scores to a few, more general variables or **factors**. **Correlation coefficients** of the original, specific scores with the factors are called **factor loadings**. Traits generated through factor analysis may be either **unipolar** (scaled from zero to some large amount) or **bipolar** (having two opposing poles, such as introversion and extraversion). Before mathematically derived factors can have psychological meaning, the axes on which the scores are plotted are rotated into either an orthogonal or an oblique relationship with each other. Eysenck favored the **orthogonal rotation** whereas Cattell used the **oblique rotation** method.

IV. Introduction to Cattell's Trait Theory

Cattell used an *inductive approach* to identify traits; that is, he began with a large body of data that he collected with no preconceived hypothesis or theory.

A.   P Technique

Cattell's P technique is a correlational procedure that uses variables collected from one person on many different occasions and is his attempt to measure individual or unique, rather than common, traits. Cattell has also used *the dR (differential R) technique,* which correlates the scores of a large number of people on many variables obtained at two different occasions. By combining these two techniques,

Cattell has measured both **states** (temporary conditions within an individual) and **traits** (relatively permanent dispositions of an individual).

B.   Media of Observation

Cattell has used three different media of observation, or sources of data: (1) **L data,** or a person's life record that comes from observations made by others; (2) **Q data,** which are based on questionnaires that require a person to respond to statements on the basis of self-observations; and (3) **T data,** or test data that either require people to perform to the best of their ability or "projective" tests that hide the test's true purpose from the subject.

V.   Source Traits

Source traits refer to the underlying factor or factors responsible for the intercorrelation among *surface traits*. They can be distinguished from surface traits, which merely provide a beginning to the factor analyst. Surface traits that consistently cluster together indicate the existence of an underlying source trait. Source traits can be identified through each of the three media of observation; that is, L, Q, and T data.

VI.   Personality Traits

Personality traits include both *common traits* (shared by many people) and *unique traits* (peculiar to one individual). Personality traits can also be classified into temperament, motivation (dynamic), and ability.

A.   Temperament Traits

Cattell identified 35 primary or first order traits. Of these, 23 are normal traits and 12 are abnormal traits. In addition, all but one of these primary traits are concerned with *how* a person behaves and are called temperament traits. The lone exception is intelligence, which is an ability trait and not a temperament trait.

1.   Normal Traits

Of the 23 normal traits, 16 were obtained through Q media and constitute Cattell's famous 16 PF scale. The additional 7 factors that make up the 23 normal traits were originally identified only through L data. Cattell believed that these 23 traits complete the picture of normal personality in terms of temperament traits.

2.   Abnormal Traits

Cattell believed that pathological people have the same 23 normal traits as other people, but, in addition, they exhibit one or more of 12 abnormal traits. Also, a person's pathology may simply be due to a normal trait that is carried to an extreme.

B.   Second-Order Traits

When Cattell factor analyzed the 35 primary source traits, he found that groups of them tended to cluster together, forming eight clearly identifiable second-order traits. The two strongest of the second-order traits might be called extraversion/introversion and anxiety. (Extraversion/introversion and anxiety are the two strongest factors in Eysenck's theory and are also part of the Big Five personality traits identified by McCrae and Costa [1999] and others.)

VII. Dynamic Traits

In addition to temperament traits, Cattell recognized motivational or dynamic traits, which include attitudes, ergs, and sems.

A.   Attitudes

An attitude refers to a specific course of action, or desire to act, in response to a given situation. Motivation is usually quite complex, so that a network of motives, or **dynamic lattice**, is ordinarily involved with an attitude. In addition, a **subsidiation chain**, or a complex set of subgoals, underlies motivation.

B. Ergs

Ergs are innate drives or motives, such as sex, hunger, loneliness, pity, fear, curiosity, pride, sensuousness, anger, and greed, that humans share with other primates. Cattell believed that ergic factors are the human equivalents of animal instinctual patterns.

C. Sems

Sems are learned or acquired dynamic traits that can satisfy several ergs at the same time. The *self-sentiment* is the most important sem in that it integrates the other sems.

D. The Dynamic Lattice

The dynamic lattice is a complex network of attitudes, ergs, and sems underlying a person's motivational structure. The self-sentiment is likely to be at the center of any dynamic lattice.

VIII. Genetic Basis of Traits

Cattell and his colleagues provided estimates of the heritability of the various source traits. Heritability is an estimate of the extent to which the variance of a given trait is due to heredity. Cattell has found relatively high heritability values for both fluid intelligence (the ability to adapt to new material) and crystallized intelligence (which depends on prior learning), suggesting that intelligence is due more to heredity than to environment.

IX. Introduction to Eysenck's Factor Theory

Compared to Cattell, Hans Eysenck (1) was more likely to theorize before collecting and factor analyzing data; (2) extracted fewer factors; and (3) used a wider variety of approaches to gather data.

X.   Biography of Hans J. Eysenck

An only child, Hans J. Eysenck was born in Berlin in 1916 to parents who had little interest in him. Eysenck was brought up mostly by his grandmother but received little discipline from any adult. As a teenager, he moved from Germany to England to escape Nazi tyranny and made London his home for more than 60 years. Eysenck was trained in the psychometrically oriented psychology department of the University of London, from which he received a bachelor's degree in 1938 and a Ph.D. in 1940. Eysenck was perhaps the most prolific writer of any psychologist in the world, and his books and articles often caused world-wide controversy. He died in 1997 at age 81.

XI.   Measuring Personality

Eysenck believed that genetic factors were far more important than environmental ones in shaping personality, and that personal traits could be measured by standardized personality inventories.

A.   Criteria for Identifying Factors

Eysenck insisted that personality factors must (1) be based on strong psychometric evidence, (2) must possess heritability and fit an acceptable genetic model, (3) make sense theoretically, and (4) possess social relevance.

B.   Hierarchy of Measures

Eysenck recognized a four-level hierarchy of behavior organization: (1) specific acts or cognitions; (2) habitual acts or cognitions; (3) traits, or personal dispositions; and (4) **types** or superfactors.

XII. Dimensions of Personality

Eysenck's methods of measuring personality limited the number of personality types to a relatively small number. Although many traits exist, Eysenck identified only three major types.

A.   What Are the Major Personality Factors?

Eysenck's theory revolves around only three general bipolar types: **extraversion**/introversion, **neuroticism**/stability, and **psychoticism**/superego function. All three have a strong genetic component.

1.   Extraversion

Extraverts are characterized by sociability, impulsiveness, jocularity, liveliness, optimism, and quick-wittedness, whereas introverts are quiet, passive, unsociable, careful, reserved, thoughtful, pessimistic, peaceful, sober, and controlled. Eysenck, however, believes that the principal difference between extraverts and introverts is one of cortical arousal level.

2.   Neuroticism

Neurotic traits include anxiety, hysteria, and obsessive compulsive disorders. Both normal and abnormal individuals may score high on the neuroticism scale of Eysenck's various personality inventories.

3.   Psychoticism

People who score high on the psychoticism scale are egocentric, cold, nonconforming, aggressive, impulsive, hostile, suspicious, and antisocial. Men tend to score higher than women do on psychoticism.

B.   Measuring Superfactors

Eysenck and his colleagues developed four personality inventories to measure superfactors, or types. The two most frequently used by current researchers are the Eysenck Personality Inventory (which measures only E and N) and the Eysenck Personality Questionnaire (which also measures P).

C.   Biological Bases of Personality

Eysenck believed that P, E, and N all have a powerful biological component, and he cited as evidence the existence of these three types in a wide variety of nations and languages.

D.   Personality and Behavior

Eysenck argued that different combinations of P, E, and N relate to a large number

of behaviors and processes, such as academic performance, creativity, and antisocial

behavior. He cautioned that psychologists can be misled if they do not consider the

various combinations of personality dimensions.

E.   Personality and Disease

For many years, Eysenck researched the relationship between personality factors

and disease. He teamed with Ronald Grossarth-Maticek to study the connection

between characteristics and both cancer and cardiovascular disease and found that

people with a helpless/hopeless attitude were more likely to die from cancer,

whereas people who reacted to frustration with anger and emotional arousal were

much more likely to die from cardiovascular disease.

XIII. Related Research

The theories of both Cattell and Eysenck have been highly productive in terms of

research, due in part to Cattell's 16 PF questionnaire and Eysenck's various

personality inventories. Some of this research has looked at personality factors and

the creativity of scientists and artists. In addition, some of Eysenck's research has

attempted to show a biological basis of personality.

A.   Personalities of Creative Scientists and Artists

Early research using the 16 PF found that creative scientists, compared with either

the general population or less creative scientists, were more intelligent, outgoing,

adventurous, sensitive, self-sufficient, dominant, and driven. Other research found

that female scientists, compared to other women, were more dominant, confident,

intelligent, radical, and adventurous. Research by Gregory J. Feist (1998) found that

writers and artists were more intelligent, dominant, adventurous, emotionally

sensitive, radical, and self-sufficient than other people. Later research found that

creative artists scored high on Eysenck's neuroticism and psychoticism scales, indicating that they were more anxious, sensitive, obsessive, impulsive, hostile, and willing to take risks than other people.

B.   Biology and Personality

If personality has a strong biological foundation, then researchers should find very similar personality types in various cultures around the world. Studies in 24 countries (Barrett & Eysenck, 1984) found a high degree of similarity among people of different cultures. Hans Eysenck's later work (Barrett, Petrides, Eysenck, & Eysenck, 1998) investigated personality factors across 35 European, Asian, African, and American cultures and found that personality factors are quite universal, thus supporting the biological nature of personality.

XIV. Critique of Trait and Factor Theories

Cattell and Eysenck's theories rate high on parsimony, on their ability to generate research, and on their usefulness in organizing data; they are about average on falsifiability, usefulness to the practitioner, and internal consistency.

XV.   Concept of Humanity

Cattell and Eysenck believe that human personality is largely the product of genetics and not the environment. Thus, both are rated very high on biological influences and very low on social factors. In addition, both rate about average on conscious versus unconscious influences and high on the uniqueness of individuals. The concepts of free choice, optimism versus pessimism, and causality versus teleology do not apply to Cattell and Eysenck.

TEACHING SUGGESTIONS

1.   Students may wish to fill out the 16 PF and the Eysenck Personality Inventory to gain some insight into their own personality traits and to compare these two approaches to measuring personality. The 16 PF is available in several forms and

can be given to children, adolescents, and adults. The 16 first-order factors measured by this inventory are warmth, intelligence, ego strength, dominance, impulsivity, group conformity, boldness, tender-mindedness, suspiciousness, imagination, shrewdness, guilt proneness, rebelliousness, self-sufficiency, compulsivity, and free-floating anxiety. In addition, the 16 PF assesses four second-order factors: extraversion, anxiety, tough poise, and independence.

The Eysenck Personality Inventory and the Junior Eysenck Personality Inventory assess two major dimensions of personality: extraversion/introversion (E) and neuroticism/stability (N). People with high E scores are usually outgoing, impulsive, and uninhibited; they like excitement, social events, and risk-taking activities. People who score high on N typically are overreactive and emotionally overresponsive, and they often complain of vague physical symptoms.

The 16 PF and the EPI may be available at a university counseling center. If not, the 16 PF can be purchased by qualified persons from

The Institute of Personality and Ability Testing

Box 188

1602 Coronado Drive

Champaign, IL 61820

The Eysenck Personality Inventory is available to qualified persons from

Educational and Industrial Testing Service

PO Box 7234

San Diego, CA 92107

2.   Students will be interested in videotapes of Richard Evans's interview with Cattell. In Part 1, Cattell presents his views on personality measurement, genetics, motivation, and the dynamic calculus. In Part 2, he talks about factor analysis, Q and P techniques, testing, and psychotherapy. Both parts are 50 minutes in length.

3.   Hans Eysenck was a self-confident, dynamic speaker. In his 32-minute interview with Richard Evans, he criticized Freud and psychoanalysis, described his approach to behavior therapy, and discussed personality measurement. Both the Cattell and Eysenck videos are for rent or sale from

> Audio-Visual Services
>
> University Division of Media and Learning Resources
>
> The Pennsylvania State University
>
> University Park, PA 16802
>
> Phone (814) 865-6314 or 1-800-826-0132

REFERENCES

Barrett, P., & Eysenck, S. B. (1984). The assessment of personality factors across 25 countries. *Personality and Individual Differences, 5*, 615–632.

Barrett, P., Petrides, K. V., Eysenck, S. B., & Eysenck, H. J. (1998). The Eysenck Personality Questionnaire: An examination of the factorial similarity of P, E, N, and L across 34 countries. *Personality and Individual Differences, 25*, 805–809.·

Feist, G. J. (1998). A meta-analysis of the impact of personality on scientific and artistic creativity. *Personality and Social Psychological Review, 2*, 290–309.

McCrae, R. R., & Costa, P. T., Jr. (1999). A five-factor theory of personality. In L. A. Pervin & O. P. John (Eds.), *Handbook of personality: Theory and research* (pp. 139–153). New York: Guilford Press.

CHAPTER 14
ALLPORT: PSYCHOLOGY OF THE INDIVIDUAL

LEARNING OBJECTIVES

After studying Chapter 14, students should be able to:

1. Discuss Allport's concept of personal dispositions and explain the difference between traits and personal dispositions.

2. Explain the distinction between motivational and stylistic dispositions.

3. Discuss Allport's idea of a proprium and explain why he used that term instead of "self."

4. Differentiate between reactive and proactive theories of motivation.

5. Review Allport's concept of functional autonomy.

6. Trace Allport's stages of development of the healthy personality.

7. Define and give examples of the morphogenic approach to the study of personality.

8. Describe the characteristics of the mature personality, according to Allport.

9. Summarize research on the Religious Orientation Scale.

10. Review Allport's concept of humanity.

LECTURE OUTLINE

I. **Overview of Allport's Psychology of the Individual**

Allport built his theory of personality as a reaction against both psychoanalysis and animal-based learning theory. He criticized these other theories as neglecting the normal and psychologically healthy individual. However, Allport was **eclectic** in his approach and borrowed ideas from both psychoanalysis and from learning theory. His major emphasis was on the uniqueness of each individual.

II. Biography of Gordon Allport

Gordon Allport was born in Indiana in 1897, the youngest son of a country doctor and a former schoolteacher. In 1915, he followed his older brother Floyd (also a famous psychologist) to Harvard, beginning a nearly continuous 50-year association with that university. Allport's undergraduate degree was in philosophy and economics, but a fortuitous meeting with Sigmund Freud in Vienna helped him decide to complete a Ph.D. in psychology. He then spent two years studying under some of the great German psychologists, but returned to teach at Harvard. After two years, he took a position at Dartmouth, but after four years at Dartmouth, he returned to Harvard, where he remained until his death in 1967.

III. Allport's Approach to Personality

Allport believed that psychologically healthy humans are motivated by present, mostly conscious drives and that they not only seek to reduce tensions but to establish new tensions. He also believed that people are capable of **proactive behavior**. The concept of proaction suggests that people can consciously behave in new and creative ways that foster their own change and growth. Allport called his study of the individual **morphogenic science** and contrasted it with traditional **nomothetic** methods that study groups of people.

IV. Personality Defined

Allport's precisely thought-out definition of personality, which remains frequently quoted, states that "personality is the dynamic organization within the individual of those psychophysical systems that determine his characteristic behavior and thought" (Allport, 1961, p. 28).

V. Structure of Personality

According to Allport, the basic units of personality are personal dispositions and the proprium.

A.   Personal Dispositions

Allport was careful to distinguish between **common traits**, which permit inter-individual comparisons, and personal dispositions, which are peculiar to the individual. He argued that one individual's personal disposition (e.g., aggressiveness) cannot be compared to that of another individual.

1.   Levels of Personal Dispositions

Allport recognized three overlapping levels of personal dispositions. The most general are the **cardinal dispositions**, which are so obvious and dominating that they cannot be hidden from others. Not everyone has a cardinal disposition, but all people have 5 to 10 **central dispositions,** or characteristics around which their lives revolve. In addition, everyone has a great number of **secondary dispositions,** which are less reliable and conspicuous than central dispositions.

2.   Motivational and Stylistic Dispositions

Allport further divided personal dispositions into motivational and stylistic dispositions. *Motivational dispositions* are more strongly felt and derive from basic needs and drives. They initiate action. *Stylistic dispositions*, which refer to the manner in which an individual behaves, guide action.

B.   Proprium

The proprium refers to all those behaviors and characteristics that people regard as warm and central in their lives. Propriate experiences and possessions are opposed to those that lie on the periphery of personality. Allport preferred the term proprium to self or ego because the latter terms could imply an object or thing within a person that controls behavior, whereas proprium suggests the core of one's personhood.

VI. Motivation

To Allport, an adequate theory of motivation must consider the notion that motives change as people mature and also that people are motivated by present drives and wants.

A. Reactive and Proactive Theories of Motivation

Allport insisted that a useful theory of personality rests on the assumption that people not only react to their environment but also shape their environment and cause it to react to them. He criticized psychoanalysis and animal-based learning theories as being reactive because they saw people as being motivated by needs to reduce tension and to react to their environment. His proactive approach emphasized that people consciously and purposefully act on their environment in a way that fosters growth toward psychological health.

B. Functional Autonomy

Allport's most distinctive and controversial concept is his theory of functional autonomy, which holds that some (but not all) human motives are functionally independent from the original motive responsible for a particular behavior. Motives that are not functionally autonomous include those that are responsible for reflex actions, basic drives, and pathological behaviors.

1. Perseverative Functional Autonomy

Allport recognized two levels of functional autonomy. Perseverative functional autonomy is the tendency of certain basic behaviors to continue in the absence of reinforcement. Addictive behaviors are examples of perseverative functional autonomy.

2. Propriate Functional Autonomy

The other level is propriate functional autonomy, which refers to self-sustaining motives that are related to the proprium. Examples of propriate functionally autonomous behaviors include pursuing interests that one holds dear and important.

3.   Criterion for Functional Autonomy

Present motives are functionally autonomous to the extent that they seek new goals. That is, functionally autonomous behaviors will continue even after the motivation behind those behaviors change.

4.   Processes That Are Not Functionally Autonomous

Allport listed eight processes that are not functionally autonomous: (1) biological drives, (2) motives directly linked to the reduction of basic drives, (3) reflexes, (4) constitutional equipment, (5) habits in the process of being formed, (6) patterns of behavior that require primary reinforcement, (7) sublimations that are linked to unpleasant childhood experiences, and (8) certain neurotic or pathological symptoms.

C.   Conscious and Unconscious Motivation

Although Allport emphasized conscious motivation more than any other personality theorist, he did not completely overlook the possible influence of unconscious motives. Pathological behaviors are often motivated by unconscious drives, but healthy individuals are ordinarily consciously in control of their behavior.

VII. The Psychologically Healthy Personality

Years before Maslow identified the characteristics of the self-actualized person, Allport listed his criteria for psychological health. To Allport, the psychologically healthy person would possess six characteristics: (1) an extension of the sense of self, (2) warm relationships with others, (3) emotional security or self-acceptance, (4) a realistic view of the world, (5) insight and humor, and (6) a unifying philosophy of life.

VIII. The Study of the Individual

Allport strongly felt that psychology should develop and use research methods that study the individual rather than groups.

A. Morphogenic Science

Traditional psychology relies on nomothetic science, which seeks general laws from a study of groups of people, but Allport used **morphogenic procedures** that study patterns of traits within the single case. Allport accepted self-reports, such as diaries, at face value.

B.   The Diaries of Marion Taylor

During the late 1930's, Allport and his wife became acquainted with personal documents, including diaries, of a woman they called Marion Taylor. Although the Allports analyzed much of this information, they never published an account of Marion Taylor's story.

C.   Letters from Jenny

A short time later, the Allports analyzed and published a series of letters they had received from an older women named Jenny. These letters constitute Allport's best-known example of morphogenic science in that they reveal one person's pattern of behavior. Two of Allport's students, Alfred Baldwin and Jeffrey Paige, used a personal structure analysis and factor analysis, respectively, whereas Allport used a commonsense approach to discern Jenny's personality structure as revealed by her letters. All three approaches yielded similar results, suggesting that morphogenic studies may be reliable.

IX. Related Research

Allport believed that a deep religious commitment was a mark of a mature person, but he also saw that many regular churchgoers did not have a mature religious orientation and were capable of deep racial and social prejudice. In other words, he saw a curvilinear relationship between church attendance and prejudice.

A.   The Religious Orientation Scale

This insight led Allport to develop and use the Religious Orientation Scale to assess both an *intrinsic orientation* and an *extrinsic orientation* toward religion. Allport and Ross (1967) found that people with an extrinsic orientation toward religion tend to be quite prejudiced, whereas those with an intrinsic orientation tend to be low on racial and social prejudice. A review of later studies (Trimble, 1997) found that prejudice is positively related to an extrinsic religious orientation but unrelated to an intrinsic religious orientation.

B.   Religious Orientation and Psychological Health

Research by Ralph Hood (1970) and others (Hansen, Vandenberg, & Patterson, 1995; Kosek, 1999; Maltby, 1999) has found that people who score high on the Intrinsic scale of the ROS tend to have overall better personal functioning than those who score high on the Extrinsic scale. In general, these studies have found that some highly religious people have strong psychological health, whereas others suffer from a variety of psychological disorders. The principal difference between the two groups is one of intrinsic or extrinsic religious orientation; that is, people with an intrinsic orientation tend to be psychologically healthy, but those with an extrinsic orientation suffer from poor psychological health.

X.   Critique of Allport

Allport wrote eloquently about personality, but his views were based more on philosophical speculation and common sense than on scientific studies. As a consequence, his theory is quite narrow, being limited mostly to a model of human motivation. Thus, it rates low on its ability to organize psychological data and to submit itself to falsification. It rates high on parsimony and internal consistency and about average on its ability to generate research and to help the practitioner.

XI. Concept of Humanity

Allport saw people as thinking, proactive, purposeful beings who are generally aware of what they are doing and why. On the six dimensions for a concept of humanity, Allport rates higher than any other theorist on conscious influences and on the uniqueness of the individual. He rates high on free choice, optimism, and teleology, and about average on social influences.

TEACHING SUGGESTIONS

1.   Can individuals be consistently described by five to eight central dispositions? Students can help answer this question with a class project that calls for them to solicit the help of three or four close acquaintances of a "target person." Students should ask these acquaintances to describe the "target person" in terms of general characteristics or traits. These descriptive terms should not be in terms of behavior (e.g., "She likes to pick fights"), but in terms of personal dispositions (e.g., "She's aggressive"). Neither should the descriptions be physical attributes (e.g., "He has an athletic build") nor should they be in terms of the acquaintance's relationship with the "target person" (e.g., "She makes me laugh" or "I like him") Acquaintances should not be told how many traits they should name. They should simply list descriptive adjectives that they feel others would also list.

     After students have gathered this data, they should group synonyms and then count the average number of central traits that others agree the "target person" possesses. The students may be interested to find whether the average number of outstanding personal dispositions is approximately the same as the number of central dispositions hypothesized by Allport, namely five to eight.

2.   A couple of years before his death, Allport was interviewed by Richard Evans. This dialogue is available on videotape in two parts, each 50 minutes long. In Part 1,

Allport discusses his famous visit with Sigmund Freud and the effect that the encounter had on his later concept of personality. He also talks about nomothetic and morphogenic approaches to the study of personality and explains his notion of functional autonomy. In Part 2, Allport speaks about the development of self, the use of personality questionnaires, and the development of human personality. These videos are available for rent or purchase from

> Audio-Visual Services
>
> University Division of Media and Learning Resources
>
> The Pennsylvania State University
>
> University Park, PA 16802
>
> Phone (814) 865-6314 or 1-800-826-0132

REFERENCES

Allport, G. W. (1961). *Pattern and growth in personality.* New York: Holt, Rinehart & Winston.

Allport, G. W., & Ross, J. M. (1967). Personal religious orientation and prejudice. *Journal of Personality and Social Psychology, 5,* 432–443.

Hansen, D. E., Vandenberg, B., & Patterson, M. L. (1995). The effects of religious orientation on spontaneous and nonspontaneous helping behaviors. *Personality and Individual Differences, 19,* 101–104.

Hood, R. W., Jr. (1970). Religious orientations and the report of religious experiences. *Journal for the Scientific Study of Religion, 9,* 285–291.

Kosek, R. B. (1999). Adaptation of the Big Five as a hermeneutic instrument for religious constructs. *Personality and Individual Differences, 27,* 229–237.

Maltby, J. (1999). Religious orientation and Eysenck's personality dimensions: The use of the amended religious orientation scale to examine the relationship between religiosity, psychoticism, neuroticism, and extraversion. *Personality and Individual Differences, 26,* 79–84.

Trimble, D. E. (1997). The Religious Orientation Scale: Review and meta-analysis of social desirability effects. *Educational and Psychological Measurement, 57,* 970–986.

CHAPTER 15
KELLY: PSYCHOLOGY OF PERSONAL CONSTRUCTS

LEARNING OBJECTIVES

After studying Chapter 15, students should be able to:

1. State Kelly's philosophical position of constructive alternativism.

2. Discuss the fundamental postulate of Kelly's theory.

3. List and explain the 11 supporting corollaries to the fundamental postulate of personal construct theory.

4. Define Kelly's concept of role, including core role and peripheral role.

5. Define threat from Kelly's point of view.

6. Define anxiety from Kelly's point of view.

7. Discuss Kelly's view of abnormal development.

8. Describe the procedure for fixed-role therapy.

9. Explain the use of the Rep test in personality assessment.

10. Discuss Kelly's concept of personality.

LECTURE OUTLINE

I. Overview of Personal Construct Theory

Kelly's theory of personality can be seen as a metatheory, or a theory about theories. It holds that people anticipate events by the meanings or interpretations that they place on those events. Kelly called these interpretations *personal constructs.* His philosophical position, called *constructive alternativism,* assumes that alternative interpretations are always available to people.

II. Biography of George Kelly

George Kelly was born on a farm in south central Kansas in 1905, the only child of a former Presbyterian minister and a former schoolteacher. During his school years and his early professional career, he dabbled in a wide variety of subjects, but eventually he took a Ph.D. in psychology from the State University of Iowa. He began his academic career at Fort Hays State College in Kansas, a state plagued both by dust storms and the Great Depression. After World War II, Kelly took a position at Ohio State, where he remained until 1965 when he joined the faculty at Brandeis University. He died two years later at age 61.

III. Kelly's Philosophical Position

Kelly believed that, although the universe is real, people construe events according to their personal constructs, rather than reality.

A.   Person as Scientist

People generally attempt to solve everyday problems in much the same fashion as scientists; that is, they observe, ask questions, formulate hypotheses, infer conclusions, and predict future events.

B.   Scientist as Person

Because scientists are people, their pronouncements should be regarded with the same skepticism as any other data. Every scientific theory can be viewed from an alternate angle, and every competent scientist should be open to changing his or her theory.

C.   Constructive Alternativism

Kelly believed that all our interpretations of the world are subject to revision or replacement, an assumption he called constructive alternativism. He further stressed that, because people can construe their world from different angles, observations that are valid at one time may be false at a later time.

IV. Personal Constructs

Kelly believed that people look at their world through templates that they create and then attempt to fit over the realities of the world. He called these templates or transparent patterns personal constructs. Kelly believed that personal constructs alone determine our behavior. A construct must have both a comparison and a contrast, both of which must occur within the same context.

A.   Basic Postulate

Kelly expressed his theory in one basic postulate and 11 supporting corollaries. The basic postulate assumes that human behavior is shaped by the way that people anticipate the future.

B.   Supporting Corollaries

The 11 supporting corollaries can all be inferred from this basic postulate.

1.   Similarities Among Events

Although no two events are exactly alike, we construe similar events as if they were the same. This is Kelly's **construction corollary**.

2.   Differences Among People

The **individuality corollary** states that, because people have different experiences, they can construe the same event in different ways.

3.   Relationships Among Constructs

The **organization corollary** assumes that people organize their personal constructs in a hierarchical system, with some constructs in a superordinate position and others subordinate to them.

4.   Dichotomy of Constructs

The **dichotomy corollary** assumes that people construe events in an either/or manner, e.g., good or bad.

5.   Choice Between Dichotomies

People tend to choose the alternative in a dichotomized construct that they see as extending the range of their future choices. Kelly called this the **choice corollary**.

6.   Range of Convenience

The **range corollary** states that constructs are limited to a particular range of convenience; that is, they are not relevant to all situations.

7.   Experience and Learning

Kelly's **experience corollary** suggests that people continually revise their personal constructs as the result of their experiences.

8.   Adaptation to Experience

Not all new experiences lead people to revise their personal constructs. Only permeable constructs lead to change; concrete constructs resist modification through experience. This is Kelly's **modulation corollary**.

9.   Incompatible Constructs

The **fragmentation corollary** states that people's behavior can be inconsistent because their construct systems can readily admit incompatible elements.

10.   Similarities Among People

To the extent that we share experiences with other people, our personal constructs tend to be similar to the construction systems of other people. This is Kelly's **commonality corollary**

11.   Social Processes

The **sociality corollary** states that people are able to communicate with other people because they can construe those people's constructions. With this corollary, Kelly introduced the concept of **role**, which refers to a pattern of behavior that stems from people's understanding of the constructs of others. Each of us has a *core role* (which gives us a sense of identity) and numerous *peripheral roles* (which are less central to our self-concept).

V.   Applications of Personal Construct Theory

Kelly's many years of clinical experience enabled him to evolve concepts of abnormal development and psychotherapy, and to develop a Role Construct Repertory (Rep) Test.

A.   Abnormal Development

Kelly saw normal people as analogous to competent scientists who test reasonable hypotheses, objectively view the results, and willingly change their theories when the data warrant it. On the other hand, unhealthy people are like incompetent scientists who test unreasonable hypotheses, reject or distort legitimate results, and refuse to amend outdated theories. Kelly identified four common elements in most human disturbances: threat, fear, anxiety, and guilt.

1.   Threat

People experience threat when they perceive that the stability of their basic constructs is likely to be shaken.

2.   Fear

Fear is more specific than threat and requires an incidental, rather than a comprehensive, restructuring of one's construct system.

3.   Anxiety

People experience anxiety when they recognize that they cannot adequately deal with a new situation. Pathological anxiety exists when people become aware that their incompatible constructs can no longer be tolerated, an awareness that breaks down one's construction system.

4.   Guilt

Kelly defined guilt as "the sense of having lost one's core role structure." This means that people will feel guilty when they behave in ways that are incompatible with their core role.

B.   Psychotherapy

Kelly insisted that clients should set their own goals for therapy and that they should be active participants in the therapeutic process. He sometimes used a procedure called *fixed-role therapy* in which clients act out a predetermined role for several weeks. By playing the part of a psychologically healthy person, clients may discover previously hidden aspects of themselves.

C.   The Rep Test

The purpose of the Rep test is to discover ways in which people construe significant people in their lives. Participants place names of people they know on a repertory grid in order to identify both similarities and differences among these people. Changes in personal constructs, as revealed by the Rep test, can reveal change during psychotherapy.

VI.   Related Research

Kelly's theory has influenced clinicians more than researchers. Nevertheless, personal construct theory and the Rep test have generated a substantial amount of empirical research with both children and adults and in both the United States and the United Kingdom.

A.   The Rep Test and Children

Wayne Hammond and David Romney (1995) used the Rep test with children and found that the self-constructs of depressed adolescents are marked by low self-esteem, pessimism, and an external locus of control. Other research with children and the Rep test (Donahue, 1994) showed that preadolescents construed themselves and others in ways consistent with the Big Five personality factors (extraversion, agreeableness, conscientiousness, emotional stability, and intelligence), thus demonstrating that the Big Five factors can come from instruments other than standard personality tests.

B.   The Rep Test and the Real Self Versus the Ideal Self

Research with adults demonstrated the usefulness of the Rep test in predicting adherence to a physical activity program (Jones, Harris, & Walter, 1998), detecting differences between the real self and the ideal self (Watson & Watts, 2001), and measuring neuroticism (Watson & Watts, 2001).

C.   The Rep Test and the Pain Patient

A number of studies from New Zealand, including the Large and Strong (1997) study, have found that the Rep test can be a reliable and valid instrument for measuring pain. Interestingly, some of this research showed that people close to the pain patient may unintentionally exacerbate their friend's pain by behaving as if the pain was more central to the pain patient's life than construed by the patient.

VII. Critique of Kelly

Kelly's theory is most applicable to relatively normal, intelligent people. Unfortunately, it pays scant attention to problems of motivation, development, and cultural influences. On the six criteria of a useful theory, we rate Kelly's theory very high on parsimony and internal consistency, about average on its capacity to generate research, and low on its ability to be falsified, to guide the practitioner, and to organize knowledge.

VIII. Concept of Humanity

Kelly saw people as anticipating the future and living their lives in accordance with those anticipations. His concept of **elaborative choice** suggests that people increase their range of future choices by the present choices they freely make. Thus, Kelly's theory rates very high in teleology and high in choice and optimism. In addition, it receives high ratings for conscious influences and for its emphasis on the uniqueness of the individual. Finally, personal construct theory is about average on social influences.

TEACHING SUGGESTIONS

1.   Students will be interested in Kelly's Rep Test, and they can fill out the test in order to assess their personal constructs. Students begin by filling out a list of role titles similar to the ones in Table 15.1 in the textbook. The number of people on the list should be around 15 to 25. Next, students take three names from the list and decide which two

people are alike and yet different from the third. Then, students report why the two are alike and yet different from the third. The reason given for judging the similarity and the contrast constitutes a personal construct.

After repeating this procedure with several other combinations, students should transfer the information on to a repertory grid similar to the one found in Figure 15.2, which is the matrix of one of Kelly's clients. This particular grid includes 19 people important to that client, but students can have a different number and may choose different people. On the first construct (belief in God), Kelly's client saw a happy person and a successful person as similar because neither believed in God, but they were contrasted to an ethical person who the client saw as very religious. After making 22 such comparisons and contrasts, the client placed checkmarks in the squares of other people seen as similar to the successful person and the happy person. In this case, an ex-flame, a rejected person, and a threatening person were seen as similar to the successful person and the happy person in that they, too, did not believe in God. The client saw the remaining people—including himself—as believing in God. By measuring personal constructs in this fashion, students will be able to see how they construe important people in their life.

2. The Rep test, of course, also yields clues concerning a student's view of self. Consider Kelly's client as seen in Figure 15.2. In looking at the "self" column, we can see that this client saw himself as similar to his brother in that they both think alike and very different from his sister (see Row 17). From Row 3, we know that he saw himself somewhat like a rejecting person and an attractive person and as not being athletic. In addition, he saw himself as being different from a pitied person, who he regarded as athletic. If we look at Row 6, we see that the client saw the accepted teacher and the happy person as both understanding him, an attitude in contrast to that of his sister, who he believed did not understand him. From this repertory grid, we can learn a good deal about the client's perception of self and others.

Similarly, students can fill out their own Rep test, which should help them gain some insight into their own personal constructs regarding other people and themselves.

REFERENCES

Donahue, E. M. (1994). Do children use the Big Five, too? Content and structural form in personality description. *Journal of Personality, 62*, 45–66.

Hammond, W. A., & Romney, D. M. (1995). Cognitive factors contributing to adolescent depression. *Journal of Youth and Adolescence, 24*, 667–683.

Jones, F., Harris, P., & Walter, H. (1998). Expectations of an exercise prescription scheme: An exploratory study using repertory grids. *British Journal of Health Psychology, 3*, 277–289.

Large, R., & Strong, J. (1997). The personal constructs of coping with chronic low back pain: Is coping a necessary evil? *Pain, 73*, 245–252.

Watson, N., & Watts, R. H., Jr. (2001). The strength of personal constructs versus conventional constructs: Self-image disparity and neuroticism. *Journal of Personality, 69*, 121–145.

CHAPTER 16
ROGERS: PERSON-CENTERED THEORY

LEARNING OBJECTIVES

After studying Chapter 16, students should be able to:

1. Describe Rogers's concepts of the formative and actualizing tendencies.

2. Discuss Rogers's concept of self and its development.

3. State the basic needs of individuals, according to Rogers's theory of personality.

4. Conceptualize Rogers's views on awareness.

5. List and describe Rogers's conception of basic needs.

6. Describe Rogers's views on psychological stagnation.

7. Name and explain the necessary and sufficient conditions for psychological growth.

8. State the characteristics of the person of tomorrow and their implications for future humanity.

9. Discuss Rogers's philosophy of science.

10. Briefly describe the methods, procedures, and results of research on the effectiveness of client-centered counseling conducted by Rogers and his colleagues at the University of Chicago.

LECTURE OUTLINE

I. **Overview of Rogers's Person-Centered Theory**

Although Carl Rogers is perhaps best known as the founder of client-centered therapy, he also developed a theory of personality that, more than any other, follows an if/then format. For example, Rogers stated that *if* certain therapeutic conditions are present, *then* predictable changes can be expected in clients.

II. **Biography of Carl Rogers**

Carl Rogers was born in a Chicago suburb in 1902, the fourth of six children of upper-middle class, devoutly religious parents. When the family moved to a farm near Chicago,

Carl became interested in scientific farming and learned to appreciate the scientific method. When he graduated from the University of Wisconsin, Rogers intended to become a minister. To realize that goal, he attended the Union Theological Seminar in New York, but he gave up this aspiration after attending education and psychology classes at neighboring Columbia University. From that point forward, he devoted his life to education and psychology. He completed a Ph.D. in 1931 and spent nearly a dozen years away from an academic life working as a clinician. In 1940, he took a position at Ohio State University, where he first elucidated his views on psychotherapy. He spent his most productive years at the University of Chicago, from 1945 to 1957. Next, he returned to the University of Wisconsin, but his stay there was less satisfying. Finally, in 1964, he moved to California, where he helped found the Center for Studies of the Person. He died in 1987 at age 85.

III. Person-Centered Theory

Rogers's person-centered personality theory, which followed from and was based on his **client-centered** approach to psychotherapy, is perhaps the only personality intentionally stated in an *if-then* framework. For example, Rogers proposed that *if* people experience certain conditions, *then* they will grow in a predictable manner.

A.   Basic Assumptions

Person-centered theory rests on two basic assumptions—the *formative tendency* and the *actualizing tendency.*

1.   Formative Tendency

The formative tendency assumes that all matter, both organic and inorganic, tends to evolve from simpler to more complex forms.

2.   Actualizing Tendency

The actualizing tendency holds that all living things, including humans, tend to move toward completion, or fulfillment of potentials. However, in order for people (or plants and animals) to become actualized, certain identifiable conditions must be present. For humans, these conditions include a relationship with another person who is genuine and who demonstrates complete acceptance and empathy.

B.   The Self and Self-Actualization

A sense of self or personal identity begins to emerge during infancy, and, once established, it allows a person to strive toward **self-actualization**, which is a subsystem of the actualization tendency and which refers to the tendency to actualize the self as perceived in awareness. The self has two subsystems: the self-concept and the ideal self.

1.   The Self-Concept

The self-concept includes all those aspects of one's identity that are perceived in awareness. Once formed, the self-concept tends to resist change, which makes psychological growth difficult.

2.   The Ideal Self

The ideal self is our view of our self as we would like to be or aspire to be. Gaps between the ideal self and the self-concept result in incongruence and various levels of psychopathology.

C.   Awareness

People are aware of both their self-concept and their ideal self, although their awareness is not always accurate or at a high level.

1.   Levels of Awareness

Rogers saw people as having experiences on three levels of awareness: (1) experiences that are **subceived**; that is, experiences symbolized below the threshold of awareness that are either *ignored* or *denied* and not allowed into the self-concept; (2) *distorted* perceptions of events, as when a person reshapes an experience to fit it into an existing self-concept; and (3) *accurately symbolized* experiences that are consistent with the self-concept and hence freely admitted into the self-structure.

2.   Denial of Positive Experiences

Any experience not consistent with the self-concept—even positive experiences—will be distorted or denied. Thus, positive comments from another person may be neutral or even threatening to the person receiving the compliments.

D.   Needs

The two basic human needs are maintenance and enhancement, but people also need positive regard and positive self-regard.

1.   Maintenance

Maintenance needs include those for food, air, and safety, but they also include our tendency to resist change and to maintain our self-concept as it is.

2.   Enhancement

In addition to maintenance, people have a need to enhance the self, to grow, and to realize their full human potential.

3.   Positive Regard

As awareness of self emerges, infants begin to receive positive regard (love and acceptance) from parents and others. As with other people, infants naturally value those experiences that satisfy their needs for positive regard, but, unfortunately, this value sometimes becomes more powerful than the reward they receive for meeting their organismic needs. This sets up the condition of *incongruence,* which is experienced when basic organismic needs are denied or distorted in favor of needs to be loved or accepted.

4.   Positive Self-Regard

As a result of their experiences with the frustration or the satisfaction of their positive regard needs, people develop the need for *self-regard*. People acquire feelings of *positive* self-regard only after they perceive that someone else cares for them and values them. Once established, however, self-regard becomes autonomous and no longer dependent on other people's continuous positive evaluation.

E.   Conditions of Worth

Unfortunately, most people are not unconditionally accepted. Instead, they receive *conditions of worth*. People experience conditions of worth when they feel that other people love and accept them only on the condition that they live up to the expectations of those other people.

F.   Psychological Stagnation

When the organismic self and the self-concept are at variance with one another, a person may experience incongruence, including vulnerability, threat, defensiveness, and even disorganization.

1.   Incongruence

Incongruence, or a discrepancy between self-concept and organismic experience, is the source of psychological maladjustment. This incongruence occurs because people experience conditions of worth, which lead to a self-concept based on distortions and denials. The greater the incongruence, the more **vulnerable** people become; that is, the more they are unaware of the discrepancy between their self-concept and their organismic experience. **Anxiety** exists whenever people become dimly aware of the discrepancy between their organismic experience and their self-concept, whereas **threat** is experienced whenever people become more clearly aware of this incongruence.

2.   Defensiveness

To prevent incongruence, people react with defensiveness, typically in the form of **distortion** and **denial**. With distortion, people misinterpret an experience so that it fits into the self-concept; with denial, people refuse to allow the experience into awareness.

3.   Disorganization

When people's defenses fail to operate properly, their behavior becomes disorganized or psychotic. With disorganization, people sometimes behave consistently with their organismic experience and sometimes in accordance with their shattered self-concept.

IV. Psychotherapy

In order for client-centered psychotherapy to be effective, certain conditions are necessary: A vulnerable client must have contact of some duration with a counselor who is congruent, and who demonstrates unconditional positive regard and listens with empathy to a client. The client, in turn, must perceive the congruence, unconditional positive regard, and empathy of the therapist. If these *conditions* are present, then the *process* of therapy will take place and certain predictable *outcomes* will result.

A. Conditions

Although these conditions are required, three are more specifically crucial to client-centered therapy. Rogers called these core conditions the *necessary and sufficient conditions* for therapeutic growth.

1. Counselor Congruence

The first necessary and sufficient condition is counselor congruence, or a therapist whose organismic experiences are matched by an awareness and by the ability and willingness to openly express these feelings. Congruence is more basic than the other two conditions because it is a relatively stable characteristic of the therapist. In contrast, the other two conditions are limited to a specific therapeutic relationship.

2. Unconditional Positive Regard

Unconditional positive regard exists when the therapist accepts the client without conditions or qualifications. The therapist does not evaluate or criticize but has a warm caring for the totality of the client.

3. Empathic Listening

Empathic listening is the therapist's ability to sense the feelings of a client and also to communicate these perceptions so that the client knows that another person has entered into his or her world of feelings without prejudice, projection, or evaluation.

B.   Process

If the conditions of therapist congruence, unconditional positive regard, and empathy are present, then the process of therapeutic change will occur.

1.   Stages of Therapeutic Change

Rogers saw the process of therapeutic change as taking place in seven stages: (1) clients are unwilling to communicate anything about themselves; (2) they discuss only external events and other people; (3) they begin to talk about themselves, but still as an object; (4) they discuss strong emotions that they have felt in the past; (5) they begin to express present feelings; (6) they freely allow into awareness those experiences that were previously denied or distorted; and (7) they experience irreversible change and growth.

2.   Theoretical Explanation for Therapeutic Change

Rogers believed that when people experience themselves as prized and unconditionally accepted, they will realize that they are lovable. This realization leads to self-acceptance, unconditional positive self-regard, congruence, and the freedom to listen with empathy to their own feelings. In other words, these people have become their own therapist.

C.   Outcomes

When client-centered therapy is successful, clients become more congruent, less defensive, more open to experience, and more realistic. The gap between their ideal self and their true self narrows, and, as a consequence, they experience less physiological and psychological tension. Finally, their interpersonal relationships improve because they are more accepting of self and others.

V.   The Person of Tomorrow

Rogers was vitally interested in the psychologically healthy person, called the "fully functioning person" or the "person of tomorrow." He listed seven characteristics of the person of tomorrow. The person of tomorrow (1) is able to adjust to change, (2) is open to experience, (3) is able to live fully in the moment, (4) is able to have harmonious relations with others, (5) is more integrated with no artificial boundaries between conscious and unconscious processes, (6) has a basic trust of human nature, and (7) enjoys a greater richness in life.

VI. Philosophy of Science

Rogers insisted that a scientist must *care* about and be involved in the phenomena being studied and that psychologists should limit their objectivity and precision to their methodology, not to the creation of hypotheses or to the communication of research findings.

VII. The Chicago Study

While at the University of Chicago, Rogers and his associates conducted a sophisticated and complex study on the effectiveness of psychotherapy. The purpose of the Chicago study was to investigate both the process and the outcomes of client-centered therapy.

A.   Hypotheses

The Chicago studies tested several broad hypotheses: (1) clients will become more aware of their feelings and experiences; (2) the gap between the real self and the ideal self will lessen as a consequence of therapy; (3) clients' behavior will become more socialized and mature; and (4) clients will become both more self-accepting and more accepting of others.

B.   Method

To assess change from an external view, the researchers used the Thematic Apperception Test, the Self-Other Attitude Scale, and the Willoughby Emotional Maturity Scale. To measure change from the client's view, they used the **Q sort** technique, which asks people to sort cards according to how they see themselves or others. Participants were adults who sought therapy at the University of Chicago counseling center. Experimenters asked half the participants to wait 60 days before receiving therapy. In addition, they tested a control group of "normals" who were matched with the therapy group. This control group was also divided into a wait group and a non-wait group.

C.   Findings

Rogers and his associates found that the therapy group—but not the control group—showed a lessening of the gap between real self and ideal self. They also found that clients who improved during therapy—but not those rated as least improved—showed changes in social behavior, as noted by their friends.

D.   Summary of Results

Although client-centered therapy was successful in changing clients, it was not successful in bringing them to the level of the fully functioning person or even to the level of "normal" psychological health.

VIII. Related Research

Other researchers have investigated Rogers's facilitative conditions both outside therapy and within therapy.

A.   Facilitative Conditions Outside Therapy

In the United Kingdom, Duncan Cramer (1989, 1990a, 1990b, 1994) has conducted a series of studies investigating the therapeutic qualities of Rogers's facilitative conditions in interpersonal relationships outside of therapy. In general, Cramer found positive relationships between self-esteem, as measured by the Rosenberg Self-Esteem Scale, and the four facilitative conditions that make up the Barrett-Lennard Relationship Inventory—level of regard, unconditionality of regard, congruence, and empathy. Moreover, the direction of the relationship strongly suggested that Rogers's facilitative conditions precede the acquisition of higher levels of self-esteem.

B.   Facilitative Conditions and Couples Therapy

In Belgium, Alfons Vansteenwegen (1996) used a revised form of the Barrett-Lennard to determine if Rogers's facilitative conditions related to success during couples therapy. He found that client-centered couples therapy can bring about positive changes in couples, and that some of these changes lasted for at least seven years after therapy.

IX.   Critique of Rogers

Rogers's person-centered theory is one of the most carefully constructed of all personality theories, and it meets quite well each of the six criteria of a useful theory. It rates very high on internal consistency and parsimony, high on its ability to be falsified and to organize knowledge, and high-average on its ability to serve as a guide to the practitioner.

X.   Concept of Humanity

Rogers believed that humans have the capacity to change and grow—provided that certain necessary and sufficient conditions are present. Therefore, his theory rates very high on optimism. In addition, it rates high on free choice, teleology, conscious motivation, social influences, and the uniqueness of the individual.

TEACHING SUGGESTIONS

1.   Throughout his career, Rogers was interviewed many times on film, and most of these are still available on videocassette. Like several other personality theorists, Rogers was interviewed by Richard Evans, and these two 50-minute videotapes give students some insight into Carl Rogers's personality, his personality theory, his approach to psychotherapy, and his views on education. These films may be rented or purchased from

       Audio-Visual Services

University Division of Media and Learning Resources

The Pennsylvania State University

University Park, PA 16802

Phone (814) 865-6314 or 1-800-826-0132

2. Psychological and Educational Films has available more than a dozen videocassettes of Rogers as counselor. Students may be interested in *Carl Rogers on Counseling: A Personal Perspective at 75*, a 25-minute video in which Rogers sums up his views on the nature of people. To see Rogers "in action" as a group therapist, we recommend *Carl Rogers Conducts an Encounter Group*, a 70-minute video of group therapy. To understand Rogers as an individual therapist, students can view *Three Approaches to Psychotherapy I, Part 1*, a session with the client Gloria, or *Three Approaches to Psychotherapy II, Part 1*, a session with the client Kathy. Both films on individual therapy are about 50 minutes, with about 30 minutes of person-to-person counseling. In the remaining time, Rogers introduces his approach, and after the counseling, he gives his immediate impression of the session. All these films are available in videocassettes from

Psychological & Educational Films

3334 East Coast Hwy, Suite 252

Corona Del Mar, CA 92625

Phone (714) 494-5079

References

Cramer, D. (1989). Self-esteem and the facilitativeness of parents and close friends. *Person-Centered Review, 4,* 61–76.

Cramer, D. (1990a). Disclosure of personal problems, self-esteem, and the facilitativeness of friends and lovers. *British Journal of Guidance and Counseling, 18,* 186–196.

Cramer, D. (1990b). Toward assessing the therapeutic value of Rogers's core conditions. *Counseling Psychology Quarterly, 3,* 57–68.

Cramer, D. (1994). Self-esteem and Rogers' core conditions in close friends: A latent variable path analysis of panel data. *Counseling Psychology Quarterly, 7,* 327–337.

Vansteenwegen, A. (1996). Individual and relational changes seven years after couples therapy. In B. J. Brothers (Ed.), *Couples and change* (pp. 95–115). New York: Haworth Press.

CHAPTER 17
MASLOW: HOLISTIC-DYNAMIC THEORY

LEARNING OBJECTIVES

After studying Chapter 17, students should be able to:

1. List and explain four assumptions Maslow made about motivation.

2. List and explain the five needs in Maslow's hierarchy of needs.

3. Distinguish among conative, aesthetic, cognitive, and neurotic needs.

4. Define instinctoid needs.

5. Describe Maslow's criteria for identifying self-actualizing people.

6. List and describe the characteristics of self-actualizing people.

7. Describe the Jonah complex.

8. Discuss Maslow's philosophy of science.

9. Critique Maslow's research methods.

10. Review research on Maslow's concept of self-actualization.

LECTURE OUTLINE

I. **Overview of Maslow's Holistic-Dynamic Theory**

Maslow's holistic-dynamic theory, sometimes called the third force in psychology, holds that people are continually motivated and that, under the proper circumstances, they can reach a level of psychological health called *self-actualization*.

II. **Biography of Abraham H. Maslow**

Abraham H. Maslow was born in New York in 1908, the oldest of seven children of Russian-Jewish immigrants. Maslow harbored great animosity toward his mother, an attitude that persisted throughout his lifetime. Although he possessed a brilliant mind, Maslow was only a mediocre student during his early years of college. However, when he transferred to the University of Wisconsin and began working with Harry Harlow, his grades greatly improved. He eventually received a Ph.D. from Wisconsin, spent a short time at Columbia University and more than a dozen years at Brooklyn College. While in New York, he met and was influenced by several important Europeans, including Alfred Adler, Erich Fromm, and Karen Horney. In 1951, Maslow became chairperson of the psychology department at Brandeis University, where he remained until poor health forced him to take a low-stress position with the Saga Administrative Corporation in California. There he died in 1970 at age 62.

III. Maslow's View of Motivation

Maslow's theory rests on five basic assumptions about motivation: (1) the whole organism is motivated at any one time; (2) motivation is complex, and unconscious motives often underlie behavior; (3) people are continually motivated by one need or another; (4) people in different cultures are all motivated by the same basic needs; and (5) needs can be arranged on a hierarchy.

A.   Hierarchy of Needs

Maslow held that lower level needs have prepotency over higher level needs; that is, they must be satisfied before higher needs become motivators.

1.   Physiological Needs

Before people can become motivated by any other needs, they must have their physiological needs relatively well satisfied; that is, they must have oxygen, food, water, and so forth. Physiological needs have prepotency over all other needs.

2.   Safety Needs

The second level of Maslow's hierarchy is the safety needs, including physical security, stability, dependency, protection, and freedom from danger. Children and neurotic adults often have difficulty satisfying safety needs and thus suffer from **basic anxiety**.

3.   Love and Belongingness Needs

Most people in first world countries are able to satisfy physiological and safety needs most of the time, but many people are only partially able to satisfy love and belongingness needs. These needs include the desire for friendship, the wish for a mate and children, and the need to belong. People who have these needs only partially satisfied are very strongly motivated by them, whereas people who have them nearly completely satisfied or who have never had them satisfied are only weakly motivated by love and belongingness.

4.   Esteem Needs

Satisfaction of love needs fosters self-esteem, self-confidence, and the recognition that one has a positive reputation. Because people are dependent on others for the satisfaction of love needs, they must also rely on others for the initial satisfaction of esteem needs. However, once people have their esteem needs relatively well satisfied, they no longer rely on others for the continual satisfaction of these needs, and they can sustain high self-esteem in the absence of a close interpersonal relationship.

5.   Self-Actualization Needs

The highest level on Maslow's hierarchy consists of self-actualization needs. Unlike other needs that automatically are activated when lower needs are met, self-actualization needs do not inevitably follow the satisfaction of esteem needs. Only psychologically healthy people who embrace the **B-values** achieve self-actualization. The five needs comprising the hierarchy are **conative needs**, but other needs exist as well.

B.   Aesthetic Needs

Aesthetic needs, which are on a different dimension than conative needs, include a desire for beauty and order. Some people have stronger aesthetic needs than do others, and when these needs are not met, these people become sick.

C.   Cognitive Needs

A third dimension includes the cognitive needs, or the desire to know, to understand, and to be curious. Knowledge is a prerequisite for each of the five conative needs. Also, people who are denied knowledge and kept in ignorance become sick, paranoid, and depressed.

D.   Neurotic Needs

With each of the three dimensions of needs listed above, physical or psychological illness results when the needs are not satisfied. Neurotic needs, however, lead to pathology regardless of whether they are satisfied or not. Neurotic needs include such motives as a desire to dominate or to inflict pain. Neurotic needs are nonproductive and do not foster health.

E.   General Discussion of Needs

Maslow believed that most people satisfy lower level needs to a greater extent than they do higher needs, and that the greater the satisfaction of one need, the more fully the next highest need is likely to emerge.

1.   Reversed Order of Needs

In certain rare cases, the order of needs might be reversed. For example, a starving father may be motivated by love needs to give up food in order to feed his starving children. Maslow believed, however, that if we understood the unconscious motivation behind many apparent reversals, we would see that they are not genuine reversals at all.

2.   Unmotivated Behavior

Maslow believed that not all behaviors are motivated, even though all of them have a cause. Expressive behaviors, such as one's handwriting or manner of talking, are unmotivated, as are drug-induced behaviors and conditioned reflexes.

3.   Expressive and Coping Behavior

Although expressive behavior is often unmotivated, coping is always motivated. Expressive behavior has no aim or goal but is merely a person's mode of expression. In comparison, coping behavior is a person's attempt to cope with the environment. The conative needs ordinarily call forth coping behaviors.

4.   Deprivation of Needs

Deprivation of any of the needs leads to pathology of some sort. For example, being deprived of physiological needs leads to malnutrition, fatigue, loss of energy, and so forth. On the other end of the scale, people who fail to reach self-actualization suffer from **metapathology**, defined as an absence of values, a lack of fulfillment, and a loss of meaning in life.

5.   Instinctoid Nature of Needs

Maslow suggested that some needs are innately determined even though they can be modified by learning. These instinctoid needs can be identified because their lack of satisfaction produces pathology. Thus, each of the conative needs is instinctoid. For example, people deprived of safety suffer basic anxiety and those deprived of love behave in self-destructive ways in order to secure love and affection.

6.   Comparison of Higher and Lower Needs

Maslow believed that higher level needs (love, esteem, and self-actualization) are later on the evolutionary scale than lower level needs and that they produce more genuine happiness and more peak experiences.

IV. Self-Actualization

Maslow believed that a very small percentage of people reach an ultimate level of psychological health called self-actualization.

A.   Values of Self-Actualizers

Maslow held that self-actualizers are motivated by such **B-values** as truth, goodness, beauty, justice, and simplicity. He called such motivation **metamotivation**.

B.   Criteria for Self-Actualization

Four criteria must be met before a person achieves self-actualization: (1) absence of psychopathology, (2) satisfaction of each of the four lower level needs, (3) acceptance of the B-values, and (4) full realization of one's potentials for growth.

C.   Characteristics of Self-Actualizing People

Maslow listed 15 qualities that characterize self-actualizing people, although not all self-actualizers possess each of these characteristics to the same extent.

1.   More Efficient Perception of Reality

Self-actualizers often have an almost uncanny ability to detect phoniness in others, and they are not fooled by sham.

2.   Acceptance of Self, Others, and Nature

They accept themselves and other people for who they are, without any need to change, convert, or rationalize.

3.   Spontaneity, Simplicity, and Naturalness

In many ways, self-actualizers are like children or animals in their spontaneity, simplicity, and naturalness. They have no need to appear complex or sophisticated.

4.   Problem-Centering

Self-actualizing people are interested in problems outside themselves. They are concerned with age-old problems, which they view from a solid philosophical position.

5.   The Need for Privacy

They also have a quality of detachment that allows them to be alone without being lonely.

6.   Autonomy

Once people reach self-actualization, they no longer are dependent on other people for their self-esteem. Neither criticism nor flattery will impinge on their self-concept.

7.   Continued Freshness of Appreciation

Unlike other people who take many things for granted, self-actualizers view everyday things with a fresh vision and appreciation. Life experiences are rich and rewarding.

8.   The Peak Experience

Although the peak experience is not limited to self-actualizers, Maslow believed that believed that self-actualizers are more likely to report peak experiences than are non-actualizers. Peak experiences are mystical and give a person a sense of transcendence and a feeling of awe, wonder, ecstasy, reverence, and humility.

9. *Gemeinschaftsgefühl*

Self-actualizing people also possess social interest, a deep feeling of oneness with all humanity. Social interest is part of each of the next two characteristics.

10. Profound Interpersonal Relations

Self-actualizers have their love and belongingness needs and their esteem needs satisfied. Therefore, they do not desperately need to make friends. However, they usually have a few close, intimate friendships.

11. The Democratic Character Structure

Self-actualizers place no importance on superficial differences between people, such as differences of gender, race, social class, or age.

12. Discrimination Between Means and Ends

Maslow's self-actualizing people have a clear sense of right and wrong, and they experience little conflict about basic values. They enjoy doing something for its own sake and not just because it is a means to an end.

13. Philosophical Sense of Humor

Maslow found that self-actualizing people have a nonhostile, nonscatological sense of humor. Their humor is intrinsic to the situation rather than contrived, spontaneous rather than planned.

14. Creativeness

Self-actualizers are creative in the broad definition of the word. They have a keen perception of truth, beauty, and reality—important ingredients in creativity.

15. Resistance to Enculturation

Although self-actualizers may have the appearance of ordinary people, they are not conformists. Their autonomy allows them to set their own standards and to resist the mold into which their culture might attempt to place them.

D.   Love, Sex, and Self-Actualization

Maslow compared **D-love** (deficiency love) to **B-love** (love for being or essence of another person). Self-actualizing people are capable of B-love because they can love without expecting something in return. B-love is mutually felt and shared and not motivated by a deficiency or incompleteness in either the lover or the loved.

V.   Philosophy of Science

Maslow criticized traditional science as being value free, with a methodology that is sterile and nonemotional. He criticized scientists who have **desacralized** science—those scientists who have removed the joy and awe from their investigations. Instead, scientists should **resacralize** their work and instill it with wonder, rapture, and ritual. Consistent with this philosophy of science, Maslow argued for a **Taoistic attitude** for psychology, one in which psychologists would be noninterfering, passive, and receptive.

VI.   Measuring Self-Actualization

Maslow's ideas have resulted in attempts to measure self-actualization through self-report. The most widely used of these measures is Everett Shostrom's (1974) **Personal Orientation Inventory (POI)**, a 150-item forced-choice inventory that is difficult to fake. The POI has 2 major scales and 10 subscales. The first major scale is Time Competence/Time Incompetence and the second is a Support Scale. The 10 subscales are (1) self-actualization values, (2) flexibility in applying values, (3) sensitivity to one's own needs and feelings, (4) spontaneity, (5) self-regard, (6) self-acceptance, (7) positive view of humanity, (8) ability to see opposites as being related, (9) acceptance of aggression, and (10) capacity for intimate contact. Because the POI is fairly lengthy, Alvin Jones and Rick Crandall (1986) developed the Short Index of Self-Actualization, a much shorter scale that possesses adequate reliability and validity. In addition, John Sumerlin and Charles Bundrick (1996, 1998) created the Brief Index of Self-

Actualization, a somewhat longer instrument than the Short Index. However, the reliability, validity, and usefulness of the Brief Index have not yet been fully determined.

VII. The Jonah Complex

Because humans are born with a natural tendency to move toward psychological health, any failure to reach self-actualization can technically be called abnormal development. One such abnormal syndrome is the **Jonah complex,** or fear of being or doing one's best. Although the Jonah complex is especially prevalent in neurotic individuals, probably all of us have some timidity about seeking perfection or greatness. People allow false humility to stifle their creativity, and therefore they prevent themselves from becoming self-actualizing.

VIII. Psychotherapy

The hierarchy of needs concept has obvious ramifications for psychotherapy. People on the two lowest levels do not need counseling; rather, they need food and safety. Most people who seek psychotherapy probably do so because they have not adequately satisfied their love and belongingness needs. For these people, the task of a therapist is to help them satisfy love and belongingness needs. Self-actualizing people, as well as those with high self-esteem, probably do not need psychotherapy.

IX. Related Research

Researchers have investigated Maslow's concept of self-actualization in many settings and for a variety of purposes.

A.   Self-Actualization and Intimate Interpersonal Relations

Michael Sheffield and his colleagues (Sheffield, Carey, Patenaude, & Lambert, 1995) used the POI as a measure of self-actualization and found that high scores on the POI were inversely related to interpersonal relations. More specifically, people who were near the threshold of self-actualization tended to be self-motivated, accepted feelings of aggression, and were able to sustain intimacy.

B.   Self-Actualization and Creativity

Mark Runco and his colleagues (Runco, Ebersole, & Mraz, 1991) used the Short Index of Self-Actualization to assess self-actualization and found a positive relationship between self-actualization scores and two measures of creativity. Although the relationships were not strong, they suggest that, as Maslow's hypothesized, creativity is at least partly related to self-actualization.

C.   Self-Actualization and Self-Acceptance

Some researchers have tested Maslow's assumption that self-actualizing people accept themselves. One study (Sumerlin & Bundrick, 2000) with African-American businessmen found that those who scored high on self-actualization tended to have increased happiness and self-fulfillment. Another study by William Compton and his colleagues (Compton, Smith, Cornish, & Qualls, 1996) found that self-actualization related to openness to experience and to seeking out new and exciting experiences.

X.   Critique of Maslow

Maslow's theory remains popular in psychology and in other disciplines, such as management, nursing, and education. The hierarchy of needs concept seems both elementary and logical, which gives Maslow's theory the illusion of simplicity. However, the theory is somewhat complex, with four dimensions of needs and the possibility of unconsciously motivated behavior. As a scientific theory, Maslow's model rates somewhat high in generating research but low in falsifiability. It rates very high on its ability to organize knowledge and high as a guide to action. In addition, it rates about average on parsimony and internal consistency.

XI.   Concept of Humanity

Maslow believed that people are structured in such a way that their activated needs are exactly what they want most. Hungry people desire food, frightened people look for safety, and so forth. Although he was generally optimistic and hopeful, he saw that people are capable of great evil and destruction. He believed that as a species, humans are becoming increasingly fully human and motivated by higher level needs. In summary, his view of humanity rates high on free choice, optimism, teleology, and uniqueness and about average on social influences.

TEACHING SUGGESTIONS

1. During his professional career, Maslow made a number of audio- and videotape cassettes that will be of interest to students. Perhaps the best of these is his two-part discussion with Everett L. Shostrom on the 15 characteristics of self-actualizing people. These two 30-minute videos can be rented or purchased from

    > Psychological & Educational Films
    >
    > 3334 East Coast Hwy, Suite 252
    >
    > Corona Del Mar, CA 92625
    >
    > Phone (714) 494-5079

2. The Personal Orientation Inventory is a nonthreatening questionnaire that students will enjoy filling out. As discussed earlier, the POI is a 150-item forced-choice test that attempts to assess levels of self-actualization. This inventory should be given to students *before* they study Chapter 17, because extensive knowledge of Maslow's concept of self-actualization may consciously or unconscious color how a person answers the questions. The POI may be available at your university counseling center, or it can be purchased from

    > Educational and Industrial Testing Service
    >
    > PO Box 7234
    >
    > San Diego, CA 92107

REFERENCES

Compton, W. C., Smith, M. L., Cornish, K. A., & Qualls, D. L. (1996). Factor structure of mental health measures. *Journal of Personality and Social Psychology, 71,* 406–413.

Jones, A., & Crandall, R. (1986). Validation of a Short Index of Self-actualization. *Personality and Social Psychology Bulletin, 12,* 63–73.

Runco, M. A., Ebersole, P., & Mraz, W. (1991). Creativity and self-actualization. *Journal of Social Behavior and Personality, 6,* 161–167.

Sheffield, M., Carey, J., Patenaude, W., & Lambert, M. J. (1995). An exploration of the relationship between interpersonal problems and psychological health. *Psychological Reports, 76,* 947–956.

Shostrom, E. L. (1974). *Manual for the Personal Orientation Inventory.* San Diego: Educational and Industrial Testing Service.

Sumerlin, J. R., & Bundrick, C. M. (1996). Brief Index of Self-Actualization: A measure of Maslow's model. *Journal of Social Behavior and Personality, 11,* 253–271.

Sumerlin, J. R., & Bundrick, C. M. (1998). Revision of the Brief Index of Self-actualization. *Perceptual and Motor Skills, 87,* 115–125.

Sumerlin, J. R., & Bundrick, C. M. (2000). Happiness and self-actualization under conditions of strain: A sample of homeless men. *Perceptual and Motor Skills, 90,* 191–203.

CHAPTER 18
MAY: EXISTENTIAL PSYCHOLOGY

LEARNING OBJECTIVES

After studying Chapter 18, students should be able to:

1.   List the common assumptions found among most existential thinkers.

2.   Define being-in-the-world and nonbeing.

3.   Distinguish between normal and neurotic anxiety.

4.   Discuss the interrelationship between care, love, and will.

5.   List and give examples of the four forms of love.

6.   Discuss May's concept of myth and explain why the Oedipus myth is important in today's world.

7.   Describe the relationship between freedom and destiny.

8.   Define existential freedom and essential freedom.

9.   Discuss George Howard's research on the effects of human agency on free will.

10. Discuss research by Jeff Greenberg and colleagues on terror management theory.

LECTURE OUTLINE

I.   **Overview of May's Existential Theory**

Existential psychology began in Europe shortly after World War II and spread to the United States, where Rollo May played a large part in popularizing it. A clinical psychologist by training, May saw people as living in the world of present experiences and ultimately being responsible for who they become. However, most people surrender their freedom and run away from assuming responsibility. On the other hand, some people are able to challenge their destiny, cherish their freedom, and live authentically with other people and with themselves.

II.   Biography of Rollo May

Rollo May was born in 1909, in Ada, Ohio, the oldest son and second born of six children. May, who was not close to either parent, spent his childhood in Michigan, where he claimed to have learned more from the St. Clair River than from school. After graduating from Oberlin College in 1930, he spent three years roaming throughout eastern and southern Europe as an itinerant artist. When he returned to the United States, he entered the Union Theological Seminary, where he met and became friends with Paul Tillich. After receiving a Master of Divinity degree, he served for two years as a pastor, but quit in order to pursue a career in psychology. He received a Ph.D. in 1949 at the age of 40. During his professional career, he served as lecturer or visiting professor at a number of universities, conducted a private practice as a psychotherapist, and wrote a number of popular books on the human condition. He died in 1994 at age 85.

III.   Background of Existentialism

Søren Kierkegaard, the Danish philosopher and theologian, is usually considered to be the founder of modern existentialism. Like later existentialists, he emphasized a balance between freedom and responsibility. People acquire freedom of action by expanding their self-awareness and by assuming responsibility for their actions. However, this acquisition of freedom and responsibility is achieved at the expense of anxiety and dread. Since Kierkegaard, existentialists have applied their ideas to art, literature, and psychology.

A.   What Is Existentialism?

Existentialist have a wide variety of beliefs, but the first tenet of existentialism is that existence takes precedence over essence, meaning that process and growth are more important than product and stagnation. Second, existentialists oppose the artificial split between subject and object. Third, they stress people's search for meaning in their lives. Fourth, they insist that each of us is responsible for who we are and what we will become. Fifth, most existentialists take an anti-theoretical position, believing that theories tend to objectify people.

B.   Basic Concepts

Existentialism rests on two basic concepts: being-in-the-world and nonbeing.

1.   Being-in-the-World

People live in a world that can best be understood from their own perspective. Thus, a basic unity exists between them and their environment, a unity expressed by the term *Dasein,* or **being-in-the-world**. Three simultaneous modes of the world characterize people in their *Dasein: **Umwelt,*** or the environment around them; ***Mitwelt,*** or their world with other people; and ***Eigenwelt,*** or people's relationship with themselves.

2.   Nonbeing

If people can be aware of themselves as living beings, then they can also be aware of the possibility of nonbeing or **nothingness**. Death is the most obvious form of nonbeing, which can also be experienced as retreat from life's experiences. People attempt to escape the dread of nonbeing by constricting their existence, compulsively using alcohol and other drugs, or engaging in promiscuous sexual behaviors.

IV. The Case of Philip

Rollo May helped illustrate his notion of existentialism with the case of Philip, a successful architect in his mid-50s. Despite his apparent success, Philip experienced severe anxiety when his relationship with Nicole (a writer in her mid-40s) took a puzzling turn. Uncertain of his future and suffering from low self-esteem, Philip went into therapy with Rollo May. Eventually, Philip was able to understand that his difficulties with women were related to his early experiences with a mother who was unpredictable and an older sister who suffered from severe mental disorders. However, he began to recover only after he accepted that his "need" to take care of unpredictable Nicole was merely part of his personal history with unstable women.

V.   Anxiety

People experience anxiety when they become aware that their existence or something identified with it might be destroyed. The acquisition of freedom inevitably leads to anxiety, which can be either pleasurable and constructive or painful and destructive.

A.   Normal Anxiety

Growth produces normal anxiety, defined as that which is proportionate to the threat, does not involve repression, and can be handled on a conscious level.

B.   Neurotic Anxiety

Neurotic anxiety is a reaction that is disproportionate to the threat and that leads to repression and defensive behaviors. It is felt whenever one's values are transformed into dogma. Neurotic anxiety blocks growth and productive action.

VI.   Guilt

Guilt arises whenever people deny their potentialities, fail to accurately perceive the needs of others, or remain blind to their dependence on the natural world. Both anxiety and guilt are **ontological**; that is, they refer to the nature of being and not to feelings arising from specific situations. Ontological guilt can stem from (1) *Umwelt,* when people become separated from nature; (2) *Mitwelt,* when people fail to anticipate the needs of others; and (3) *Eigenwelt,* when people deny their own potentialities or fail to fulfill them.

VII. Intentionality

The structure that gives meaning to experience and allows people to make decisions about the future is called intentionality. May believed that intentionality permits people to overcome the dichotomy between subject and object, because it enables them to see that their intentions are a function of both themselves and their environment.

VIII. Care, Love, and Will

Care is an active process that suggests that things matter. Love means to care, to delight in the presence of another person, and to affirm that person's value as much as one's own. Care is also an important ingredient in will, defined as a conscious commitment to action.

A.   Union of Love and Will

May believed that our modern society has lost sight of the true nature of love and will, equating love with sex and will with will power. He further held that psychologically healthy people are able to combine love and will because both imply care, choice, action, and responsibility.

B.   Forms of Love

May identified four kinds of love in Western tradition: sex, eros, philia, and agape.

1.   Sex

May believed that Americans no longer view sex as a natural biological function, but have become preoccupied with it to the point of trivialization. During the past century or so, we have gone from an overly repressive attitude toward sex to an over-concern with having as many sexual escapades as possible.

2.   Eros

Eros is a psychological desire that seeks an enduring union with a loved one. It may include sex, but it is built on care and tenderness. Eros can lead to the psychological growth of both partners.

3.   Philia

Philia is an intimate nonsexual friendship between two people. It takes time to develop and is not contingent on the actions of the other person.

4.   Agape

Agape is an altruistic or spiritual love that carries with it the risk of playing God. Agape is both undeserved and unconditional.

IX. Freedom and Destiny

Psychologically healthy individuals are comfortable with freedom, able to assume responsibility for their choices, and willing to face their destiny.

A. Freedom Defined

Freedom comes from an understanding of our destiny. We are free when we recognize that death is a possibility at any moment and when we are willing to experience changes, even in the face of not knowing what those changes will bring.

B. Forms of Freedom

May recognized two forms of freedom: freedom of doing, which he called existential freedom, and freedom of being, or essential freedom.

1. Existential Freedom

Existential freedom is the freedom of action, as exemplified by the ability to move from place to place, to voice one's opinions, to change jobs, and so forth.

2. Essential Freedom

Essential freedom is the freedom of being, an inner freedom, a type of liberty that is only achieved if we face our destiny and recognize our mortality.

C. Destiny Defined

May defined destiny as "the design of the universe speaking through the design of each one of us." In other words, our destiny includes the limitations of our environment and our personal qualities, including our mortality, gender, and genetic predispositions. Freedom and destiny constitute a paradox, because freedom gains vitality from destiny, and destiny gains significance from freedom.

D. Philip's Destiny

After some time in therapy, Philip was able to stop blaming his mother for not doing what he thought she should have done. The objective facts of his childhood had not changed, but Philip's subjective perceptions had. As he came to terms with his destiny, Philip began to be able to express his anger, to feel less trapped in his relationship with

Nicole, and to become more aware of his possibilities. In other words, he gained his freedom of being.

X. The Power of Myth

May believed that the people of Western civilization have an urgent need for **myths** and, because they have lost many of their traditional myths, they turn to religious cults, drugs, and popular culture to fill the vacuum. May compared myths to the structural beams of a house—not easily visible but the strength that holds the house together. The Oedipus myth, for example, has had a powerful effect on our culture because it deals with such common existential crises as birth, separation from parents, sexual union with one parent and hostility toward the other, independence in one's search for identity, and finally death.

XI. Psychopathology

May saw apathy and emptiness—not anxiety and guilt—as the chief existential disorders of our time. People have become alienated from the natural world (*Umwelt*), from other people (*Mitwelt*), and from themselves (*Eigenwelt*). Psychopathology is a lack of connectedness and an inability to fulfill one's destiny.

XII. Psychotherapy

The goal of May's psychotherapy was not to cure patients of any specific disorder, but to make them more fully human. May said that the purpose of psychotherapy is to set people free, to allow them to make choices and to assume responsibility for those choices. Existential psychotherapy de-emphasizes techniques while stressing the personal qualities of the therapist, who is both a friend and an interpreter of the client's private meanings.

XIII. Related Research

May's theory of personality does not lend itself to easily testable hypotheses and, therefore, it has not generated much research. Nevertheless, Jeff Greenberg and colleagues (Goldenberg et al., 2000; Greenberg et al., 1994; Greenberg et al., 1992; McGregor et al., 1998; Pyszczynski, Greenberg, & Solomon, 2000; Schimel et al., 1999) have investigated the concept of terror management, which is based on the notion of existential anxiety. In general, the findings of Greenberg and his colleagues are consistent with May's definition of existential anxiety, but they can also be explained by other psychological theories.

XIV. Critique of May

May's psychology has been legitimately criticized as being anti-theoretical and unjustly criticized as being anti-intellectual. May's anti-theoretical approach calls for a new kind of science—one that considers uniqueness and personal freedom. However, according to the criteria of present science, May's theory rates low on most standards. Currently, his theory is very low on its ability to generate research and to guide action; low on internal consistency (because it lacks operationally defined terms), average on parsimony, and high on its organizational powers due to its consideration of a broad scope of the human condition.

XV. Concept of Humanity

May viewed people as complex beings, capable of both tremendous good and immense evil. People have become alienated from the world, from other people, and, most of all, from themselves. On the dimensions of a concept of humanity, May rates high on free choice, teleology, social influences, and uniqueness. On the issue of conscious or unconscious forces, his theory takes a middle position.

TEACHING SUGGESTIONS

1. Students will be interested in seeing and hearing Rollo May discuss his views of existential and humanistic psychology. Several videos with May are available from different vendors.

A. In the video *Rollo May: Discovery of Being*, May discusses his concept of humanity and the role of "being" in integrating the individual. This video can be purchased from

> Insight Media
>
> 2162 Broadway
>
> New York, NY 10024-6620
>
> Phone (212) 721-6316 or (1-800) 233-9910

B. May was one of several personality theorists interviewed by Richard Evans. The interview is in three parts, each slightly less than 30 minutes. In Part 1, May talks about existential anxiety, love, will, responsibility, and the psychology of dying. In Part 2, he discusses maturity and creativity and responds to his critics. In Part 3, May gives his reactions to the views of Freud, Otto Rank, Sullivan, Adler, and Jung. These videocassettes can be rented or purchased from

> Audio-Visual Services
>
> University Division of Media and Learning Resources
>
> The Pennsylvania State University
>
> University Park, PA 16802
>
> Phone (814) 865-6314 or 1-800-826-0132

C. Several videocassettes on May's psychology are available from Psychological and Educational Films. Perhaps the most appropriate one is *Rollo May on Humanistic Psychology*, a 24-minute tape in which May discusses basic concepts of his existential/humanistic psychology. These videos may be rented or purchased from

> Psychological & Educational Films
>
> 3334 East Coast Hwy, Suite 252

Corona Del Mar, CA 92625

Phone (714) 494-5079

REFERENCES

Goldenberg, J. L., McCoy, S, K., Pyszczynski, T., Greenberg, J., & Solomon, S. (2000). The body as a source of self-esteem: The effects of mortality salience on identification with one's body, interest in sex, and appearance monitoring. *Journal of Personality and Social Psychology, 79*, 118–130.

Greenberg, J., Pyszczynski, T., Solomon, S., Simon, L., & Breus, M. (1994). Role of consciousness and accessibility of death-related thoughts in mortality salience effects. *Journal of Personality and Social Psychology, 67*, 627–637.

Greenberg, J., Simon, L., Pyszczynski, T., Solomon, S., & Chatel, D. (1992). Terror management and tolerance: Does mortality salience always intensify negative reactions to others who threaten one's worldview? *Journal of Personality and Social Psychology, 63*, 212–220.

McGregor, H. A., Lieberman, J. D., Greenberg, J., Solomon, S., Arndt, J., Simon, L., & Pyszczynski, T. (1998). Terror management and aggression: Evidence that mortality salience motivates aggression against worldview-threatening others. *Journal of Personality and Social Psychology, 74*, 590–605.

Pyszczynski, T., Greenberg, J., & Solomon, S. (2000). Proximal and distal defense: A new perspective on unconscious motivation. *Current Directions in Psychological Science, 9*, 156–160.

Schimel, J., Simon, L., Greenberg, J., Pyszczynski, T., Solomon, S., Waxmonsky, J, & Arndt, J. (1999). Stereotypes and terror management: Evidence that mortality salience enhances stereotypic thinking and preferences. *Journal of Personality and Social Psychology, 77*, 905–926.

TEST BANK

CHAPTER 1
INTRODUCTION TO PERSONALITY THEORY

ESSAY QUESTIONS

1. What is the relationship between theory and each of the following terms:
(a) philosophy, (b) speculation, (c) hypothesis, and (d) taxonomy?

   A. A theory is a set of related assumptions capable of generating hypotheses. As such, it is narrower than a philosophy and more general than a hypothesis.
   B. Philosophy deals with what should be, whereas theories are built on scientific evidence. Theory relates to a branch of philosophy called epistemology, or the nature of knowledge, because theory is an essential tool of science, an important means of gaining knowledge.
   C. Although theories are built partially on speculation, they do not stem from baseless speculation. Theorists combine scientifically derived data with thoughtful speculation to construct theories that will lead to further scientific experimentation.
   D. A useful theory is capable of generating multiple hypotheses, or educated guesses. Hypotheses can be tested through scientific experimentation, whereas theories are not directly testable.
   E. Theories should include a careful taxonomy, or classification system. A taxonomy is merely part of a useful theory. Unlike a theory, a taxonomy is not dynamic; that is, it is not capable of generating hypotheses.

2. What is the relationship between theory and observation?

   A. Theories and observations have a mutual and dynamic interaction. A newly born theory is built on tentative observations. Hypotheses spawned by that theory can be tested, leading to new observations. As more observations become available, the theory can grow to include a greater number of hypotheses, which, in turn, can be tested, providing additional observations.

3. List and briefly discuss six criteria for a useful theory.

   A. A useful theory should generate both descriptive research and hypothesis testing. A theory that fails to spark research falls into disuse and will be discarded by scientists.
   B. A theory must be open to falsifiability. It must suggest research that is capable of either supporting or refuting its major tenets. Theories that can explain opposing data are not falsifiable.
   C. Theories should organize observations. A theoretical framework allows scientists to make sense of their findings.
   D. A theory should guide action. It provides people with a road map for making day-to-day decisions.
   E. A useful theory is internally consistent. It has a set of operational definitions that are used consistently and does not offer opposing answers to the same questions.
   F. A theory should be as parsimonious as possible. Other things being equal, the simpler of two theories is preferred.

MULTIPLE CHOICE QUESTIONS

c   *4.   The word personality comes from the Latin word "persona," meaning
         a.   that which one truly is.
         b.   the evil side of people.
         c.   theatrical mask.
         d.   soul.

c   *5.   Psychologists generally agree that personality
         a.   refers mostly to surface traits.
         b.   is largely inherited.
         c.   can be explained by several different theories.
         d.   can best be explained by a single theory.

b   *6.   The word "theory" is most closely associated with
         a.   philosophy.
         b.   science.
         c.   armchair speculation.
         d.   taxonomy.

a   7.   Theories are built primarily on
         a.   scientific observations.
         b.   philosophical speculation.
         c.   unique definitions of terms.
         d.   sociological models.

b   *8.   A set of related assumptions from which, by logical deductive reasoning,
         testable hypotheses can be drawn is
         a.   a philosophy.
         b.   the definition of theory.
         c.   the definition of taxonomy.
         d.   an armchair speculation.

c   9.   Statements formed in an if-then framework are most likely
         a.   taxonomies.
         b.   philosophies.
         c.   theories.
         d.   definitions of personality.

b   10.   What is the proper place of theory within science?
         a.   Theories enable scientists to know how they should live their lives.
         b.   Theories are tools used by scientists to give meaning to observations.
         c.   Theory building is the ultimate aim of science.
         d.   Theories play no role in scientific pursuits.

d   *11. Which statement best characterizes the relationship between a theory and
         a hypothesis?
         a.   A theory is narrower than a hypothesis.
         b.   A theory is directly verifiable, a hypothesis is not.
         c.   A theory is logically deduced from a specific hypothesis.
         d.   A theory may generate one or more hypotheses.

b   *12. An educated guess that can be scientifically tested is a definition of
            a.   theory.
            b.   hypothesis.
            c.   philosophy.
            d.   taxonomy.

d   *13. A taxonomy is best defined as
            a.   an educated guess.
            b.   a set of if-then statements.
            c.   the study of the nature of reality.
            d.   a classification system.

a   14.   The basic data of science are
            a.   observations.
            b.   facts.
            c.   theories.
            d.   hypotheses.

d   15.   What is the relationship between theory and observation?
            a.   They are mutually exclusive.
            b.   Several theories make up an observation.
            c.   Several observations make up a theory.
            d.   There is a mutual and dynamic interaction between them.

d   16.   A theory may be set aside when it
            a.   generates testable hypotheses.
            b.   explains a set of observations.
            c.   is proven by experimentation.
            d.   loses its usefulness.

a   17.   The ultimate value of any theory depends on its
            a.   usefulness.
            b.   truthfulness.
            c.   reliability.
            d.   simplicity.

d   *18. The personalities, cognitive processes, developmental histories, and social
            experiences of personality theorists help shape their theories. The discipline
            that deals with these factors is called
            a.   personology.
            b.   psychology.
            c.   sociology.
            d.   psychology of science.
            e.   psychobiology.

b   19.   According to the authors of the text, personality theories
            a.   are former principles that have been proven true.
            b.   originate from the historical, social, and psychological world of
                 their originators.
            c.   are useful tools of science to the extent that they are value free.
            d.   should not be open to falsification.

b   20.   Descriptive research
            a.   is designed to test hypotheses.
            b.   contributes to expanding a theory.
            c.   is that which uses an experimental design.
            d.   is expressed by if-then statements.

c   21.   The two MOST important functions of a theory are its
            a.   internal consistency and accuracy.
            b.   logic and its consistency with established theories.
            c.   ability to generate research and organize observations.
            d.   ability to be proven true and to become a doctrine.

a   *22.   A useful theory must be falsifiable, which means that
            a.   it must be precise enough to suggest research that may either support or fail
                 to support its major tenets.
            b.   it will eventually be proven false.
            c.   it should be flexible enough to encompass opposing data into its framework.
            d.   it must be either true or false.

b   *23.   Which of these is NOT a function of a useful theory?
            a.   It will generate research.
            b.   It will be consistent with one's philosophy of life.
            c.   It organizes observations.
            d.   It serves as a guide to action.

a   24.   Which statement is most nearly true?
            a.   A theory can be a practical guide for a psychotherapist.
            b.   Theory and practice are mutually exclusive.
            c.   Other things being equal, the more complex a theory the better.
            d.   A good theory gives opposing answers to a single question.

b   25.   Part of the internal consistency of a theory is
            a.   a taxonomy.
            b.   a set of operational definitions.
            c.   its agreement with older, more established theories.
            d.   its empirical validity.

a   26.   A researcher uses the number of times a person smiles at others as a measure of
            friendliness. This an example of
            a.   an operational definition.
            b.   hypothesis testing.
            c.   parsimony.
            d.   internal consistency.

c   *27.   A useful theory should be parsimonious, meaning that it should be
            a.   based on empirical research.
            b.   complex.
            c.   simple.
            d.   verifiable.

b   28.   Which of the following is NOT a dimension used by the authors to assess a theorist's concept of humanity?
          a. determinism versus free choice
          b. order versus disorder
          c. pessimism versus optimism
          d. conscious versus unconscious

a   29.   The variety of personality theories at the present time is due to
          a. the different personal and philosophical perspectives that each theorist has of human nature.
          b. the use of different terminology for the same basic concepts.
          c. different translations of theories originally written in other languages.
          d. the reluctance of psychologists to accept any theory except their own.

d   30.   Personality theorists have evolved different systems because
          a. they have different conceptions as to the nature of humanity.
          b. they have had a variety of childhood and professional experiences.
          c. they begin with different assumptions concerning personality.
          d. any or all of the above.

d   31.   Personality theorists who adopt a teleological approach generally believe that people's behavior is a function of
          a. early childhood experiences.
          b. genetic makeup.
          c. environment.
          d. people's expectations of future events.
          e. both a and c.

c   32.   A high positive reliability coefficient indicates
          a. validity for two sets of test scores.
          b. parsimonious test scores.
          c. similar test scores.
          d. different test scores.

d   *33. A reliable test
          a. is always valid.
          b. measures what it purports to measure.
          c. correlates positively with its validity.
          d. yields consistent results.

a   34.   If scores on an instrument that measures introversion correlate highly with a number of other measures of introversion—for example, shyness and inhibition—then that instrument is said to have
          a. discriminant validity.
          b. convergent validity.
          c. divergent validity.
          d. test-retest reliability.
          e. concurrent reliability.

e   35.   A test that can accurately divide extraverts from introverts is said to have
           a.   test-retest reliability.
           b.   internal consistency.
           c.   divergent validity.
           d.   convergent validity.
           e.   discriminant validity.

CHAPTER 2
FREUD: PSYCHOANALYSIS

ESSAY QUESTIONS

1.   Describe how Freud's three levels of mental life relate to his concept of the provinces of the mind.

   A. Freud developed his concept of the unconscious, preconscious, and conscious several years before he formulated the notion of the id, ego, and superego.
   B. The unconscious is a dynamic aspect of mental life responsible for many of our behaviors. It consists of both repressed experiences and experiences that have never been conscious. Childhood sexual and aggressive experiences are most likely to be repressed and thus enter into the unconscious in a disguised form.
   C. The preconscious consists of those experiences that are less threatening than those of the unconscious. Preconscious ideas can become conscious with varying degrees of difficulty, depending on their potential threat to the ego.
   D. The conscious mind plays a relatively minor role in Freudian psychology. It refers to those ideas that are in our awareness at any given time.
   E. The id is the amoral, animal side of human nature and is completely unconscious. The id serves the pleasure principle.
   F. The ego is the sense of "I" or "me" that children develop at an early age. The ego, which can be unconscious, preconscious, or conscious, serves the reality principle.
   G. The superego comes into existence after the resolution of the Oedipus complex and serves both the moral and the idealistic principles. The superego, like the id, is completely unconscious, meaning that its moralistic and idealistic demands are incessant and out of contact with reality.

2.   Trace the development of both the male and the female phallic stages and explain why Freud believed that they follow different paths.

   A. Freud believed that the male and female phallic stages take different routes because male and female anatomies are different.
   B. The male phallic stage begins with the little boy's sexual desire for his mother and hostility for his father—a condition called the male Oedipus complex. Fearing his father's retribution, the boy develops a castration complex, which takes the form of castration anxiety, or a fear of losing his penis. Because castration anxiety is extremely traumatic, the little boy quickly resolves this dilemma by giving up his incestuous feelings for his mother and identifying with his father. His identification with his father leads to his developing a strong male superego—one based on his perception of his father's morals and ideals.
   C. The female phallic stage begins with the castration complex, which for little girls takes the form of penis envy. Holding her mother responsible for her lack of a penis, the girl turns to her father for sexual love and generates hostility for her mother This condition, called the female Oedipus complex, is more difficult to resolve than the male Oedipus complex because the girl has no traumatic experience (such as castration anxiety) to shatter it. Gradually, the girl sees the futility of her position and turns to her mother for nonsexual love. The girl's identification with her mother leads to the

development of the female superego—a superego based on the little girl's perception of her mother's morals and ideals.

3.   How does Freud's early therapeutic technique relate to recent reports of childhood abuse?

   A. Some observers have criticized Freud for abandoning the seduction theory, which placed responsibility for childhood sexual abuse on a parent, usually the father. When Freud substituted the Oedipus complex for the seduction theory, he switched responsibility from the parent onto the child.
   B. Freud's early therapeutic technique was quite active, forceful, and suggestive. He placed his hands on his patients' heads and told them that they would think of something. This procedure usually led to precisely the results that Freud was looking for, namely, the confession of a childhood seduction.
   C. Freud's highly suggestive technique tended to yield stories of childhood seduction that had been repressed for years. Many current therapists, using somewhat different but equally suggestive procedures, have been able to "recover" patients' long-lost experiences of being sexually or physically abused by an older person, often a parent.
   D. Elizabeth Loftus and other researchers have argued that therapists have unwittingly planted suggestions—just as Freud did a century ago. Loftus has presented evidence indicating that 80 percent of women who reported childhood sexual abuse had remembered the abuse throughout their whole life; that is, they never had a period when they could not remember the experience.

MULTIPLE CHOICE QUESTIONS

a   *4.   Freud's psychoanalysis rests on which two cornerstones?
   a.   sex and aggression
   b.   sex and hunger
   c.   security and safety
   d.   security and sex

b   5.   Freud saw himself primarily as a
   a.   psychologist.
   b.   scientist.
   c.   philosopher.
   d.   writer of fiction.
   e.   general practitioner.

a   6.   Freud's lifelong optimism and self-confidence may have stemmed from
   a.   being his mother's favorite child.
   b.   his father's outstanding business success.
   c.   the death of his younger brother.
   d.   the presence of much older half-brothers.

b   *7.   During the first 35 years of his life, Freud had a strong desire to
   a.   live in the United States.
   b.   win fame by making a great discovery.
   c.   treat the poor and destitute of Vienna.
   d.   practice medicine.

c   8.   Freud's free association technique evolved from
        a.   Charcot's hypnotic technique.
        b.   his use of cocaine.
        c.   Breuer's cathartic method.
        d.   the periodicity theory of Wilhelm Fliess.

a   9.   Freud abandoned his _____ theory in 1897, the year after his father died.
        a.   seduction
        b.   Oedipal
        c.   dream
        d.   childhood sexuality
        e.   anal

a   10. After World War I, Freud made which revision to his theory of personality?
        a.   He placed greater emphasis on the aggression instinct.
        b.   He identified the three levels of mental life.
        c.   He rejected repression as an ego defense mechanism.
        d.   He rejected the notion of a female Oedipus complex.

a   *11. Freud began his famous self-analysis
        a.   at about the time that his father died.
        b.   as a reaction to his experiences during World War I.
        c.   as a reaction to the death of his wife.
        d.   while still a schoolboy.
        e.   as a reaction to the death of his mother.

d   12. Among Freud's personal qualities were
        a.   a lifelong acceptance and loyalty to those followers who broke away from psychoanalysis.
        b.   an inability to learn languages other than German.
        c.   an unromantic and dispassionate disposition, especially toward his close friends.
        d.   an intellectual curiosity and high moral courage.

e   13. The event that eventually led to Freud's achievement of fame was his
        a.   partnership with Jung.
        b.   use of cocaine.
        c.   insistence on the existence of male hysteria.
        d.   marriage to Martha Bernays.
        e.   publication of *The Interpretation of Dreams.*

a   14. Freud's three levels of mental life are
        a.   unconscious, preconscious, and conscious.
        b.   id, ego, and superego.
        c.   aim, object, and impetus.
        d.   Thanatos, Eros, and Oedipus complexes.

c. *15. According to Freud, most of our mental life is
        a.   conscious.
        b.   preconscious.
        c.   unconscious.
        d.   a function of the superego.
        e.   a product of phylogenetic endowment.

c   16. Freud believed that unconscious ideas
          a. influence behavior only when one is aware of them.
          b. have no influence on behavior.
          c. influence behavior even when one is unaware of them.
          d. are learned only after birth.

a   17. Freud claimed that an important function of repression is to
          a. protect a person against the pain of anxiety.
          b. convert superego functions into ego functions.
          c. protect a person against public disgrace.
          d. convert id functions into ego functions.
          e. convert ego functions into id functions.

c   18. Which of these progressions is most consistent with psychoanalytic theory?
          a. Anxiety leads to repression, which leads to suppression of sexual feelings,
              which leads to a reaction formation.
          b. Punishment of a child's sexual behavior leads to repression, which leads to
              anxiety, which leads to suppression of sexual activity.
          c. Punishment of a child's sexual behavior leads to suppression of sexual
              behavior, which leads to anxiety, which leads to repression.
          d. Anxiety leads to suppression of sexual feelings, which leads to repression,
              which leads to punishment of sexual behaviors.

c   19. Freud's notion of phylogenetic endowment refers to
          a. anatomical differences between the sexes that lead to psychological
              differences.
          b. the physical structure of the brain where the unconscious is located.
          c. our ancestor's experiences that we inherit and that form part of
              our unconscious.
          d. the social rules we learn from our parents that form the superego.

b   20. According to Freud, ideas that slip in and out of awareness with greater or lesser
          degrees of ease are
          a. unconscious.
          b. preconscious.
          c. conscious.
          d. repressed.
          e. censored.

c   21. Freud held that ideas in the preconscious originate from
          a. the conscious.
          b. the unconscious.
          c. both the conscious and the unconscious.
          d. neither the conscious nor the unconscious.

c   *22. Freud believed that the id
          a. serves the reality principle.
          b. serves the moral or idealistic principle.
          c. constantly seeks to increase pleasure and reduce tension.
          d   is the executive branch of personality.
          e. is reasonable and logical.

c   23. The id is primarily involved in which of the following activities, according
          to Freud?
          a. solving problems in geometry
          b. contemplating the meaning of life
          c. salivating at the sight of food
          d. convincing a friend to plant a garden

a   24. Freud claimed that pleasure-seeking people with no thought of what is
          reasonable or proper are dominated by the
          a. id.
          b. ego.
          c. superego.
          d. ego-ideal.

b   25. Freud held that the secondary process functions through
          a. the id.
          b. the ego.
          c. the superego.
          d. the conscience.
          e. the ego-ideal.

d   26. According to Freud, the ego is
          a. conscious only.
          b. preconscious only.
          c. unconscious only.
          d. conscious, preconscious, and unconscious.
          e. conscious and preconscious only.

d   27. Freud believed that the ego begins to evolve from the id soon after birth. While
          the ego is developing, the id
          a. begins to diminish.
          b. develops parallel to the ego.
          c. disappears completely.
          d. remains stationary.

b   28. Freud believed that the superego develops from the
          a. id.
          b. ego.
          c. ego-ideal.
          d. conscience.
          e. preconscious.

d   *29. Freud's notion of the superego includes
          a. conscious and preconscious levels.
          b. pleasure and reality principles.
          c. the ego and the id.
          d. a conscience and an ego-ideal.

d   30. In psychoanalytic theory, unacceptable drives and impulses are repressed by the
          a. id.
          b. aggressive drive.
          c. superego.
          d. ego at the urging of the superego.
          e. ego-ideal.

b   *31.   According to Freud, which of these regions of the mind is (are) in contact with the external world?
- a. id
- b. ego
- c. superego
- d. ego and superego
- e. id, ego, and superego

b   32.   The superego, said Freud,
- a. is rational.
- b. strives for perfection.
- c. is the executive branch of personality.
- d. strives for pleasure.
- e. does all of the above.

e   33.   According to Freud, feelings of inferiority stem from the
- a. id.
- b. ego.
- c. superego.
- d. conscience.
- e. ego-ideal.

a   34.   According to Freud, a guilt-ridden, timid person is most likely dominated by
- a. the superego.
- b. the ego.
- c. the id.
- d. the Oedipus complex.
- e. phylogenetic endowment.

a   35.   The function that fights against id impulses regardless of what is realistic or possible is what Freud called the
- a. superego.
- b. ego.
- c. preconscious.
- d. conscious.

b   36.   According to Freud, a psychologically healthy person has a dominant
- a. id.
- b. ego.
- c. superego.
- d. conscience.
- e. ego-ideal.

e   *37.   According to Freud, all people possess two major instincts or drives. They are
- a. ego and id.
- b. id and superego.
- c. hunger and safety.
- d. self-defense and self-enhancement.
- e. sex and aggression.

a   38. Freud believed that instincts are characterized by all of the following EXCEPT
        a. depth.
        b. impetus.
        c. source.
        d. aim.
        e. object.

b   39. Freud contended that the object of the sexual instinct is
        a. the region of the body in a state of tension.
        b. the person or thing that is capable of bringing about sexual pleasure.
        c. the amount of force that sexual pleasure exerts on a person.
        d. to seek pleasure by removing a state of sexual tension.
        e. to seek pleasure by building up a state of sexual tension.

e   40. Freud called areas of the body especially capable of producing sexual pleasure
        a. aim-impetus areas.
        b. instinct zones.
        c. genital organs.
        d. pleasure-principle areas.
        e. erogenous zones.

a   41. A young man gets sexual gratification by kissing and caressing women's shoes.
        What statement best describes this situation, according to Freud?
        a. The sexual object has been displaced.
        b. The sexual aim has been changed.
        c. The path of the sexual instinct is inflexible.
        d. The sexual instinct is permanently inhibited.

b   42. According to Freud, a teenager preoccupied with self and personal appearance
        is exhibiting
        a. primary narcissism.
        b. secondary narcissism.
        c. aim-inhibited love.
        d. moral masochism.

c   43. Freud called the nonsexual love a child has for a sibling
        a. primary narcissism.
        b. secondary narcissism.
        c. aim-inhibited love.
        d. masochism.

c   44. In Freud's aim-inhibited love, that which is inhibited is
        a. the strength of the drive.
        b. the overt, open expression of love.
        c. the sexual aspect of the instinct.
        d. the aggressive aspect of the instinct.

d   *45. Freud called an expression of both the sexual and the aggressive instinct
        a. narcissism.
        b. love.
        c. superego.
        d. masochism.

d   46.   According to Freud, a masochist may receive sexual pleasure from
              a.   inflicting pain on others.
              b.   inflicting pain on self.
              c.   receiving pain inflicted by others.
              d.   both b and c.

c   47.   The aim of Freud's destructive instinct is
              a.   self-preservation.
              b.   self-assertion.
              c.   self-destruction.
              d.   self-hatred.

a   48.   Freud regarded precepts such as "Love thy neighbor as thyself" as
              a.   reaction formations.
              b.   worthless relics from an ancient religion.
              c.   expressions of the erotic drive.
              d.   expressions of neurotic anxiety.

a   49.   According to Freud, the apprehension a person feels when physically threatened
              is _____ anxiety.
              a.   realistic
              b.   neurotic
              c.   masochistic
              d.   moral

d   *50.   Ashley feels uneasy after violating her personal standards of honesty
              and cheating on a test. Freud might suggest that she is suffering from
              _____ anxiety.
              a.   aim-inhibited
              b.   realistic
              c.   neurotic
              d.   moral

d   51.   According to Freud, the ego's dependency on the superego results in
              a.   basic anxiety.
              b.   realistic anxiety.
              c.   neurotic anxiety.
              d.   moral anxiety.
              e.   traumatic.

e   52.   Which anxiety does Freud claim most nearly resembles fear?
              a.   neurotic
              b.   traumatic
              c.   moralistic
              d.   aim-inhibited
              e.   none of the above

a   53.   The apprehension one feels while in the presence of a teacher is what Freud
              called _____ anxiety.
              a.   neurotic
              b.   psychotic
              c.   realistic
              d.   moral
              e.   none of the above

d   *54. In psychoanalytic theory, anxiety
    a. is produced and felt by the ego.
    b. often signals that some undesirable, unconscious impulse is threatening to become conscious.
    c. is produced by repression.
    d. both a and b are correct.
    e. a, b, and c are all correct.

b   55. Freud held that the pain of anxiety is most likely to result in
    a. psychotic behavior.
    b. defensive behavior.
    c. neurotic behavior.
    d. realistic behavior.

a   56. The use of Freudian defense mechanisms requires an
    a. expenditure of psychic energy.
    b. extremely strong superego.
    c. immediate return to primary narcissism.
    d. exposure of the superego to prolonged anxiety.

a   57. The most basic Freudian defense mechanism is
    a. repression.
    b. reaction formation.
    c. fixation.
    d. projection.
    e. regression.

c   58. Which statement is correct, according to Freud?
    a. Repression produces anxiety.
    b. Anxiety reduces repression.
    c. Repression reduces anxiety.
    d. All of the above are correct.
    e. None of the above are correct.

c   *59. According to Freud's theory, anxiety
    a. results from repression of libidinal impulses.
    b. represents one type of defense mechanism.
    c. instigates repression.
    d. is a property of the superego.
    e. is felt by the id.

e   60. Shakespeare's account of Lady Macbeth ceremonially rubbing her hands to erase her guilt of Duncan's murder is an example of what Freud called
    a. reaction formation.
    b. sublimation
    c. regression
    d. isolation
    e. undoing.

b   61.   Compulsive actions are part of Freud's undoing defense mechanism. Obsessive thoughts are associated primarily with
a.   displacement.
b.   isolation.
c.   reaction formation.
d.   fixation.

d   62.   A mother who has deep-seated hostility toward her only child but who shows overprotection and hyper-concern for the physical well-being of her child illustrates which Freudian defense mechanism?
a.   identification
b.   displacement
c.   projection
d.   reaction formation
e.   sublimation

d   63.   Madison is frequently berated by his domineering employer. Madison is too timid to confront his employer, but he takes out his frustration by mistreating his dog, children, and wife. According to Freud, this is an example of
a.   reaction formation.
b.   identification.
c.   projection.
d.   displacement.
e.   regression.

b   64.   Robin protects herself against the threat of change by constantly clinging to objects and behaviors left from her early childhood. It thus appears that Robin is relying primarily on which Freudian defense mechanism?
a.   reaction formation
b.   fixation
c.   projection
d.   regression
e.   sublimation

d   *65.   Amy, an 18-month-old child, resorts to taking her baby sister's bottle even though she has previously been completely weaned. This behavior illustrates which Freudian defense mechanism?
a.   stubbornness
b.   fixation
c.   repression
d.   regression

c   66.   Seeing deficiencies in others that one unconsciously feels within oneself is an example of which Freudian defense mechanism?
a.   reaction formation
b.   undoing
c.   projection
d.   isolation

d   *67.   When carried to extremes, which Freudian defense mechanism can become
           paranoid behavior?
           a.   reaction formation
           b.   rationalization
           c.   fixation
           d.   projection

c   68.   An example of Freud's notion of projection might be
           a.   "Things will be better tomorrow."
           b.   "The only reason I failed is because I had a headache."
           c.   "I like him fine, but for some reason he hates me."
           d.   "I didn't really want that job anyway."

d   69.   A man goes into a gay bar and initiates a fight with a homosexual man as a
           result of his own unconscious homosexual impulses. This is an example of
           which Freudian defense mechanism?
           a.   sublimation
           b.   introjection
           c.   fixation
           d.   projection

a   *70.   Tyler greatly admires his geometry teacher and tries to copy his mannerisms
           and lifestyle. This is an example of which Freudian defense mechanism?
           a.   introjection
           b.   fixation
           c.   projection
           d.   sublimation

c   *71.   Which of the following distinguishes sublimation from the other Freudian
           defense mechanisms?
           a.   Sublimation is directly related to the superego.
           b.   Sublimation is always destructive.
           c.   Sublimation is constructive to society.
           d.   Sublimation involves the Oedipus complex.

c   72.   The transformation of instinctual drives into socially productive forces such as
           art, science, and religion is what Freud called
           a.   regression.
           b.   rationalization.
           c.   sublimation.
           d.   acting out.
           e.   isolation.

d   73.   The paintings and sculpture of Michelangelo best exemplify Freud's concept of
           a.   Thanatos.
           b.   regression.
           c.   paranoia.
           d.   sublimation.

c   74.   Freud's oral-sadistic stage is characterized by
           a.   early attempts at toilet training.
           b.   unambivalent feelings toward the mother.
           c.   the emergence of teeth.
           d.   rivalry toward younger siblings.
           e.   rivalry toward one or both parents.

c   75.   The principle source of frustration during Freud's anal phase is
           a.   weaning.
           b.   learning to dress one's self.
           c.   toilet training.
           d.   suppression of masturbation.

a   76.   Freud hypothesized that a permissive, accepting attitude of parents during toilet
           training is likely to lead to which behaviors as the child grows to adulthood?
           a.   generosity and benevolence
           b.   stubbornness, compulsiveness, and miserliness
           c.   masochism and/or sadism
           d.   sexual dysfunction and aggression

c   77.   A compulsively neat person who is also stubborn and miserly is what
           Freud called an
           a.   oral-receptive character.
           b.   oral-sadistic character.
           c.   anal character.
           d.   ego-defense character.

b   *78.   The classical Freudian anal character possesses all EXCEPT which of
           the following traits?
           a.   orderliness
           b.   passivity
           c.   obstinacy
           d.   stinginess

a   79.   According to Freud, male and female personality development is
           a.   similar until the phallic stage.
           b.   similar until the genital stage.
           c.   different during the anal stage.
           d.   different during the oral stage.

d   *80.   Freud believed that boys and girls have a different psychosexual development
           because of
           a.   cultural influences.
           b.   parental attitudes.
           c.   fantasies that originate soon after birth.
           d.   anatomical differences between the genders.
           e.   hormonal differences between the genders.

c   81.   Freud claimed that during the Oedipal period, a boy
           a.   feels sexual love only toward his father.
           b.   feels sexual love only toward his mother.
           c.   may feel sexual love toward each parent.
           d.   is not capable of sexual love toward either parent.

b   82.   According to Freud, a boy who feels strong hostility toward his father and
           sexual love for his mother is experiencing
           a.   moral masochism.
           b.   the simple male Oedipus complex.
           c.   the complete Oedipus complex.
           d.   the castration complex.
           e.   penis envy.

b   83.   Freud held that castration anxiety
           a   results in penis envy.
           b.   dissolves the male Oedipus complex.
           c.   dissolves the female Oedipus complex.
           d.   triggers penis envy, which then dissolves the female Oedipus complex.

d   84.   According to Freud, normally, in post-Oedipal identification with his father,
           a boy
           a.   accepts homosexual feelings toward his father.
           b.   rejects the hated and feared father.
           c.   wants to be his father.
           d.   identifies with his father's morals and ideals.

d   85.   Freud said that in girls, the castration complex
           a.   shatters the Oedipus complex.
           b.   takes the form of penis envy.
           c.   precedes the Oedipus complex.
           d.   both b and c are correct.

c   86.   According to Freud, a girl's wish to be a boy or to have a baby
           a.   indicates feminine identification.
           b.   results from a mature superego.
           c.   is an expression of penis envy.
           d.   is called the complete Oedipus complex.
           e.   is an unnatural condition.

e   87.   Freud believed that a little girl's Oedipal wish for a baby is a substitute for the
           a.   father.
           b.   nipple.
           c.   feces.
           d.   mother.
           e.   phallus.

c   88.   After the female Oedipus complex is resolved, Freud claimed that it is
           replaced by
           a.   the sadistic-anal phase.
           b.   rationalizations.
           c.   the superego.
           d.   the wish to be a boy.

c   89.   Freud believed that a girl's superego
     a.   developed before the phallic stage.
     b.   was more severe than a boy's superego.
     c.   was not as fully developed as a boy's superego.
     d.   leads to castration anxiety.

b   90.   Concerning the male and female Oedipus complexes, Freud felt
     a.   more confident of his views on the female Oedipus complex.
     b.   more confident of his views on the male Oedipus complex.
     c.   strongly confident of his views on both complexes.
     d.   little or no confidence with his views of either complex.

b   91.   Freud's notion of the Oedipus complex is compounded, or made more complicated, by the
     a.   latency period.
     b.   bisexual nature of the child.
     c.   Electra complex.
     d.   castration complex.
     e.   influence of culture.

a   92.   Freud suggested that the latency period was rooted in
     a.   our phylogenetic endowment.
     b.   anatomical differences between the sexes.
     c.   an increase in psychic energy from the id.
     d.   decreased activity of the superego.
     e.   increased activity of the superego.

c   93.   According to Freud, the genital period
     a.   ends with the development of the superego.
     b.   is a result of penis envy.
     c.   begins at puberty.
     d.   is marked by an autoerotic sexual aim.
     e.   begins immediately after the anal stage.

b   94.   Freud's hypothesis that during prehistoric times a group of brothers, denied the right to have sexual relations with their mother or sisters, joined together to kill their father, felt guilty, and thus instigated strong prohibitions against sexual relations with and murder of family members could best be used to explain
     a.   anxiety dreams.
     b.   the latency period.
     c.   the origin of the ego.
     d.   the current prevalence of sadism.

a   95.   From a Freudian perspective, psychological maturity might be characterized by
     a.   minimal repression and maximal consciousness.
     b.   a maximum number of defense mechanisms.
     c.   a heavily repressed id and an overwhelming superego.
     d.   minimal libido directed toward others.

c   96. In Freudian psychology, the psychologically mature person would be
         characterized by
         a. an absence of id impulses.
         b. a superego strong enough to control the ego.
         c. an ego strong enough to incorporate the ego-ideal and the id.
         d. strong Oedipal feelings.

a   97. Freud gave four reasons why he abandoned his seduction theory. Which of the
         following was NOT a reason?
         a. He realized that his highly suggestive therapeutic tactics had elicited false
             memories of seduction.
         b. The seduction theory had not helped him treat patients.
         c. He realized that the unconscious memories of severely disturbed patients
             almost never revealed childhood sexual experiences.
         d. He believed that the unconscious mind could not distinguish reality
             from fiction.
         e. He realized that even his own father would have had to be guilty of sexually
             abusing some of Freud's siblings.

a *98. In Freudian theory, dreams are seen as
         a. wish-fulfillments.
         b. being prophetic in nature.
         c. having importance primarily on the manifest level.
         d. expressions of human's phylogenetic endowment.

d   99. According to Freud, dreams have meaning on two levels. The more important
         level concerns the
         a. conscious level.
         b. the preconscious level.
         c. manifest content.
         d. latent content.

b 100. Dreams of patients suffering from traumatic neuroses, or posttraumatic stress
         disorder, follow the Freudian principle of
         a. wish-fulfillments.
         b. repetition compulsion.
         c   parapraxis.
         d. aim inhibition.
         e. phylogenetic endowment.

c 101. Freud believed that condensation and displacement
         a. change latent dream level into manifest level.
         b. expand the latent dream level.
         c. are ways of distorting dream content.
         d. expand the manifest dream level.
         e. expand the latent dream level.

b 102. Trained psychoanalysts can interpret dreams
         a. by knowing the meaning of a standard set of symbols.
         b. most accurately by asking the dreamer for his or her associations to the
             material.
         c. without talking personally to the patient.
         d. by concentrating on the manifest meaning of the dream.

d   103. The "royal road to the unconscious" was thought by Freud to be
      a. the preconscious.
      b. meditation.
      c. parapraxes.
      d. dreams.
      e. Route 66.

d   104. "Freudian slips" are a product of
      a. dreamwork.
      b. free association.
      c. conscious and unconscious forces.
      d. preconscious and unconscious forces.

a   105. Freud believed that parapraxes, or "Freudian slips,"
      a. revealed unconscious intent.
      b. had no psychological meaning.
      c. demonstrated a dominant preconscious intention.
      d. were due to fatigue.

a   106. The goal of psychoanalytic therapy is to
      a. transform unconscious material into consciousness.
      b. eliminate all neurotic symptoms.
      c. bring about self-actualization.
      d. uncover archetypes.

a   107. Asking a patient to verbalize thoughts, no matter how absurd, irrelevant, or embarrassing, is the Freudian technique of
      a. free association.
      b. displacement.
      c. condensation.
      d. dream analysis.
      e. transference.

d   108. According to Freud, transference is necessary to
      a treat psychoses and other constitutional illnesses.
      b. understand the latent content of dreams.
      c. prevent the development of neuroses after treatment.
      d. free the libido from neurotic symptoms.
      e. understand the manifest level of dreams.

d   109. After successful psychoanalytic treatment
      a. neurotic symptoms are repressed.
      b. psychic energy strengthens the superego.
      c. positive transference toward the analyst increases.
      d. the ego is expanded with previously repressed material.
      e. the ego is incorporated into the superego.

c   110. George Vaillant reported some evidence that _____ is a mature and adaptive defense mechanism.
      a. reaction formation
      b. isolation
      c. sublimation
      d. projection
      e. undoing

d   111. Gilleard, Eskin, and Savasir found some evidence that
a. men and women who are chronic nail-biters tend to score low on aggression.
b. men and women who are chronic nail-biters tend to score high on aggression.
c. men, but not women, who are chronic nail-biters tend to score high on aggression.
d. women, but not men, who are chronic nail-biters tend to score high on aggression.

e   112. Although Freud's theory rates high on its ability to generate research, it rates low on
a. biological influences on personality.
b. falsifiability.
c. unconscious determinants of behavior.
d. operational definitions.
e. both b and d.

c   113. Bettelheim argued that psychoanalysis should be seen as a
a. natural science.
b. learning theory.
c. human science.
d. humanistic religion.

b   114. Freud's enduring popularity is most likely due to his
a. careful experimental analyses.
b. gifts as a writer and his emphasis on sex and aggression.
c. commonsense model of human development, especially during the infantile stage.
d. determination to reverse 19th-century scientific methods.

d   115. Which label best fits Freud's theory of personality?
a. scientific
b. sterile
c. parsimonious
d. comprehensive

a   116. Freud's concept of humanity can be described as
a. deterministic and pessimistic.
b. deterministic and optimistic.
c. goal directed and purposive.
d. purposive and optimistic.

CHAPTER 3
ADLER: INDIVIDUAL PSYCHOLOGY

ESSAY QUESTIONS

1. Differentiate the striving for superiority and the striving for success in Adler's theory of personality.

    A. Originally, Adler spoke of the striving for superiority as the final goal for all people, but after he placed more emphasis on social interest, he made a distinction between striving for superiority and striving for success.
    B. In Adler's final theory, the striving for superiority was seen as an attempt to gain personal superiority over other people. As such, it is pathological and devoid of a high level of social interest. For example, a person may give money to a street beggar to convey a message of superiority over the beggar.
    C. After Adler began to see the importance or social interest, he talked about striving for success, defined as success for all humanity. The striving for success is thus motivated by a high level of social interest and not by personal gain. A person who strives for success may give money to a street beggar out of interest in the beggar as part of humanity. A person with high social interest would genuinely care about the beggar and may extend that care beyond merely giving money.

2. Describe the role of subjective perceptions in Adler's theory of personality.

    A. To Adler, objective reality (such as a deformed hand) does not determine style of life; rather, style of life is shaped by one's view of realty.
    B. People are motivated more by fictions, or expectations of the future, than by experiences of the past. Fictions influence people as if they really existed. Expectations of the future reflect the concept of teleology and are opposed to the influence of past events, which emphasizes causality.
    C. Adler believed that the people are "blessed" by organ inferiorities. The inferiority itself does not determine the direction of a person's striving, but one's view of one's inferiority can lead to either healthy or unhealthy striving.

3. List and describe three Adlerian safeguarding tendencies.

    A. Safeguarding tendencies take the form of neurotic symptoms and are designed to protect an inflated self-image against public disgrace.
    B. The most common of Adlerian safeguarding tendencies are excuses, which can take the form of either the "Yes, but" excuse or the "If only" excuse. With either excuse, a person is attempting to protect a real sense of self-worth by deceiving other people into believing that he or she is a worthy person.
    C. A second safeguarding tendency is aggression, which may take the form of depreciation, accusation, or self-accusation. In all three cases, the person aggresses against others or self in order to gain personal superiority.
    D. The third safeguarding tendency is to withdraw, or run away from life's difficulties. People can withdraw by (1) moving backward, or reverting to a more secure period of life; (2) standing still, which avoids responsibility for growing up; (3) hesitating, which gives people the excuse that "It's too late now;" and (4) constructing obstacles so that they can demonstrate their superiority by overcoming the obstacle.

MULTIPLE CHOICE QUESTIONS

c   4.   Unlike Freud's psychoanalysis, Adler's individual psychology assumed that
a.   behavior is shaped by past experiences.
b.   people are motivated largely by aggression.
c.   people are mostly responsible for their own personality.
d.   most behavior is motivated by unconscious forces.
e.   the sexual instinct is the basis for most human behavior.

a   5.   Adler's earliest memories concerned
a.   comparisons with his older and healthier brother.
b.   an active interest in helping others.
c.   neglect by his mother.
d.   his desire to become a famous psychologist.

c   6.   The death of Adler's younger brother resulted in Adler
a.   withdrawing from other family members.
b.   developing a severe childhood neurosis.
c.   deciding to become a doctor.
d.   turning to his older brother for protection.

e   7.   From Adler's biography, we know that he
a.   came from a Jewish background.
b.   had a younger brother who died in infancy.
c.   was second born.
d.   none of the above.
e.   a, b, and c are all correct.

c   8.   Adler's break with Freud was due to the fact that
a.   Freud believed that psychoanalysis should change to keep up with society.
b.   Adler was extremely deferent to Freud.
c.   Adler could not accept Freud's strong emphasis on sexual factors as motivators of behavior.
d.   Freud lacked organizational skills, leaving Adler with the responsibility of directing the Wednesday Psychological Society.

e   9.   During the time that Freud and Adler were members of the Wednesday Psychological Society,
a.   Adler considered Freud to be his mentor.
b.   Freud prevented Adler from holding office in the organization.
c.   they shared a warm personal relationship.
d.   they conspired to prevent Carl Jung from joining the organization.
e.   none of the above.

b   10.   Adler's concern for the whole person led to his
a.   development of treatments for cancer.
b.   study of psychiatry.
c.   becoming a rabbi.
d.   advocating revolution.

c   11.   In response to World War I, Adler
            a.   enlisted in the army.
            b.   became a conscientious objector.
            c.   changed his theoretical views.
            d.   moved to a neutral country.

d   12.   Unlike other psychiatrists of his time, Adler treated
            a.   large numbers of schizophrenics.
            b.   mentally retarded children.
            c.   patients without medical insurance.
            d.   large numbers of middle- and lower-class patients.

a   13.   One of Adler's strongest beliefs was in
            a.   the equality of the two sexes.
            b.   his Jewish faith.
            c.   his Protestant faith.
            d.   the communist doctrine.

a   14.   Which of the following assumptions is NOT part of Adler's theory?
            a.   All motives are unconscious.
            b.   The dynamic force behind a person's activity is the striving for
                 superiority or success.
            c.   All psychological phenomena are unified within the individual in a
                 self-consistent manner.
            d.   The subjective opinions of people shape their behavior and personality.

c.   15.   Adler believed that the dynamic force motivating all human activity is
            a.   organ dialect.
            b.   a feeling of superiority.
            c.   the striving for superiority or success.
            d.   inferior physical endowment.

d   16.   Early in his career, Adler used which term to refer to the single force behind all
            human motivation?
            a.   compensation
            b.   Eros
            c.   striving for success
            d.   will to power

a   17.   Adler first postulated the aggressive drive and the will to power as the
            fundamental motivations that shape human personality. He later extended his
            view to include the
            a.   striving for superiority or success.
            b.   will to knowledge.
            c.   search for meaning.
            d.   striving for self-actualization.

c   18.   Adler felt that every individual is striving to reach the same goal of
            a.   self-fulfillment.
            b.   a perfect society.
            c.   superiority or success.
            d.   reduction of anxiety.

b   19. The tendency toward completion, Adler believed,
          a. was a result of birth order.
          b. was innate but needed to be developed.
          c. was learned during preadolescence.
          d. resulted from the masculine protest.

a   20. Adler believed that people strive for superiority
          a. in order to compensate for feelings of inferiority.
          b. in order to survive in a competitive society.
          c. as a means of attaining sexual satisfaction.
          d. in imitation of parents and other authority figures.

a   21. Concerning feelings of inferiority, Adler held that
          a. all individuals possess them.
          b. only neurotics develop them.
          c. they always lead to the development of social interest.
          d. they only develop when organ inferiorities are present.

b.   22. According to Adler, the behavior of psychologically healthy individuals is
          a. unmotivated.
          b. motivated mostly by conscious goals and drives.
          c. motivated mostly by unconscious goals and drives.
          d. motivated by exaggerated feelings of inferiority.

c   *23. Adler believed that there are two general routes by which people strive. One is
          the path of exaggerated personal superiority and the other is the road of
          a. power.
          b. masculine protest.
          c. social interest.
          d. individuation.
          e. aggression.

c   24. According to Adler, children who feel pampered
          a. are generally conscious of their final goal.
          b. typically become loving parents.
          c. are usually neglected by their parents.
          d. are frequently unaware of their final goal.

a   25. Jade is a 20-year-old college junior who "checks in" daily with her out-of-state
          mother by e-mail or telephone. Jade, who makes no decisions without
          consulting her mother, is a pre-med major because her mother insists that she
          become a doctor. Adler would see Jade's relationship with her mother as a
          _____ one.
          a. parasitic
          b. casual
          c. loving
          d. sadistic

b   26. Adler would see an individual's inconsistent behavior as
          a. evidence of a variety of basic motives.
          b. a person's attempt to strive for superiority.
          c. a symptom of schizophrenia.
          d. a conscious means of acquiring social interest.

d   27.   From an Adlerian perspective,
            a.   all behavior is inconsistent.
            b.   psychological conflict leads to inconsistent behavior.
            c.   inconsistent behavior serves multiple purposes.
            d.   inconsistent behavior serves a single purpose.

d   28.   According to Adler, unconscious thoughts and behaviors are
            a.   essential to healthy psychological functioning.
            b.   understood only by the individual who has them.
            c.   regarded as helpful but not essential to healthy psychological functioning.
            d.   not clearly understood by the individual.

a   29.   Jared develops tension headaches while trying to meet a deadline at work.
            This tactic allows him to escape responsibility for meeting the deadline
            and to receive sympathy from his boss and coworkers. According to Adler,
            Jared's headaches are examples of
            a.   an organ dialect.
            b.   an organ inferiority.
            c.   an as-if illness.
            d.   a fiction.

c   *30.   Adler believed that behavior and personality are shaped by
            a.   early childhood experiences.
            b.   organ inferiorities.
            c.   subjective perceptions.
            d.   sexual and aggressive impulses.
            e.   birth order.

c   31.   Ideas that have no real existence yet influence people as if they really existed
            are what Adler referred to as
            a.   delusions.
            b.   hallucinations.
            c.   fictions.
            d.   hypothetical constructs.
            e.   objective certainty.

b   32.   Adler said that all humans are "blessed" at birth with
            a.   well developed social interest.
            b.   inferior bodies.
            c.   superior intellect.
            d.   the need to become superior to other people.

a   *33.   According to Adler, the goal toward which a psychologically healthy person
            strives is
            a.   fictional.
            b.   the creation of conscious thought.
            c.   largely known to that person.
            d.   shaped mostly by the person's birth order.
            e.   all of the above are correct.

a   *34. Teleology
           a. is the doctrine that motivation must be considered according to its final
               purpose or aim.
           b. considers behavior as springing from a specific cause.
           c. is more accurately associated with Freud than with Adler.
           d. is the study of telescopes.

d   35. Adler borrowed his ideas on fictionalism from
           a. Sigmund Freud.
           b. Karl Marx.
           c. John Calvin.
           d. Hans Vaihinger.

c   *36. According to Adler, organ inferiorities
           a. cause inferior personalities.
           b. cause superior personalities.
           c. are important because they stimulate subjective feelings of inferiority.
           d. are important because they bestow purpose on all behavior.

a   37. Social interest
           a. exists in everyone to some degree.
           b. exists only in psychologically healthy people.
           c. requires personal gain by the individual.
           d. is much stronger in pampered children than in neglected ones.

d   *38. Adler believed that social interest
           a. develops early in the mother–child relationship.
           b. is characteristic of all people to some degree.
           c. is the English translation of *Gemeinschaftsgefühl*.
           d. all of the above.
           e. none of the above.

e   39. Adler said that the usefulness or uselessness of all human activity should be seen
          from the point of view of
           a. the masculine protest.
           b. the ego.
           c. the superego.
           d. the society.
           e. social interest.

a.   40. According to Adler, social interest is strongest in people who strive for
           a. success.
           b. personal gain.
           c. superiority.
           d. inferiority.

d   41. According to Adler, _____ is the bond that holds society together.
           a. fiction
           b. the sex drive
           c. a feeling of incompleteness
           d. social interest

d   *42.   The "sole criterion of human values," Adler said, is
      a.   style of life.
      b.   creative power.
      c.   subjectivity of perception.
      d.   social interest.

a   43.   According to Adler, _____ is the "barometer of normality."
      a.   social interest
      b.   creative power
      c.   subjectivity of perception
      d.   fictional finalism

c   44.   Adler maintained that social interest is
      a.   inborn.
      b.   acquired through experience.
      c.   inborn, but brought to expression through experience.
      d.   inborn in some people but acquired by others.

d   45.   Unlike Freud, Adler believed that
      a.   people are basically narcissistic.
      b.   narcissism is an inherent human characteristic.
      c.   sublimation is necessary for social interest.
      d.   narcissism is a form of neurosis.

e   *46.   Adler believed that creative power
      a.   shapes an individual's style of life.
      b.   guides the method of striving toward the final goal.
      c.   implies individual freedom.
      d.   none of the above.
      e.   a, b, and c are all correct.

a   47.   As a dynamic concept, Adler's notion of creative power implies
      a.   movement.
      b.   adjustment.
      c.   social interest.
      d.   conflict.
      e.   cooperation.

d   48.   Adler believed that the essence of maladjustment is a person's
      a.   fictional goals.
      b.   creative power.
      c.   safeguarding tendencies.
      d.   underdeveloped social interest.
      e.   psychic conflict.

b   49.   Adler believed that maladjusted people
      a.   set their goals too low.
      b.   set their goals too high.
      c.   set too many goals.
      d.   set too few goals.

b 50. Which factor does NOT describe maladjusted people, according to Adler?
        a. a dogmatic style of life
        b. a high level of social interest
        c. exaggerated goals
        d. a private world of experience

c 51. Adler held that exaggerated physical deficiencies
        a. cause abnormal psychological development.
        b. are the result of abnormal psychological development.
        c. lead to abnormal psychological development when they trigger strong
            feelings of inferiority.
        d. are unrelated to abnormal psychological development.

d 52. According to Adler's theory of abnormal development, the goals of
        neurotic people
        a. originate in the id.
        b. are exaggerated and unrealistic.
        c. are overcompensations for exaggerated feelings of inferiority.
        d. both b and c.
        e. none of the above.

c *53. Adler believed that children who are pampered
        a. develop high levels of social interest.
        b. are well prepared for life's problems.
        c. often feel neglected.
        d. have mothers who love them too much.
        e. none of the above.

a 54. Adler held that children who received love and affection from their parents
        typically develop
        a. strong social interest.
        b. a pampered style of life.
        c. a neglected style of life.
        d. a variety of safeguarding tendencies.
        e. a parasitic style of life.

c *55. Although similar to Freud's defense mechanisms, Adler's concept of
        safeguarding tendencies differs in several respects. One difference is that
        safeguarding tendencies are
        a. completely conscious.
        b. completely unconscious.
        c. sometimes conscious.
        d. used by everyone.

d 56. According to Adler, two commonly used safeguarding tendencies are excuses and
        aggression. A third is
        a. regression.
        b. fixation.
        c. social interest.
        d. withdrawal.
        e. early recollections.

b   *57. Adlerian safeguarding tendencies protect _____ against public disgrace and
     loss of self-esteem.
     a. the ego
     b. exaggerated superiority feelings
     c. creative power
     d. fictional finalism

b   58. Envy, gossip, and intolerance are manifestations of which Adlerian
     safeguarding tendency?
     a. excuses
     b. depreciation
     c. accusation
     d. self-accusation
     e. withdrawal

e   59. Adler's notion of moving backward is similar to Freud's notion of
     a. sublimation.
     b. fixation.
     c. progression.
     d. repression.
     e. regression.

a   60. Adler's concept of standing still is similar to Freud's concept of
     a. fixation.
     b. repression.
     c. regression.
     d. sublimation.
     e. projection.

c   61. Vacillating, procrastinating, or behaving compulsively are examples of which
     Adlerian safeguarding tendency?
     a. moving backward
     b. standing still
     c. hesitating
     d. constructing obstacles
     e. excuses

e   *62. According to Adler,
     a. the psychic lives of men and women are fundamentally different.
     b. only men overemphasize the importance of being manly.
     c. women's inferior place in society is biological.
     d. only a and c are correct.
     e. none of the above are correct.

a   63. Adler refers to the overemphasis on the importance of being manly as the
     a. masculine protest.
     b. sexist imperative.
     c. sexual safeguarding tendency.
     d. gender excuse.

a   64. Adler's notion of the masculine protest
          a. is a reaction to feelings of inferiority.
          b. applies only to women.
          c. is genetically determined.
          d. is the precursor to the feminine protest.

c   65. Firstborn children, according to Adler, are likely to
          a. suffer from organ inferiorities.
          b. communicate in organ dialect more than secondborn children do.
          c. have intensified feelings of power and superiority.
          d. have very little anxiety.

a   66. Adler believed that the typical secondborn child
          a. develops moderate competitiveness.
          b. becomes extremely competitive.
          c. becomes easily discouraged.
          d. is fearful of authority.

e   67. The most important factor for the child in Adler's family constellation is
          a. rank order of siblings.
          b. gender of siblings.
          c. spacing of siblings.
          d. number of siblings.
          e. subjective perception of self and environment.

b   *68. According to Adler, _____ is the most reliable means of revealing style of life.
          a. the word association test
          b. early recollections
          c. free association
          d. hypnosis

d   *69. Adler believed that early recollections
          a. have no objective validity.
          b. are inconsistent with present style of life.
          c. are psychologically meaningless.
          d. yield clues to understanding one's style of life.

b   70. Adlerians believe that if style of life changes, early recollections
          a. are forgotten.
          b. also change.
          c. are objectively verified.
          d. cause the changes in style of life.

d   71. Adler hypothesized that early recollections
          a. are complex daydreams.
          b. cause or determine one's style of life.
          c. are usually unpleasant and traumatic.
          d. are shaped by one's present style of life.
          e. all of the above.

b *72. Adler believed that dreams
    a. are expressions of infantile wishes.
    b. provide clues for solving future problems.
    c. are prophetic.
    d. can be easily understood by the dreamer.

a 73. The night before Adler made his first trip to the United States, he dreamed that
    a. his ship capsized and that he had to courageously swim to safety.
    b. he saw Freud on board the ship and that Freud asked him to hold his coat.
    c. he saw a smiling Freud on board the ship and that Freud admitted that individual psychology was superior to psychoanalysis.
    d. a huge American audience was applauding loudly after one of his speeches.

a 74. Adler used the therapeutic relationship to
    a. increase social interest.
    b. increase private intelligence.
    c. increase personal superiority.
    d. increase safeguarding tendencies.
    e. decrease safeguarding tendencies.

c 75. A unique aspect of early Adlerian therapy was
    a. self hypnosis.
    b. its use of patients' drawings and sketches.
    c. treating children in front of an audience.
    d. its emphasis on returning patients to the workforce.

b 76. Manaster and Perryman have developed several instruments to measure Adler's concept of
    a. social interest.
    b. early recollections.
    c. style of life.
    d. family constellations.

a 77. Nichols and Feist found that the early recollections of optimists, compared with those of pessimists, included
    a. more people.
    b. scenes in which they were passive rather than active.
    c. unpleasant experiences.
    d. more vague recollections.

b 78. Research on early recollections by Buchanan, Kern, and Bell-Dumas suggests that
    a. early recollections may be reliable, but not valid.
    b. made-up early recollections yield about the same content as do actual early recollections.
    c. early recollections do not tend to change during the course of psychotherapy.
    d. early recollections are valid predictors of psychopathology.

c   79.   Research by Statton and Wilborn found that children who received counseling
          a. had essentially the same quality of early recollections as those who did not
             receive counseling.
          b. tended to forget their earliest recollections.
          c. showed more changes in early recollections than did students who did not
             receive counseling.
          d. tended to recall more vivid early recollections.

a   80.   Although Adler's theory is optimistic, it can be criticized for its
          a. inability to be falsified.
          b. inconsistency.
          c. parsimony.
          d. inability to generate research.
          e. inability to organize knowledge.

d   *81. Which of the following statements best expresses Adler's concept of humanity?
          a. Personality is basically determined by the environment.
          b. People are by nature good.
          c. Early childhood experiences are the single most important factor in   ·
             shaping personality.
          d. People's interpretations of experiences are more important than the
             experiences themselves.

b   82.   Adler's concept of humanity is most accurately summarized in which phrase?
          a. Childhood experiences determine adult personality.
          b. People are motivated by their goals for the future.
          c. People's experiences are more important than their interpretations
             of experience.
          d. Genetic factors are more influential than social factors in
             shaping personality.

CHAPTER 4
JUNG: ANALYTICAL PSYCHOLOGY

ESSAY QUESTIONS

1. Describe Jung's levels of the psyche.

    A. Jung divided the psyche into two levels: the conscious and the unconscious. The unconscious, in turn, is divided into the personal unconscious and the collective unconscious.
    B. The conscious psyche plays a relatively minor role in analytical psychology. When people rely too heavily on their conscious, to the exclusion of the unconscious, they become shallow and unbalanced. The ego is the center of consciousness.
    C. The personal unconscious in Jungian theory is comparable to the unconscious in Freudian theory. It is a storehouse for repressed memories. The contents of the personal unconscious are called complexes, or emotionally tinged ideas that spring from personal experiences.
    D   Jung's most distinctive and controversial concept is that of a collective unconscious. The collective unconscious is the psychological counterpart to an instinct. It stems from the repeated experiences of our ancestors and is passed from one generation to the next as psychic potential. The collective unconscious does not consist of inherited ideas, but of predispositions to act. Before people react to these inherited predispositions, however, they must have a personal experience that sparks the collective unconscious. The contents of the collective unconscious are called archetypes.

2. List and briefly describe Jung's most important archetypes.

    A. The persona is the side of personality that we show to the outside world. It is the role we adopt in society.
    B. The shadow is the archetype of darkness and repression and represents the evil side of our personality. Rather than hiding their shadow, self-realized people become acquainted with it and thus learn to control their dark side. Jung believed the realization of the shadow is our first test of courage on the road to self-realization.
    C. The anima is the feminine side of men. Psychologically healthy men recognize their feminine disposition, become comfortable with it, and do not project it onto the women in their lives. The anima influences the feeling side of men.
    D. The animus is a woman's masculine side, and it influences her thinking and reasoning. Jung also believed the animus is also responsible for some women's irrational moods and unfounded opinions.
    E. The great mother is the archetype of both nourishment and destruction. It represents our ancestors' collective experiences with a mother who was capable of either nurturing or destroying them. Today, the great mother archetype is symbolized by gardens, plowed fields, a grandmother, Mother Nature, or a witch.
    F. The wise old man is the archetype of wisdom and meaning, but his wisdom and meaning is superficial and deceptive. The wise old man archetype is symbolized by a father, grandfather, teacher, rabbi, or priest.

G. The hero archetype is represented as a powerful man, sometimes part god. However, the hero has a tragic flaw, or weakness. Without such a weakness, no one could be heroic; that is, one must be vulnerable to be a hero. The hero archetype is represented in legends and fairy tales by a strong person who conquers a villain using great personal courage. The hero is also symbolic of ancient humanity's conquering darkness and achieving consciousness.

H. The self is an all-inclusive archetype that includes all aspects of personality, both conscious and unconscious. The self is manifested by our quest for perfection, completion, and self-realization. It is symbolized by the mandala, or a perfect geometric figure.

3. Discuss Jung's notion of extraversion and introversion.

A. Jung's ideas of extraversion and introversion are not the same as most people's views of extraversion and introversion. To Jung, an extravert is not necessarily someone who is socially outgoing; rather, it is someone who looks at things objectively—in much the same way that others look at them.

B. An introvert, in Jung's psychology, is someone who takes a personalized or individualistic view of the world, An introvert is in tune with his or her subjective world, including dreams, unique opinions, biases, and fantasies. Introverts have a minority view of things and look to their own standards rather than socially popular standards.

C. Both extraversion and introversion can combine with each of the four functions to create eight general types.

MULTIPLE CHOICE QUESTIONS

d 4. Carl Jung believed that people are influenced by
   a. repressed experiences.
   b. experiences inherited from their ancestors.
   c. conscious sexual and aggressive urges.
   d. all of the above.

b 5. Jung came from a
   a. large close-knit family.
   b. family of two children with parents who had many disagreements.
   c. French farm family.
   d. single-parent family.

b 6. Like Freud, Jung was
   a. an Austrian.
   b. a physician.
   c. Jewish.
   d. an archaeologist.

b   7.   Both Jung and Freud underwent a personal crisis and a profound change during their late 30s or early 40s. In contrast to Freud, Jung
    a.   began his self-analysis as a reaction to his father's death.
    b.   was relatively unproductive in terms of publications and external accomplishments.
    c.   was primarily concerned with his personal unconscious rather than the collective unconscious.
    d.   increased his social contacts and became more extraverted.

a   8.   As a boy, Jung became aware of a No. 1 and a No. 2 personality. His No. 2 personality was
    a.   in touch with feelings and intuitions that were unavailable to the No. 1 personality.
    b.   a reflection of the Egyptian queen Cleopatra.
    c.   his persona, or face, that he showed to other people.
    d.   extraverted and in tune with the objective world.

e   9.   Because Jung was _____, Freud groomed him to be his successor.
    a.   Jewish
    b.   unmarried
    c.   Viennese
    d.   a lawyer
    e.   none of the above

b   10.   Jung's warm relationship with Freud began to collapse when
    a.   Jung learned of Freud's love affair with his sister-in-law.
    b.   the two men began to interpret one another's dreams.
    c.   Freud learned of Jung's frequent affairs.
    d.   Jung refused to travel with Freud to the United States.

e   11.   After Jung broke from Freud, he developed an approach to theory and therapy called
    a.   psychoanalysis.
    b.   archetype analysis.
    c.   complex counseling.
    d.   individuation analysis.
    e.   none of the above.

a   12.   Jung, like Freud, assumed that the mind, or psyche,
    a.   has both conscious and unconscious aspects.
    b.   draws psychic energy from the ego.
    c.   is dominated by archetypes.
    d.   remains inactive during the latency period.
    e.   begins to develop during late infancy.

a   *13. According to Jung, the unconscious can be divided into the
    a.   personal and collective.
    b.   animalistic and humanistic.
    c.   amoral and moralistic.
    d.   asocial and social.
    e.   preconscious and unconscious proper.

c   14. Jung believed that the conscious mind should be balanced by the
          a. ego.
          b. anima.
          c. unconscious mind.
          d. shadow.
          e. id.

b   *15. In Jungian theory, the ego
          a. is completely unconscious.
          b. is the center of consciousness.
          c. develops after individuation.
          d. has the same characteristics as the self.

d   16. According to Jung, a complex is
          a. the unconscious feminine side of a man.
          b. the part of personality turned toward the outside world.
          c. the center of the self.
          d. an emotionally toned conglomeration of associated ideas.

c   17. In Jungian psychology, repressed, forgotten, or subliminally perceived
          experiences are part of the
          a. ego.
          b. persona.
          c. personal unconscious.
          d. collective unconscious.
          e. archetypal unconscious.

d   18. Jung called contents of the personal unconscious
          a. fantasies.
          b. archetypes.
          c. instincts.
          d. complexes.
          e. none of the above.

c   19. Jung's notion of the collective unconscious refers to
          a. repressed childhood experiences.
          b. repressed experiences from adolescence.
          c. ideas inherited from our ancestors.
          d. people's tendency to react to biologically inherited response patterns.

d   20. Jung called the contents of the collective unconscious
          a. extraverted images.
          b. introverted affect.
          c. word associations.
          d. archetypes.
          e. complexes.

a   21. Jung claimed that both archetypes and instincts
          a. impel a person to act.
          b. are consciously determined.
          c. represent physiological drives.
          d. are learned during infancy.

d 22. According to Jung, when a personal experience corresponds to a latent primordial image
    a. self-realization and individuation occur.
    b. an instinct is discharged.
    c. psychotic behavior intensifies.
    d. an archetype is activated.
    e. the anima touches the animus.

a 23. Jung cited _____ as evidence for the existence of a collective unconscious.
    a. big dreams
    b. early recollections
    c. the word association test
    d. both a and b

e 24. Freud's concept of phylogenetic endowment is similar to Jung's idea of
    a. the ego.
    b. the self.
    c. the personal unconscious.
    d. archetypes.
    e. the collective unconscious.

d 25. Jung's "man-eater" dream expressed his
    a. childhood psychosis.
    b. sexual neurosis.
    c. personal unconscious.
    d. collective unconscious.

a *26. According to Jung, the archetype that manifests itself as one's social role is the
    a. persona.
    b. individual.
    c. shadow.
    d. self.

a 27. Jung believed that psychologically healthy people would
    a. recognize their persona but not confuse it with the self.
    b. have no persona.
    c. use their persona as a shield against self-realization.
    d. identify with their persona and use it as a guideline for effective interpersonal relations.

a 28. According to Jung, the shadow
    a. is the archetype of darkness and repression.
    b. springs from the personal conscious.
    c. represents humanity's search for transcendence.
    d. all of the above.

c *29. The first test of a person's courage, according to Jung, is to
    a. recognize one's inheritance.
    b. recognize the animus.
    c. realize the shadow.
    d. submit one's self to the ego.

e   30. Jung claimed that to overcome moral obstacles and admit the inferior side of
          one's nature may lead to the realization of the
          a. persona.
          b. anima.
          c. animus.
          d. wise old man.
          e. shadow.

b   31. Like Freud, Jung believed that
          a. the collective unconscious is more important than the personal
              unconscious.
          b. all humans are psychologically bisexual.
          c. the ego should be the master of personality.
          d. motivation is largely conscious.
          e. the first four or five years of life are most crucial in shaping personality.

c   *32. Jung called the feminine side of males the
          a. shadow.
          b. persona.
          c. anima.
          d. animus.

a   *33. Jung held that the anima influences
          a. irrational moods and feelings in men.
          b. irrational moods and feelings in women.
          c. irrational thinking and illogical opinions in men.
          d. irrational thinking and illogical opinions in women.

b   34. According to Jung, the realization of the anima
          a. must come before the realization of the shadow.
          b. would involve a man recognizing his feminine disposition rather than
              projecting it onto the women in his life.
          c. would result in a man conquering his homosexual ideation.
          d. is accomplished by nearly all men during old age.
          e. must follow the realization of the self.

c   35. Jung would say that a man who finds women alluring and mysterious may be
          projecting his _____ archetype onto women.
          a. self
          b. shadow
          c. anima
          d. animus   .

a   36. During his period of self-analysis, Carl Jung claimed to have carried on a
          conversation with
          a. his anima.
          b. his animus.
          c. his grandfather.
          d. Goethe.
          e. his shadow.

b   37.   Jung said that the animus
     a.   is an instinct.
     b.   represents the masculine side of women.
     c.   represents the evil side of men.
     d.   both a and b are correct.

b   38.   Jung believed that in a woman's relationship to the men in her life, she is most likely to project her _____ on to those men.
     a.   anima
     b.   animus
     c.   persona
     d.   shadow

b   *39.   The great mother is Jung's archetype of
     a.   farmers and ranchers.
     b.   nourishment and destruction.
     c.   children.
     d.   thinking and opinions.

c   40.   Symbols for Jung's great mother archetype include
     a.   baseball bats, balls, and gloves.
     b.   politicians, priests, and rabbis.
     c.   trees, gardens, and plowed fields.
     d.   the moon and stars.

d   *41.   Jung's archetype of wisdom and meaning is the
     a.   anima.
     b.   animus.
     c.   self.
     d.   wise old man.
     e.   great mother.

a   42.   The wizard in the *Wizard of Oz* symbolizes which Jungian archetype?
     a.   wise old man
     b.   self
     c.   great mother
     d.   animus
     e.   anima

c   43.   Certain political and religious leaders rely on charisma and verbal persuasions to influence multitudes of people. Jung would say that the spell these individuals cast over others may be due to the _____ archetype within people.
     a.   animus
     b.   shadow
     c.   wise old man
     d.   persona

e   44.   In dreams, figures such as a teacher, philosopher, doctor, or priest may personify the _____ archetype, according to Jung.
     a.   ego
     b.   self
     c.   anima
     d.   shadow
     e.   wise old man

d   *45. According to Jung, the hero archetype, as represented in myth and legend,
           a. is sometimes part god.
           b. fights to conquer evil.
           c. frequently has a tragic flaw.
           d. all of the above.

e   46.   Mythical characters such as Achilles and Superman personify which
           Jungian archetype?
           a. shadow
           b. persona
           c. wise old man
           d. animus
           e. hero

a   47.   Which of these people is most likely to represent Jung's hero archetype?
           a. a frightened person who overcomes fear to save another person from harm
           b. an immortal person who fights to keep another person from harm
           c. a man who overcomes his anima and thus becomes more desirable
               to women
           d. a woman who overcomes her animus and thus becomes more desirable
               to men

d   48.   According to Jung, the achievement of consciousness by our distant ancestors is
           reflected in the hero's
           a. divine birth.
           b. tragic flaw.
           c. superhuman strength.
           d. conquest of darkness.

a   *49. The mandala represents Jung's _____ archetype.
           a. self
           b. hero
           c. ego
           d. wise old man
           e. great mother

d   50.   In Jungian psychology, the ego is to consciousness as the _____ is to the
           whole personality.
           a. unconscious
           b. collective unconscious
           c. libido
           d. self
           e. conscious

b   51.   Which Jungian archetype includes the other archetypes and also represents
           wholeness or completion?
           a. ego
           b. self
           c. persona
           d. shadow

a   *52. In Jungian psychology, _____ is the essence of personality.
             a. the self
             b. the id
             c. consciousness
             d. the persona

a   *53. To Jung, the two basic attitudes are
             a. introversion and extraversion.
             b. thinking and feeling.
             c. conscious and unconscious.
             d. sensing and intuiting.
             e. sensing and feeling.

c   54. In Jungian psychology, the psychologically healthy person has a
             a. predominance of introversion.
             b. predominance of extraversion.
             c. balance of introversion and extraversion.
             d. lack of both introversion and extraversion.

b   55. Jung called an inclination to act or react in a characteristic direction
             a. a function.
             b. an attitude.
             c. a type.
             d. a complex.
             e. an archetype.

c   *56. According to Jung, introversion is basically
             a. feminine.
             b. masculine.
             c. subjective.
             d. objective.
             e. none of these.

c   57. According to Jung, if people's introversion is conscious, then their
             a. shadow is realized.
             b. mandala is conscious.
             c. extraversion is unconscious.
             d. extraversion is also conscious.

a   58. In Jungian theory, types include
             a. both attitudes and functions.
             b. only attitudes.
             c. only functions.
             d. neither attitudes nor functions.

b   59. In Jungian psychology, a person primarily concerned with external matters such
           as financial success, competition, and material possessions would be
             a. introverted.
             b. extraverted.
             c. dominated by his or her persona.
             d. self-realized.
             e. neurotic.

a   60. In Jungian theory, extraverted feeling types are more likely than other types to
         a. become businessmen or politicians.
         b. become artists and to rely on subjective evaluations.
         c. suffer from pathological guilt.
         d. suffer from extreme mood swings.

e   61. Jung would consider a person who relies blindly on thoughts and ideas that have
         been transmitted from others to be an _____ type.
         a. extraverted feeling
         b. introverted sensing
         c. introverted feeling
         d. extraverted intuiting
         e. extraverted thinking

a   62. In Jungian psychology, a withdrawn accountant with a strong interest in
         numbers and things and with little knowledge of his or her internal strivings
         would be classified as
         a. extraverted.
         b. introverted.
         c. psychotic.
         d. intuitive.

b   63. In Jungian psychology, introverted thinking types
         a. would not react to external stimuli.
         b. would react to external stimuli, but their interpretation of an event would be
             more important than the "facts."
         c. base their decisions primarily on objective phenomena.
         d. are concerned only with subjective phenomena because they have no
             contact with external world.

a   64. Which function tells us the value of something, according to Jung?
         a. feeling
         b. introversion
         c. extraversion
         d. thinking

c   *65. In Jungian psychology, introverted feeling types
         a. follow traditional beliefs.
         b. rely primarily on objective facts.
         c. are relatively indifferent to the opinions of others.
         d. value highly the opinion of others.

c   66. Pablo Picasso's abstract art best represents an _____ type person, in Jungian
         psychology.
         a. extraverted feeling
         b. introverted feeling
         c. introverted sensing
         d. extraverted sensing

d   67. Which function involves perception beyond consciousness, according to Jung?
         a. thinking
         b. feeling
         c. sensation
         d. intuition

a   68.   In Jungian psychology, religious fanatics swept up in a strongly felt cause are frequently _____ types.
     a.   introverted intuiting
     b.   introverted thinking
     c.   introverted sensing
     d.   introverted judging

a   *69.   According to Jung, the rational functions include
     a.   thinking and feeling.
     b.   sensation and intuition.
     c.   judgment and perception.
     d.   introversion and extraversion.
     e.   Yin and Yang.

b   70.   Sensation and intuition were regarded by Jung as
     a.   rational functions.
     b.   irrational functions.
     c.   extraverted attitudes.
     d.   introverted attitudes.

c   *71.   Jungian psychology
     a.   is basically causal.
     b.   is essentially teleological.
     c.   emphasizes a balance of causality and teleology.
     d.   assumes the validity of Freud's position on causality versus teleology.

d   72.   Jung's anarchic phase of childhood is
     a.   easily recalled by most adults.
     b.   the source of adult dreams.
     c.   characterized by a highly differentiated consciousness.
     d.   characterized by a chaotic and sporadic consciousness.

a   73.   The ego is divided into objective and subjective aspects during the _____ phase of childhood, according to Jung.
     a.   dualistic
     b.   monarchic
     c.   anarchic
     d.   bimodal

c   *74.   Jung believed that the crucial time in life when one should move from an extraverted attitude toward an introverted one is
     a.   infancy.
     b.   childhood.
     c.   middle life.
     d.   old age.

c   75.   Jung believed that
     a.   motivation should remain consistent throughout life.
     b.   infancy and childhood are the most important stages of development.
     c.   the goals and behaviors of early life are not appropriate for the second half of life.
     d.   people should develop an extraverted attitude during the second half of life.

c   76. According to Jung, individuation, or self-realization,
          a. is common among young people.
          b. requires inflating the ego.
          c. involves replacing the ego with the self.
          d. develops one function exclusively.

a   *77. In Jung's theory, the process of actualizing the various components of
          personality best describes
          a. individuation.
          b. introversion.
          c. extraversion.
          d. style of life.
          e. active imagination.

b   78. Jung used the word association test to
          a. measure intelligence.
          b. uncover complexes.
          c. activate archetypes.
          d. interpret "big dreams."

d   *79. Jung disagreed with Freud's belief that dreams
          a. were both causal and teleological.
          b. originated in strivings for superiority.
          c. had a latent meaning.
          d. were wish fulfillments.

d   80. The ultimate goal of Jungian dream interpretation is to
          a. enhance the persona.
          b. uncover hidden sexual urges.
          c. conquer unconscious fears.
          d. facilitate the process of self-realization.

a   81. An introverted person has extraverted dreams. Jung would say this demonstrates
          which purpose of dreams?
          a. compensatory
          b. prophetic
          c. entropic
          d. equivalent
          e. progressive

e   82. Jung developed the _____ technique during his self-analysis and then later
          used it with many of his patients.
          a. free association
          b. word association test
          c. bibliotherapy
          d. rational-emotive therapy
          e. active imagination

a   83. According to Jung, the confession of a pathogenic secret in psychotherapy
          involves the
          a. cathartic method.
          b. psychoanalytic approach.
          c. development of social interest.
          d. stage of transformation.

c   84.   The Myers-Briggs Type Indicator adds which dimension to Jungian typology?
          a.   extraversion versus introversion
          b.   aggression versus passivity
          c.   judgment versus perception
          d.   tough mindedness versus tender mindedness

a   85.   According to research by Nancy Marioles and her associates, a high level of
          marital satisfaction tend to exist when
          a.   the partners have similar types of personality.
          b.   the partners have opposite types of personality.
          c.   the man is extraverted and the woman is introverted.
          d.   the woman is extraverted and the man is introverted.

b   86.   Colleen Hester found that extraverts are more likely than introverts to
          a.   prefer partners they can dominate.
          b.   prefer partners with high self-confidence.
          c.   have extraverted dreams.
          d.   be attracted to highly creative people.

d   87.   Terry Schurr and his associates found that _____ college students were most
          likely to eventually graduate.
          a.   Intuitive and Perceiving
          b.   Introverted and Intuitive
          c.   Extraverted and Feeling
          d.   Judging and Sensing.

c   88.   One criticism of Jungian theory is that
          a.   it has failed to spawn any Jungian therapists.
          b.   it has generated no research.
          c.   it is nearly impossible to falsify.
          d.   it lacks popular appeal.

a   89.   On the dimension of causality versus teleology, Jung
          a.   adopted a middle position.
          b.   favored causality.
          c.   favored teleology.
          d.   took no position.

a   90.   Jung's theory sees humans as
          a.   a composite of opposing forces.
          b.   evolved animals but with no animal instincts.
          c.   destined to destroy themselves or others with modern warfare.
          d.   biological creatures trapped in a social environment.
          e.   helpless to shape our own behavior and personality.

CHAPTER 5
KLEIN: OBJECT RELATIONS THEORY

ESSAY QUESTIONS

1.   Compare and contrast Klein's object relations theory and Freud's psychoanalytic theory.

   A. In contrast to Freud's emphasis on the first 4 to 6 years of life, object relations theory stresses the first 4 to 6 months.
   B. Klein believed that an infant's drives are directed to an object such as a breast, penis, or vagina. These early childhood drives give an infant's experiences an unrealistic, fantasy-like quality that affects later interpersonal relations.
   C. Compared with Freud, Klein placed more emphasis on interpersonal relations and less emphasis on biology.
   D. Whereas Freud's theory emphasized the importance of the father during the male Oedipus complex, Klein's theory is built on the importance of the mother.
   E. Object relations theory holds that human contact and relatedness—not sexual pleasure—are the principal motivators of human behavior.

2.   Discuss Klein's concept of the paranoid-schizoid position.

   A. During the first few months of life, an infant experiences both a good breast (one that offers nourishment and contentment) and a bad breast (one that frustrates the infant).
   B. When these opposing experiences threaten the existence of the infant's vulnerable ego, the infant tries to gain control of the breast by both harboring the breast and destroying it.
   C. To tolerate these opposing feelings, the ego splits itself and deflecting parts of both the life and death instincts onto the breast.
   D. The infant wishes to retain and control the good breast as a defense against annihilation by persecutors.
   E. This paranoid-schizoid position allows the infant to organize experiences into both good and bad experiences.

3.   List and discuss Klein's psychic defense mechanisms.

   A. According to Klein, infants adopt several psychic defense mechanisms to protect their ego against anxiety aroused by their own destructive fantasies.
   B. Introjection refers to the infants' fantasizing about incorporating external objects (such as their mother's breast) into their own body.
   C. Projection is the fantasy that one's own impulses are within another person rather than within one's own body. By projecting destructive urges onto external objects or other people, infants protect themselves from unpleasant anxiety.
   D. Splitting allows infants to keep apart the good and bad aspects of themselves or of external objects.
   E. Projective identification is a means of reducing anxiety by splitting off unacceptable parts of one's self and projecting them onto another object, and then introjecting them back into the self in a disguised form.

MULTIPLE CHOICE QUESTIONS

d   4.   Klein extended Freud's psychoanalysis by emphasizing
          a. adolescence.
          b. young adulthood.
          c. old age.
          d. very early infancy.

a   *5. According to Klein, the child's first model for interpersonal relations is the
          a. breast.
          b. mother.
          c. father.
          d. self.

e   6.   Klein came to psychoanalysis as
          a. a historian.
          b. a physician.
          c. a sociologist.
          d. a psychologist.
          e. none of the above.

b   *7. Among the people that Klein psychoanalyzed was
          a. Anna Freud.
          b. her son Erich.
          c. Erich Fromm.
          d. Albert Ellis.
          e. Erik Erikson.

d   8.   Melanie Klein had an especially warm relationship with
          a. her daughter Mellita.
          b. Anna Freud.
          c. both of the above.
          d. neither of the above.

d   9.   Object relations theory differs from Freud's theory in that it
          a. places more emphasis on interpersonal relations.
          b. stresses the importance of a nurturing mother.
          c. places less emphasis on sexual pleasure.
          d. all of the above.
          e. none of the above.

a   *10. According to Klein, the person or part of a person through which the aim of an
          instinct is satisfied is called
          a. an object.
          b. an impetus.
          c. the source.
          d. a motivator.

c   11. According to Klein, the fantasies of an infant are
          a. of little importance.
          b. mostly conscious.
          c. unconscious.
          d. both a and b.

b 12. Klein believed that children introject their mother into their psychic structure. This means that they
        a. believe that they are inside their mother.
        b. believe that their mother is inside their own body.
        c. reject their mother's authority.
        d. adopt their mother's standards of morality.

a 13. Klein assumed that infants come into the world with
        a. an active fantasy life.
        b. a desire to have sexual relations with their mother.
        c. a desire to have sexual relations with their father.
        d. a blank slate.

c 14. If a hungry infant cries and kicks, Klein would say that it is
        a. motivated by the death instinct.
        b. inventing a sign language to communicate distress with its mother.
        c. fantasizing about kicking or destroying the "bad" breast.
        d. engaging in random behavior.

d *15. Klein agreed with Freud that people can be motivated by
        a. phylogenetic endowment.
        b. a life instinct.
        c. a death instinct.
        d. all of the above.
        e. none of the above.

b 16. To Klein, an introjected object
        a. is an internal thought about an external object.
        b. is a fantasy about internalizing the object in a physical form.
        c. desires to escape from an infant's mind.
        d. loses its dynamic power to influence an infant's psychic life.

b *17. According to Klein, the two basic positions are
        a. introjection and projection.
        b. the paranoid-schizoid and the depressive.
        c. ego and superego.
        d. the mature and the mature.
        e. the ideal and the real.

d 18. Klein's conception of a "position" is different from "stage of development" in that "positions" are
        a. completely psychological.
        b. due largely to social influences.
        c. determined by chronological age.
        d. not periods of time.

d *19. Klein claimed that infants use the paranoid-schizoid position to
        a. strengthen their attachment to their mother.
        b. escape from reality.
        c. fight off threats from older siblings.
        d. control the good breast and fight off its persecutors.

a   20.   Klein's depressive position includes
           a.   feelings of anxiety over losing a loved object and a sense of guilt for
                wanting to destroy that object.
           b.   feelings of persecution for wanting to destroy the bad breast.
           c.   a desire to devour and harbor the good breast.
           d.   fear of being bitten by animals.

b   *21. Klein suggested that psychic defense mechanisms
           a.   protect the child against public ridicule.
           b.   protect the ego against anxiety aroused by destructive fantasies.
           c.   safeguard the superego against uncontrollable id impulses.
           d.   prevent unconscious fantasies from reaching consciousness.

c   22.   Klein contended that when introjected, dangerous objects
           a.   lose their danger.
           b.   increase their danger.
           c.   become internal persecutors.
           d.   are projected onto the father.

a   23.   Klein called the fantasy that one's own feelings actually reside in
           another person
           a.   projection.
           b.   introjection.
           c.   splitting.
           d.   rejection.
           e.   introjective identification.

d   *24. According to Klein, infants use splitting as a means of
           a.   controlling conscious fantasies.
           b.   destroying the bad breast.
           c.   gaining control over their parents by dividing them against one another.
           d.   controlling good and bad aspects of themselves.

b   25.   Klein called the process in which infants split off unacceptable parts of
           themselves, project these parts onto another object, and finally introject these
           parts back into themselves
           a.   introjective identification.
           b.   projective identification.
           c.   repression.
           d.   incorporation.
           e.   regression.

c   26.   Klein believed that before a unified ego can emerge, it must first
           a.   assimilate the id.
           b.   learn syntaxic language.
           c.   split itself into the "good me" and the "bad me."
           d.   gain control over the repressive superego.

d   *27. In contrast to Freud, Klein believed that the superego
           a.   emerged during adolescence.
           b.   grows out of the Oedipus complex.
           c.   precedes the development of the ego.
           d.   is much more harsh and cruel.

a   28. Klein's notion of the Oedipus complex differed from Freud's in that it
    a. includes fear of retaliation from parents for fantasies of emptying
       their bodies.
    b. takes place at a later time.
    c. includes hostile feelings only.
    d. includes sexual feelings only.
    e. is the origin of the superego.

d   29. Klein believed that the male Oedipus complex is resolved mostly when the boy
    a. identifies with his father and adopts a feminine position with his mother.
    b. identifies with his mother and adopts a feminine position with his father.
    c. adopts a masculine position toward both parents.
    d. establishes positive relationships toward both parents.

b   30. Klein believed that during the female Oedipus complex, the girl
    a. sees only the good aspects of the mother's breast.
    b. fantasizes that the father's penis feeds the mother with babies.
    c. sees only the bad aspects of the mother's breast.
    d. adopts a masculine position toward both parents.
    e. holds her mother responsible for her lack of a penis.

d   *31. According to Klein, when the female Oedipus complex is successfully resolved,
    the little girl will
    a. see her mother as a rival.
    b. fantasize about robbing her mother of the father's penis and of her babies.
    c. adopt a homosexual attitude toward her mother.
    d. develop positive feelings toward both parents.
    e. develop negative feelings toward her mother and neutral feelings toward
       her father.

b   *32. Which object relations theorist spent much time observing normal babies as
    they bonded with their mothers during the first 3 years of life?
    a. Melanie Klein
    b. Margaret Mahler
    c. Otto Kernberg
    d. Heinz Kohut

a   *33. Mahler's principal concern was with
    a. the psychological birth of the child.
    b. the effects of the Oedipus complex on psychological health.
    c. the child's symbiotic relationship with the father.
    d. narcissistic needs of infants.

c   34. Mahler believed that when infants realize that they cannot satisfy their own
    basic needs, they
    a. reject those needs and introject a new set of learned needs.
    b. become autistic.
    c. seek a symbiotic relationship with their mother.
    d. merge their ego with their superego.

b   35.   Mahler believed that children begin to develop feelings of personal identity during which developmental stage?
      a.   normal symbiosis
      b.   separation-individuation
      c.   normal autism
      d.   preadolescence

d   *36.   Which object relations theorist strongly emphasized the process by which the self evolves?
      a.   Freud
      b.   Klein
      c.   Mahler
      d.   Kohut

a   37.   Kohut's narcissistic needs include
      a.   the need to exhibit the grandiose self.
      b.   the need to be first in the eyes of one's parents.
      c.   the need to acquire a sense of self-identity.
      d.   the needs for power and authority.

b   *38.   Kernberg believes that the key to understanding personality is
      a.   inherited dispositions.
      b.   the early mother-child relationship.
      c.   a person's family constellation.
      d.   one's earliest recollections.

c   39.   Which of these is NOT one of Kernberg's internalized object relationships?
      a.   affect
      b.   self-image
      c.   Oedipus complex
      d.   object-image

a   40.   According to Kernberg, splitting allows infants to
      a.   separate "good" and "bad" images of their mother.
      b.   keep emotions and thoughts separate.
      c.   control their parents by dividing them against themselves.
      d.   introject negative images of the mother.

a   41.   Kernberg is LEAST concerned with
      a.   narcissistic needs of infants.
      b.   the child's ego identity.
      c.   the defense mechanisms of introjection and identification.
      d.   internalized object relationships.

a   42.   Bowlby's attachment theory was based on studies of
      a.   infants and primates.
      b.   adolescents.
      c.   middle-age adults.
      d.   elderly adults.

c *43. According to Bowlby, infants who become separated from their primary
         caregivers experience separation anxiety. The first stage of separation is the
         a. detachment stage.
         b. attachment stage.
         c. protest stage.
         d. despair stage.
         e. anal stage.

a   44. According to Bowlby, both humans and other primates experience separation
         anxiety. The stage unique to humans is the _____ stage.
         a. detachment
         b. protest
         c. attachment
         d. despair
         e. anal

a   45. Bowlby's theory assumes that
         a. the relationship between infant and caregiver becomes a model for
             future interpersonal relations.
         b. the bonding relationship between infant and caregiver leads to
             infantile narcissism.
         c. the bonding relationship between infant and caregiver results in a neurotic
             symbiotic relationship.
         d. the infant need not be responsive to the caregiver, because a devoted
             caregiver will satisfy the infant's needs unconditionally.
         e. all of the above.

b   46. An infant remains calm when her mother exits the room, leaving her with a
         stranger. When the mother returns, the infant ignores her. According to
         Ainsworth, this infant is displaying the _____ attachment style.
         a. anxious-resistant
         b. anxious-avoidant
         c. secure
         d. insecure

b   47. Which issue became part of a bitter debate between Melanie Klein and Anna
         Freud during the 1920s and 1930s?
         a. the male Oedipus complex
         b. the idea of childhood psychoanalysis
         c. the notion of unconscious defense mechanisms
         d. the importance of symbolic language in young children

c   48. The aim of Kleinian therapy is to
         a. resolve the Oedipus complex.
         b. uncover repressed sexual feelings toward one's parents.
         c. reduce depressive anxieties and persecutory fears.
         d. increase social skills.
         e. enhance feelings of self-esteem and self-worth.

c   49.   Research by Kirsh and Cassidy (1997) found that insecure-ambivalent children, when placed in Ainsworth's Strange Situation,
a.   tended to fix their gaze on drawings of mother-child dyads interacting in a positive manner.
b.   tended to fix their gaze on drawings of mother-child dyads interacting in a negative manner.
c.   looked away from different mother-child dyads engaging in a variety of positive interactions.
d.   recalled helpful stories better than did secure attachment children.

a   *50.   Research by Sroufe and colleagues found that securely attached children, compared with insecurely attached children, were
a.   more independent and more socially skilled.
b.   more independent but less popular and socially skilled.
c.   more impulsive and extraverted.
d.   less likely to form friendship groups during middle childhood.

c   51.   Fury and colleagues found that _____ may tap into unconscious ways in which children represent themselves and their families.
a.   home movies
b.   sociograms
c.   family drawings
d.   hypnotic episodes

c   52.   Research by Hazan and Shaver found that people whose adult love relationships include trust, closeness, and positive emotions had which early childhood attachment style?
a.   neurotic symbiotic
b.   anxious-resistant
c.   secure
d.   anxious-avoidant

d   53.   On the dimensions for a concept of humanity, Klein's theory rates lowest on
a.   unconscious motivation.
b.   causality.
c.   social influences.
d.   free choice and uniqueness.

CHAPTER 6
HORNEY: PSYCHOANALYTIC SOCIAL THEORY

ESSAY QUESTIONS

1. Discuss Horney's criticism of Freud.

   A. Horney believed that Freud's psychoanalysis was too rigid and that strict adherence to it would lead to stagnation in both theory and practice.
   B. Horney's strongest difference with Freud was on the issue of feminine psychology. To Horney, psychic differences between women and men are not due to anatomy or to instincts but to cultural and social expectations.
   C. Horney recognized the possibility of an Oedipus complex, but she insisted that it is not universal and not due to biology. To her, the Oedipus complex resulted from environmental conditions and is found only in those people who have a neurotic need for love.
   D. Horney objected to the notion of penis envy, but she recognized that many women have a masculine protest, or a pathological belief that men are superior to women.
   E. Horney believed that people are not ruled by the pleasure principle but by the needs for safety and satisfaction.

2. Discuss Horney's concepts of neurotic needs and neurotic trends.

   A. Horney originally identified 10 categories of neurotic needs that underlie the attempts of neurotics to combat basic anxiety. One person may use several neurotic needs in an attempt to deal with other people.
   B. The 10 neurotic needs are (1) the need for affection and approval, (2) the need for a powerful partner, (3) the need to restrict one's life within narrow borders, (4) the need for power, (5) the need to exploit others, (6) the need for social recognition or prestige, (7) the need for personal admiration, (8) the need for ambition and personal achievement, (9) the need for self-sufficiency and independence, and (10) the need for perfection and unassailability.
   C. Later, Horney grouped these 10 neurotic needs into three basic attitudes, or neurotic trends. The three neurotic trends are (1) moving toward people, which includes neurotic needs 1, 2, and 3; (2) moving against people, which includes neurotic needs 4, 5, 6, 7, and 8; and (3) moving away from people, which includes neurotic needs 9 and 10.
   D. Each of the three neurotic trends has a normal analog. Moving toward people translates as a friendly, loving attitude in normal people; moving against people has a normal analog of survivability in a competitive society; and the normal analog for moving away from people is an autonomous and serene attitude.

3. Summarize the chief findings of Lyon and Greenberg's 1991 study and discuss how it relates to Horney's theory.

   A. Lyon and Greenberg hypothesized that college women with an alcoholic parent would offer more help to a person they saw as exploitative than to a person they perceived as nurturing.
   B. They compared women with one alcoholic parent to women with no alcoholic parent and found that the former group (codependent women)

volunteered more than twice as much time to help a person perceived as exploitative than to the same person portrayed as nurturing.
C. The codependent women liked the exploitative person better than the nurturing one, and saw him as needing to be nurtured.
D. These findings support Horney's contention that people with morbid dependency and strong needs to move toward others will go out of their way to win the approval of other people.

MULTIPLE CHOICE QUESTIONS

d *4. According to Horney, the underlying cause of human neuroses is
   a. the Oedipus complex.
   b. physiological deficiencies.
   c. restrictive toilet training.
   d. human relations.

a 5. Horney believed that children develop _____ as a reaction to unfilled needs for love and affection.
   a. basic hostility toward their parents
   b. codependence with their parents
   c. independence from their parents
   d. an Oedipus complex

d 6. Horney believed that people combat basic anxiety by adopting which mode of relating to people?
   a. moving against others
   b. moving toward others
   c. moving away from others
   d. any of the above

c *7. Karen Horney, like _____, was the youngest child of a middle-age father, had older siblings who were favored by her parents, and felt unwanted and unloved.
   a. Sigmund Freud
   b. Carl Jung
   c. Melanie Klein
   d. Eric Fromm

c 8. Horney came to psychoanalysis from
   a. art.
   b. music.
   c. medicine.
   d. sociology.

a *9. In Horney's view, _____ is (are) largely responsible for the development of basic anxiety and subsequent unhealthy interpersonal relations.
   a. cultural conditions
   b. the existential dilemma
   c. the idealized self image
   d. neurotic pride

c   10. According to Horney, normal and neurotic individuals differ in their use of the
        three basic styles of relating to people in that
        a. neurotics use deceit to relate to others.
        b. normals only use one mode of relating to others.
        c. neurotics only use one mode of relating to others.
        d. neurotics use the three basic styles, but normals do not.

b   11. Horney's theory is built mainly on her writings about
        a. psychoses and psychotic people.
        b. neuroses and neurotic people.
        c. normality and normal people.
        d. self-actualizing people.
        e. women rather than men.

a   *12. Horney criticized Freudian theory on several accounts. Which of these was one
         of her major criticisms?
         a. inadequate understanding of feminine psychology
         b. too little emphasis on biological factors
         c. too little emphasis on ego functioning
         d. too flexible in theory and practice

c   *13. Horney believed that people are governed by which two guiding principles?
         a. sex and aggression
         b. avoidance and attraction
         c. safety and satisfaction
         d. superiority and inferiority
         e. love and hate

c   14. Horney was most critical of Freud's
        a. research methods.
        b. observations.
        c. interpretations of observations.
        d. lack of scientific data.
        e. honesty of interpretation.

e   *15. Feelings of isolation, Horney said, stem from
         a. anatomical differences between the two genders.
         b. early childhood rejection by parents.
         c. peer rejection during adolescence.
         d. lack of courage and assertiveness.
         e. a competitive society.

b   16. Needs for affection, Horney contended, result in
        a. an undervaluation of love.
        b. an overvaluation of love.
        c. isolation.
        d. self-esteem.

c   17. According to Horney, the attempts of neurotics to find love typically result in
        a. increased self-esteem.
        b. decreased hostility.
        c. basic anxiety.
        d. success.

d   18.   According to Horney, Western society hinders people's attempts to find
            love by
            a.   rewarding aggressiveness and competitiveness.
            b.   rewarding failure.
            c.   instilling feelings of free choice.
            d.   both a and c.
            e.   none of the above.

d   19.   Horney contended that modern society is based on _____ between individuals.
            a.   cooperation
            b.   altruism
            c.   dependence
            d.   competition
            e.   estrangement

a   20.   Horney believed that the cultural contradictions of society
            a.   lead to intrapsychic conflict.
            b.   result in achievement and success.
            c.   are a result of anatomical differences between the sexes.
            d.   can never be successfully resolved.

d   21.   For Horney, adult attitudes toward others are
            a.   a result of an unresolved Oedipus complex.
            b.   repetitions of infantile attitudes.
            c.   directly tied to instinctual needs.
            d.   a product of the individual's character structure.

a   22.   According to Horney, most neuroses stem from
            a.   childhood.
            b.   adolescence.
            c.   an unhappy marriage.
            d.   genetic factors.

c   23.   Horney believed that people are
            a.   innately healthy.
            b.   innately neurotic.
            c.   born with a potential for psychological health, but that this potential must
                 be developed in a warm and loving atmosphere.
            d.   born with the potential for psychological health, but that this potential
                 must be developed in an atmosphere of competition.

d   *24.   "A feeling of being isolated and helpless in a potentially hostile world" is
            Horney's definition of
            a.   basic dread.
            b.   basic threat.
            c.   basic fear.
            d.   basic anxiety.
            e.   innate inferiority.

b   *25. Neuroses, Horney said, grow out of the "nutritive soil" of
           a. failure.
           b. basic anxiety.
           c. exaggerated feelings of superiority.
           d. an unresolved Oedipus complex.
           e. an agrarian culture.

a   26. Horney asserted that the primary adverse influence inhibiting a child's potential
           for healthy development is
           a. parental failure to love the child.
           b. rivalry and competitiveness between children.
           c. the unconscious instinctual urges of the child.
           d. the lack of proper socialization of the child.

b   27. Horney saw the tendency to humiliate others in order to protect oneself against
           humiliation as
           a. power.
           b. prestige.
           c. possession.
           d. dominance.

d   28. According to Horney, neurotic strategies differ from normal ones by their
           a. aggressiveness.
           b. ineffectiveness.
           c. effectiveness.
           d. compulsivity.

d   *29. Horney saw neurotic behavior as a protection against
           a. low self-esteem.
           b. self-hated.
           c. psychoses.
           d. basic anxiety.

b   30. Kip seeks out powerful people to be his friends. Horney would say that Kip's
           needs for a powerful partner
           a. are an indication of high self-esteem.
           b. are neurotic.
           c. produce basic anxiety.
           d. will result in shame and guilt.

b   31. Which of these is NOT one of Horney's 10 neurotic needs?
           a. affection and approval
           b. order and direction
           c. power
           d. perfection

c   32. Parker is constantly belittling his own accomplishments. He also dreads asking
           others for favors. These behaviors illustrate Horney's neurotic need
           a. for affection and approval.
           b. for a partner.
           c. to restrict one's life within narrow borders.
           d. for self-sufficiency and independence.

e   33.   Tami is proud of her intellectual skills and abilities, and she is pleased when
           others notice and admire her superior intelligence. These characteristics reflect
           Horney's neurotic need for
           a.   power.
           b.   affection and approval.
           c.   independence.
           d.   prestige.
           e.   personal admiration.

e   34.   According to Horney, neurotics differ from normals in that they
           a.   are unconscious of their basic attitude.
           b.   are free to choose their actions.
           c.   experience severe, insoluble conflicts.
           d.   both a and b.
           e.   both a and c.

b   35.   According to Horney, an important difference between the neurotic trends of
           normal individuals and those of neurotic people is that neurotics
           a.   are usually conscious of their strategies.
           b.   are compelled to follow a single rigid strategy.
           c.   experience little conflict from their strategies.
           d.   enjoy their misery.

a   36.   Horney believed that neurotics move toward people because they experience
           a.   deep feelings of helplessness.
           b.   painful feelings of inferiority.
           c.   painful feelings of isolation.
           d.   deep feelings of love and affection.

c   37.   Some people move toward other people by seeking a powerful partner. Horney
           referred to this search for a powerful partner as
           a.   a neurotic symbiotic need.
           b   basic desire for food and shelter.
           c.   morbid dependency.
           d.   moving against people.

b   *38. Children who feel isolated from others are likely to develop Horney's neurotic
           trend of moving
           a.   with others.
           b.   away from others.
           c.   against others.
           d.   toward others.

b   39.   According to Horney, aggressive people assume that other people are
           a.   helpless.
           b.   hostile.
           c.   superior to them.
           d.   inferior to them.

d   40. Those individuals who adopt Horney's neurotic trend of moving away from
          people typically fear
          a. needing others.
          b. dependence upon others.
          c. competition.
          d. all of the above.
          e. only a and b.

b   41. Horney believed that intrapsychic processes originate from
          a. anatomical differences between the sexes.
          b. interpersonal experiences.
          c. the collective unconscious.
          d. the neurotic trends.
          e. instinctual strivings.

a   42. Each of Horney's neurotic trends has a normal analog. The ability to survive in
          a competitive society is a healthy extension of which neurotic trend?
          a. moving against people
          b. moving toward people
          c. moving with people
          d. moving away from people

b   *43. An outstanding characteristic of people who adopt Horney's trend of moving
          toward people is
          a. self-confidence.
          b. compliance.
          c. aggressiveness.
          d. detachment.

d   44. According to Horney, the principal behavior of neurotics who move away from
          people is
          a. self-confidence.
          b. compliance.
          c. aggressiveness.
          d. detachment.

c   *45. According to Horney, two important intrapsychic conflicts are
          a. guilt and remorse.
          b. competition and cooperation.
          c. self-hatred and the idealized self-image.
          d. moving away from people and moving toward people.
          e. moving against people and moving toward people.

b   46. Horney predicted that people who experience a positive, loving relationship
          will move
          a. away from people.
          b. toward self-realization.
          c. toward people.
          d. toward a pampered style of life.
          e. toward a neglected style of life.

d   47. Horney believed that an idealized self-image is established in order to
      a. achieve self-actualization.
      b. overcome feelings of inferiority.
      c. convince others of one's worth.
      d. combat a sense of self-alienation.

a   48. The normal analog of Horney's neurotic trend of moving away from people is
      a. autonomy.
      b. competition.
      c. compliance.
      d. indifference.
      e. hostility.

b   49. In Horney's view, neurotics
      a. use the real self as the standard for self-evaluation.
      b. use the idealized self as the standard for self-evaluation.
      c. move toward actualizing the real self.
      d. are unable to form an idealized self.

c   50. Horney referred to the neurotic's compulsive drive toward actualizing the ideal self as
      a. self-realization.
      b. the neurotic trend.
      c. the neurotic search for glory.
      d. the tyranny of the should.
      e. neurotic ambition.

c   51. In their need for perfection, neurotics often set up complex rules and outrageous standards that they feel they must follow. Horney refers to this as
      a. self-realization.
      b. neurotic claims.
      c. the tyranny of the should.
      d. neurotic ambition.
      e. vindictive triumph.

d   52. According to Horney, the most destructive element of the neurotic search for glory is
      a. neurotic ambition.
      b. neurotic claims.
      c. neurotic pride.
      d. the drive toward a vindictive triumph.
      e. the tyranny of the should.

a   53. Which of these is LEAST characteristic of people Horney regarded as neurotic?
      a. high self-esteem
      b. feelings of perfection
      c. self-hatred
      d. a need to be first in everything

b   *54. Horney insisted that the Oedipus complex
      a. did not exist.
      b. was the result of cultural forces.
      c. was the result of anatomy.
      d. was universal.

a   55. Horney believed that the core of men's need to subjugate women and women's
           wish to humiliate men is
           a. basic anxiety.
           b. self hatred.
           c. neurotic pride.
           d. a vindictive triumph.
           e. the tyranny of the should.

d   56. For Horney, psychic differences between men and women result from
           a. anatomical differences between the sexes.
           b. differences in superego development.
           c. the resolution of the Oedipus complexes.
           d. cultural and social expectations.

c   57. Horney recognized that some women may wish to be a man due to
           a. penis envy.
           b. womb envy.
           c. cultural privileges for men.
           d. anatomical differences between the sexes.

e   *58. The general goal of Horneyian therapy is to help the patient
           a. enhance the trend of moving toward people.
           b. reject the trend of moving against people.
           c. actualize the idealized self.
           d. increase the needs for safety and security.
           e. grow in the direction of self-realization.

d   59. Which technique(s) did Horney use in her psychotherapy?
           a. dream analysis
           b. free association
           c. hypnosis
           d. a and b

b   60. Using Horney's definition of morbid dependency, Lyon and Greenberg (1991)
           found that women with an alcoholic parent, compared to those with no
           alcoholic parent,
           a. tended to marry alcoholic men.
           b. offered more help to an exploitative person than to a nurturant one.
           c. offered less help to an exploitative person than to a nurturant one.
           d. tended to delay marriage.

a   61. Ryckman and colleagues found that _____ is a predictor of
           hypercompetitiveness.
           a. narcissism
           b. basic hostility
           c. the need to move toward people
           d. the need to move away from people
           e. the need to move against people

d   *62. According to Ryckman and colleagues, a healthy form of competitiveness is
           a. hypercompetitiveness.
           b. hypocompetitiveness.
           c. compliance.
           d. personal development competitiveness.

d   63.   Ryckman and colleagues found that hypercompetitive people tend to value
          a.   social concern.
          b.   conformity.
          c.   security.
          d.   power.

d   64.   Research suggests that hypercompetitive women, compared with women low on
          competitiveness, tend to
          a.   have higher academic performance.
          b.   be more career oriented.
          c.   be substantially overweight.
          d.   have a greater chance of developing an eating disorder.
          e.   both c and b.

a   65.   The major strength of Horney's theory is her
          a.   comprehensive description of the neurotic personality.
          b.   concern with the biological determinants of behavior.
          c.   description of psychic conflict.
          d.   innovative psychotherapy techniques.
          e.   support for Freud's ideas on the importance of the Oedipus complex.

c   66.   According to Horney, the principal difference between a psychologically
          healthy person and a neurotic person is the degree of _____ with which each
          moves toward, against, or away from people.
          a.   force
          b.   basic hostility
          c.   compulsivity
          d.   aggression

a   67.   Horney's concept of humanity was based mostly on her
          a.   clinical experiences with neurotic patients.
          b.   reaction against Freud's psychoanalysis.
          c.   search for the self-actualizing person.
          d.   training in sociology.

CHAPTER 7
FROMM: HUMANISTIC PSYCHOANALYSIS

ESSAY QUESTIONS

1.   Discuss Fromm's basic assumptions about personality and include his three existential dichotomies.

   A. Fromm's most fundamental assumption is that individual personality can be understood only in the light of human history.
   B. Humans, unlike other animals, have been torn away from their prehistoric union with nature.
   C. Having no powerful instincts to adapt to the world, humans have had to acquire the ability to reason. Fromm called this condition the human dilemma.
   D. Human's ability to reason sets up three existential dichotomies to which people must react according to their individual personalities.
   E. The first existential dichotomy is that between life and death. Although we desire life, our ability to reason tells us that we will die.
   F. Second, we are capable of setting goals for individual growth that we know we can never reach.
   G. Third, we recognize that we are ultimately alone, yet we cannot tolerate isolation.

2.   Discuss Fromm's five human, or existential, needs.

   A. Our human dilemma cannot be satisfied by needs we have in common with other animals. Only our human, or existential, needs can move us toward a reunification with the natural world.
   B. Relatedness is the human need of uniting with another person or persons. We can do this by (1) submission, (2) power, and (3) love.
   C. Another existential need is transcendence, or the urge to rise above our passive and accidental existence. We can transcend our passive nature by either creating life or by destroying it.
   D. A third human need is for rootedness, or the need to establish roots and to feel at home again in the world. We can either relate to the world creatively of become fixated and fail to move beyond our mother's care.
   E. A fourth human need is for a sense of identity, or the capacity to be aware of ourselves as a separate entity. The productive component of this need is individuality; the nonproductive component is adjustment to the group.
   F. The final existential need is a frame of orientation, or a road map to make our way through the world. The productive component of this need is rational goals; the nonproductive component is irrational goals.

3.   List and discuss Fromm's nonproductive and productive character orientations.

   A. By character orientation, Fromm meant a person's relatively permanent way of relating to people and things.
   B. People relate to the world by acquiring and using things (assimilation) and by relating to self and others (socialization).
   C. The four nonproductive orientations are: (1) receptive, (2) exploitative, (3) hoarding, and (4) marketing.

D. Receptive characters believe that all good lies outside themselves, so they relate to the world by receiving things, including love and material possessions.

E. Exploitative characters also feel that all good is outside themselves, but they act aggressively to take what they want.

F. Hoarding characters value things or people they have already obtained, so they hold on and do not let go of things and people.

G. Marketing characters are a relatively new orientation, having developed as an outgrowth of modern commerce. These personalities see themselves as being in constant demand and change their values to match whatever they think others want them to be.

H. The two productive orientations are love (socialization) and work (assimilation). Productive personalities possess biophilia, or a passionate love of life. Their work is directed toward attaining positive freedom.

MULTIPLE CHOICE QUESTIONS

a   4.   Compared with Freud, Fromm placed more emphasis on
    a.   social influences on personality.
    b.   biological determinants of psychic conflict.
    c.   the influence of the Oedipal situation.
    d.   dream interpretation during therapy.

b   *5.   Fromm held that our culture's current feelings of anxiety, isolation, and powerlessness stem from
    a.   the collective unconscious.
    b.   the rise of capitalism.
    c.   a lack of religious values.
    d.   the basic nature of humans.

d   6.   Fromm's view of human nature was influenced by
    a.   Jewish family life.
    b.   the suicide of a young woman.
    c.   the extreme nationalism of the German people.
    d.   all of the above.
    e.   only a and c.

c   7.   Fromm regarded his parents as
    a.   ideal models.
    b.   sinful.
    c.   quite neurotic.
    d.   overburdened with too many children.
    e.   overly religious.

b   8.   Fromm's most basic assumption is that personality must be understood in the light of
    a.   biology.
    b.   history.
    c.   geography.
    d.   literature.
    e.   determinism.

a   *9.   Fromm's human dilemma includes the notion that
          a. people have acquired the ability to reason yet have few animal instincts.
          b. people have lost the ability to love yet desperately seek it.
          c. people are unable to prevent war.
          d. people are torn by the forces of an unrelenting unconscious.

d   10.   According to Fromm, existential needs
          a. emerge during the evolution of human culture.
          b. grow out of people's attempts to find answers to their existence.
          c. represent attempts to avoid insanity.
          d. all of the above.
          e. a and b only.

e   11.   For Fromm, the drive for union with another person or persons reflects the
          human need of
          a. transcendence.
          b. rootedness.
          c. a sense of identity.
          d. a frame of orientation.
          e. none of the above.

a   12.   According to Fromm, submission, power, and love are the three basic modes of
          a. relatedness.
          b. transcendence.
          c. existential dichotomies.
          d. the frame of orientation.

b   13.   Fromm believed that a symbiotic relationship
          a. is the ideal form of relatedness.
          b. can be gratifying to the participants.
          c. enhances growth towards integrity and psychological health.
          d. a and b.
          e. b and c.

b   *14. Fromm called the urge to rise above one's passive and accidental existence
          a. relatedness.
          b. transcendence.
          c. rootedness.
          d. a sense of identity.
          e. a frame of orientation.

b   15.   For Fromm, productive and caring creation reflects the need for
          a. relatedness.
          b. transcendence.
          c. rootedness.
          d. love.
          e. a frame of orientation.

c   16.   From J. J. Bachofen, Fromm borrowed the idea that
          a. malignant aggression underlies all human motivation.
          b. early societies were patriarchal.
          c. the mother was the central figure in early societies.
          d. a sense of identity and a sense of communion with other people result in
              the human dilemma.

b   17.   Fromm believed that killing members of one's species for reasons other than survival is peculiar to humans. He called such killings
    a.   transcendence.
    b.   malignant aggression.
    c.   the syndrome of decay.
    d.   existential identity.

c   *18.   Fromm called the need to feel at home again in the world
    a.   relatedness.
    b.   transcendence.
    c.   rootedness.
    d.   a sense of identity.
    e.   a frame of orientation.

a   19.   In Fromm's productive strategy of attaining rootedness, people
    a.   are weaned from the protective orbit of the mother or mother substitute.
    b.   establish strong and lifelong ties with their mother or mother substitute.
    c.   see their spouse as a new mother or mother substitute.
    d.   crave the security of a mother or mother substitute.

b   20.   Fromm called our capacity to be aware of ourselves as a separate entity
    a.   self-awareness.
    b.   a sense of identity.
    c.   transcendence.
    d.   a frame of orientation.

b   *21.   Fromm referred to our human need for a guide or map to make our way through the world as a need for
    a.   rootedness.
    b.   a frame of orientation.
    c.   relatedness.
    d.   transcendence.

a   22.   Adrianna's frame of orientation is constantly challenged by inconsistent information. Fromm would predict that Adrianna will
    a.   force the information into an organization that she can understand.
    b.   make a major revision in her philosophy of life.
    c.   judge any information inconsistent with her life's philosophy as common sense.
    d.   lose her sense of identity.

c   23.   According to Fromm, to keep from going insane, one's frame of orientation must include
    a.   consistent information.
    b.   inconsistent information.
    c.   a final goal.
    d.   a simple structure.

e   *24. Fromm believed that the lack of satisfaction of existential needs
        a. has little effect on modern, post-marketing individuals.
        b. leads to the development of an individual's willpower.
        c. is unimportant in the post-capitalistic world.
        d. can only be helped through psychotherapy.
        e. results in insanity.

c   *25. Fromm believed that humans, as the only animal to possess self-awareness,
        imagination, and reason, are the
        a. masters of the universe.
        b. deal animal.
        c. freaks of the universe.
        d. children of destiny.

d   *26. In Fromm's view, the burden of freedom results in
        a. primal guilt.
        b. narcissistic shame.
        c. rootedness.
        d. basic anxiety.

a   27. Fromm asserted that as people gained more economic and political freedom,
        they felt more
        a. isolation.
        b. dominance.
        c. transcendence.
        d. malignant aggression.

b   28. For Fromm, basic anxiety is a feeling of
        a. malignant aggression.
        b. being alone in the world.
        c. being judged by others.
        d. being unable to achieve one's goals.

c   *29. Fromm believed that authoritarianism takes two forms:
        a. normal and neurotic.
        b. fear and anxiety.
        c. masochism and sadism.
        d. obsessive and compulsive.

d   30. According to Fromm, both masochism and sadism aim at
        a. increasing basic anxiety through unity with others.
        b. decreasing basic anxiety through destruction of others.
        c. increasing basic anxiety through destruction of others.
        d. decreasing basic anxiety through unity with others.

a   31. Which did Fromm NOT list as a sadistic tendency?
        a. the need to accept criticism from others
        b. the need to gain power over others
        c. the need to exploit and use others
        d. the desire to see others suffer
        e. none of the above

d   32.   Fromm believed that people who use conformity as a mechanism of escape
          a.   lack authenticity and individuality.
          b.   often behave in a stiff, predictable manner.
          c.   lose their identity as a unique person.
          d.   all of the above.

d   33.   Fromm contended that people can break the cycle of conformity and
          powerlessness only by
          a.   political revolution against authority.
          b.   rejecting existential needs.
          c.   adopting the receptive orientation.
          d.   achieving positive freedom.

e   *34. For Fromm, positive freedom consists of
          a.   conforming to society's rules.
          b.   choosing to accept authoritarianism.
          c.   doing what one wishes and with no regard for others.
          d.   seeking safety and security within the social structure.
          e.   acting spontaneously to express one's emotional potentialities.

b   35.   Fromm believed that _____ is the successful solution to the human dilemma
          of being part of the natural world and yet separate from it.
          a.   conformity
          b.   positive freedom
          c.   authenticity
          d.   receptive awareness
          e.   political revolution

b   *36. Fromm held that the twin components of positive freedom are
          a.   hope and charity.
          b.   love and work.
          c.   duty and desire.
          d.   faith and spirituality.
          e.   productivity and marketing.

a   37.   For Fromm, the relatively permanent way in which people relate to themselves
          and to the world is called
          a.   character.
          b.   transcendence.
          c.   personality.
          d.   reception.

d   38.   Fromm believed that people relate to the world in two basic ways:
          a.   love and hate.
          b.   receiving and exploiting.
          c.   passively and actively.
          d.   assimilation and socialization.

e   39.   According to Fromm, the exploitative character, like the receptive character,
          a.   is a productive orientation.
          b.   achieves positive freedom.
          c.   seeks to preserve what has already been obtained.
          d.   is an outgrowth of modern capitalism.
          e.   sees the source of good as lying outside himself or herself.

b   40.   Nell is careful with her money and rarely shares her thoughts or emotions with
           others. Her behavior illustrates Fromm's _____ orientation.
           a. marketing
           b. hoarding
           c. receptive
           d. exploitative

c   *41.   Fromm's hoarding character is similar to Freud's _____ character.
           a. hysterical.
           b. oral.
           c. anal.
           d. phallic.

d   *42.   Fromm believed that the _____ orientation is an outgrowth of modern
           commerce.
           a. productive
           b. receptive
           c. exploitative
           d. marketing
           e. hoarding

b   43.   From her salary as an elementary school teacher, Jennifer has accumulated a
           very large bank account. In addition, she has seldom thrown away any teaching
           aids. It thus appears that Jennifer has Fromm's _____ orientation.
           a. receiving
           b. hoarding
           c. marketing
           d. exploiting

c   44.   In Fromm's view, the marketing character's personal value is dependent upon
           the ability to
           a. drive a hard bargain.
           b. earn a profit.
           c. sell themselves to others.
           d. preserve their possessions.
           e. cash a check.

d   45.   For Fromm, healthy people value work as
           a. an end in itself.
           b. a source of money.
           c. a source of anxiety.
           d. a means of creative self-expression.

c   *46.   Fromm called the healthy individual's passionate love of life and all
           living things
           a. libido.
           b. eros.
           c. biophilia.
           d. megaphilia.
           e. life lust.

d   47.   Fromm believed that healthy people's survival is dependent on
      a. the productive orientation.
      b. one productive and one nonproductive orientation.
      c. all four unproductive orientations.
      d. some combination of all character orientations.

b   48.   Fromm believed that serious psychopathology has roots in
      a. modes of assimilation.
      b. modes of socialization.
      c. biochemical abnormalities.
      d. childhood trauma.
      e. biophilia.

b   49.   For Fromm, psychologically disturbed people have
      a. received too much love from their mothers.
      b. have failed to establish union with others.
      c. have failed to resolve their normal Oedipus complex.
      d. a and c.
      e. a and b.

e   50.   Fromm used the term "necrophilia" to refer to
      a. a sexual perversion involving contact with animals.
      b. a sexual perversion involving contact with feces.
      c. a sexual perversion involving contact with a corpse.
      d. an irrational desire to die.
      e. any attraction to death.

b   *51.   Tracy perceives everything that belongs to her as valuable and everything that belongs to others as having little value. Fromm would say Tracy is suffering from
      a. necrophilia.
      b. malignant narcissism.
      c. incestuous symbiosis.
      d. moral hypochondriasis.
      e. existential dilemma.

b   52.   Omar is preoccupied with guilt about previous transgressions. Fromm would say that Omar suffering from
      a. hypochondriasis.
      b. moral hypochondriasis.
      c. incestuous symbiosis.
      d. necrophilia.
      e. malignant aggression.

c   53.   Lorilee, a college junior, is extremely dependent on her mother to make both major and minor decisions for her. According to Fromm, Lorilee's behavior is characterized by
      a. necrophilia.
      b. moral hypochondriasis.
      c. incestuous symbiosis.
      d. the syndrome of decay.
      e. symbiotic nurturing.

a   54. Fromm's syndrome of decay consists of all the following EXCEPT
          a. malignant aggression.
          b. malignant narcissism.
          c. necrophilia.
          d. incestuous symbiosis.

d   55. Fromm believed that the therapist should try to understand the patient by using
          a. a scientific attitude.
          b. objective psychological tests.
          c. projective tests.
          d. an attitude of relatedness.

b   56. What was the most common character type found in Fromm's research on
          social character in a Mexican village?
          a. productive-marketing
          b. nonproductive-receptive
          c. productive-hoarding
          d. unproductive-exploitative
          e. productive-exploitative

e   57. Fromm regarded Adolf Hitler as the world's most conspicuous example of a
          person suffering from
          a. psychoses.
          b. moral hypochondriasis.
          c. the existential dilemma.
          d. a receptive orientation.
          e. the syndrome of decay.

a   58. Fromm suggested that Hitler's obsession with "superiority" of the German
          people reflects his
          a. incestuous symbiosis.
          b. receptive orientation.
          c. malignant narcissism.
          d. necrophilic orientation.

d   59. According to Fromm, Hitler's neurotic need to annihilate his enemies shows his
          a. incestuous symbiosis.
          b. receptive orientation.
          c. malignant narcissism.
          d. necrophilic orientation.

c   *60. Saunders and Munro's Consumer Orientation Index is a measure of Fromm's
          a. hoarding character.
          b. receptive character.
          c. marketing character.
          d. exploitative character.

b   61. As a scientific theory, Erich Fromm's humanistic psychoanalysis rates
          a. high on falsifiability.
          b. low as a generator of empirical research.
          c. high as a guide to parents and teachers.
          d. high in parsimony.

b   62.   Fromm's concept of humanity includes the notion that
    a.   people are basically evil.
    b.   people are the freaks of nature.
    c.   most people achieve positive freedom.
    d.   personality is shaped largely by experiences during childhood and preadolescence.

CHAPTER 8
SULLIVAN: INTERPERSONAL THEORY

ESSAY QUESTIONS

1. Distinguish between Sullivan's concepts of intimacy and lust.

    A. Both intimacy and lust are dynamisms, meaning that they are relatively stable behavior patterns or habits.
    B. In an ideal situation, intimacy should develop during preadolescence when a child can safely form a meaningful friendship with another person who is more or less like himself or herself.
    C. Once children form an intimate relationship, usually with someone of equal status and of the same gender, they are able to feel confident in their ability to love and be loved, even with regard to members of the other gender.
    D. However, if children have no preexisting capacity for intimacy, they may confuse lust with love (intimacy) and develop sexual relationships that are devoid of true intimacy. Sullivan believed that people who emerge from early adolescence in command of both their intimacy and lust dynamisms will have few serious interpersonal difficulties later in life.

2. Enumerate and discuss the basic Sullivanian epochs.

    A. Sullivan theorized seven epochs or stages of development, each crucial to personality formation. Interpersonal relations are important during each of the stages.
    B. Personality change can take place at any time, but it is most likely to occur during the transitional periods dividing the stages.
    C. The first stage is infancy, from birth until the child develops meaningful (syntaxic) language. The mothering one is the most important other during this stage. Infants who see their mothering one mostly as positive have a strong good-mother personification and will have many of their needs for tenderness satisfied.
    D. Childhood lasts from the beginning of syntaxic language until the child experiences a need for playmates of equal status, or from about 18 to 24 months until 5 or 6 years old. The mother and father (and other nurturing persons) are now seen as individuals. The child has a relationship not only with parents, but frequently with an imaginary playmate as well. These playmates allow children to have a safe interpersonal relationship with a friend who will not punish them.
    E. The juvenile stage begins with the need for peers of equal status and ends with the need for intimacy with a single chum. In American society, this stage corresponds with the first 3 or 4 years of school. An important challenge for children of this age is the learning of cooperation, compromise, and competition.
    F. Having learned cooperation, compromise, and competition, the child establishes an orientation toward living and enters into the most crucial of all stages—preadolescence. During this stage, a child should develop intimacy with a single friend of more or less equal status. This period, from about 8 or 9 years of age until adolescence, is, perhaps, the most untroubled and carefree time in a person's life. He or she can form a close interpersonal relationship without the encumbrance of sexual desires.

G. Early adolescence comes to young people regardless of whether they are socially and psychologically ready for it. This stage begins with puberty and ends with the need for sexual love with one person. Ideally, children should retain the intimate friendships they formed during preadolescence while seeking lasting relationships with others.

H. Late adolescence is marked by the union of lust and intimacy; that is, it begins when young people are able to feel both lust and intimacy toward the same person. Late adolescence may begin around age 16 to 18, but some people experience it because they are not able to love the person for whom they feel the most sexual attraction or they are not able to feel sexual attraction toward the person for whom they feel the strongest love.

I. People who combine lust and intimacy continue into the stage of adulthood. Sullivan wrote very little about adulthood because people who attain it are beyond the realm of interpersonal psychiatry.

MULTIPLE CHOICE QUESTIONS

b *3. The outstanding feature of Sullivan's theory of personality is its strong emphasis on
    a. conscious thought.
    b. interpersonal relationships.
    c. environmental reinforcers.
    d. unconscious cognition.

d 4. Sullivan's belief in the therapeutic power of an intimate relationship during the preadolescent years
    a. was based on his scientific observations of children and adolescents.
    b. is true of male but not female relationships.
    c. grew out of his psychiatric work with male schizophrenics.
    d. appeared to grow out of his own childhood experiences.

b 5. As a child, Sullivan
    a. twice was elected most popular boy in his class.
    b. had few friends or acquaintances his age.
    c. fought in religious wars in Ireland.
    d. aspired to become a farmer and move to Kansas.
    e. experienced a warm, intimate relationship with his father.

a 6. Sullivan's Zodiac group served as
    a. an informal discussion group of professionals interested in the social sciences.
    b. a research group to investigate his interest in astrology.
    c. a forum for training hospital attendants in the care of schizophrenics.
    d. a source of financial support for his research on treating schizophrenia.

a *7. "The relatively enduring pattern of recurrent interpersonal situations which characterized a human life" is Sullivan's definition of
    a. personality.
    b. dynamism.
    c. personification.
    d. interpersonal relations.
    e. energy transformations.

e   8. Sullivan believed that people develop their personality
        a. independent of environmental influences.
        b. through the clash of unconscious motives.
        c. through the actualization of innate biological drives.
        d. only within the context of the family.
        e. none of the above.

e   9. Sullivan, like Freud and Jung, saw personality as
        a. consisting of three levels of consciousness.
        b. resulting from childhood trauma.
        c. a product of the collective unconscious.
        d. relatively fixed and unchanging.
        e. an energy system.

a   10. Sullivan postulated two kinds of experience:
        a. tensions and energy transformations.
        b. parataxic and syntaxic.
        c. real and therapeutic.
        d. mental and physical.

c   *11. In Sullivan's theory, tensions are of two kinds: needs and
        a. metaneeds.
        b. wants.
        c. anxiety.
        d. satisfaction of needs.
        e. tenderness.

a   12. According to Sullivan, a potentiality for action that may or may not be
        conscious is called
        a. a tension.
        b. an energy transformation.
        c. a personification.
        d. a dynamism.
        e. a self-system.

a   13. To Sullivan, the most basic interpersonal need is
        a. tenderness.
        b. euphoria.
        c. food.
        d. lust.
        e. intimacy.

d   14. Which Sullivanian needs must be satisfied for the general well-being of
        the organism?
        a. survival
        b. dynamic
        c. interpersonal
        d. general
        e. zonal

a   15.   To Sullivan, a 12-month-old infant boy who enjoys playing with his genitals
            would be
            a. satisfying zonal needs.
            b. satisfying general needs.
            c. increasing anxiety.
            d. experiencing the Oedipus complex.

d   16.   According to Sullivan, anxiety differs from tensions of needs in that anxiety is
            a. felt as an unpleasant state.
            b. a product of the physiochemical system.
            c. sometimes helpful.
            d. disjunctive.

d   17.   Sullivan believed anxiety was different from other tensions because an infant
            a. associates anxiety only with zonal needs.
            b. always experiences it in relationship to general needs.
            c. seldom experiences it with the mothering one.
            d. has no capacity to reduce it.

b   18.   According to Sullivan, _____ incapacitates learning, blocks memory, and
            narrows perception.
            a. tenderness
            b. anxiety
            c. lust
            d. empathy
            e. tensions of needs

b   19.   In Sullivan's personality theory, anxiety in an infant is induced through the
            process of
            a. euphoria.
            b. empathy.
            c. personification.
            d. parataxia.

b   *20.   Sullivan believed that _____ was the chief disruptive force blocking
            interpersonal relations.
            a. intimacy
            b. anxiety
            c. prototaxic cognition
            d. syntaxic cognition

d   21.   Sullivan distinguished fear from anxiety in several ways. One difference is that
            a. anxiety ordinarily facilitates learning.
            b. anxiety is experienced more or less the same way by everyone, whereas fear
                is individualized.
            c. the origin of fear is more difficult to determine.
            d. anxiety is more likely to stem from an interpersonal situation.
            e. fear is always disjunctive

b   22.   An energy transformation in Sullivanian theory can best be described as
            a. a dynamism.
            b. an action or behavior.
            c. a trait or habit.
            d. a tension.

b   23. The term Sullivan used to describe those behavioral patterns that consistently
         characterize a person throughout life is
         a. personification.
         b. dynamism.
         c. prototaxic.
         d. proprium.

a   *24. According to Sullivan, the _____ is characterized by the feeling that one is
         living among one's enemies.
         a. malevolent transformation
         b. isolating dynamism
         c. pseudo-intimacy dynamism
         d. paranoid personification
         e. schizoid self-system

a   25. Sullivan believed that timidity, mischievousness, and cruelty could be ways of
         expressing
         a. malevolence.
         b. anxiety.
         c. isolating dynamisms.
         d. tensions of needs.

d   26. Sullivan believed that
         a. society prevents people from killing each other.
         b. people are possessed of something wonderful called sadism.
         c. the malevolent attitude is inherited.
         d. malevolence in adults can be traced to early childhood experiences.
         e. none of the above.

b   27. Sullivan referred to _____ as a close interpersonal relationship between two
         people of more or less equal status.
         a. tenderness.
         b. intimacy.
         c. lust.
         d. agape.

d   *28. Sullivan categorized lust as
         a. a parataxic distortion.
         b. a tenderness need.
         c. a conjunctive dynamism.
         d. an isolating dynamism.

c   29. In Sullivan's terminology, _____ is UNLIKELY to mark a relationship
         between an adolescent girl and her father.
         a. love.
         b. tenderness.
         c. intimacy.
         d. anxiety.
         e. fear

d 30. 15-year-old Carter has strong sexual feelings for Lynne, who does not return his interest. Sullivan would say that the term best describing Carter's feelings for Lynne is
  a. love.
  b. agape.
  c. intimacy.
  d. none of the above.

c 31. Sullivan's dynamism of intimacy grows out of which earlier need?
  a. lust
  b. security
  c. tenderness
  d. euphoria
  e. malevolence

d 32. Sullivan believed that intimacy should develop during
  a. infancy.
  b. childhood.
  c. the juvenile era.
  d. preadolescence.
  e. early adolescence.

a 33. According to Sullivan, when intimacy first develops, it typically involves
  a. same-sex peers.
  b. opposite-sex peers.
  c. the same-sex parent.
  d. an opposite-sex sibling.
  e. an imaginary playmate.

a 34. A Sullivanian dynamism that tends to evoke loving reactions from others and that decreases loneliness is
  a. intimacy.
  b. tenderness.
  c. lust.
  d. malevolence.
  e. dissociation.

e 35. The most complex and inclusive of Sullivan's dynamisms is
  a. malevolence.
  b. intimacy.
  c. lust.
  d. euphoria.
  e. the self-system.

a 36. Sullivan's self-system arises out of the interpersonal situation when an infant
  a. is approximately 12 to 18 months of age.
  b. has developed intimacy with the mothering one.
  c. is exposed to the malevolent attitude of the mothering one.
  d. has been successfully trained.

d   37. Sullivan believed that the self-system's ability to detect and protect
         against anxiety
         a. leads to adaptive personality change.
         b. is a transactional defense mechanism.
         c. usually develops after the juvenile era.
         d. makes favorable personality change difficult.

a   38. Sullivan believed that personality is most likely to change
         a. at the beginning of each developmental stage.
         b. during preadolescence.
         c. during the development of tenderness.
         d. at the end of late adolescence.

b   39. Sullivan believed that people attempt to defend themselves against
         interpersonal tensions by means of
         a. anxiety.
         b. security operations.
         c. intimacy.
         d. personifications.
         e. malevolence.

d   40. According to Sullivan, dissociation
         a. leads to the pursuit of satisfaction.
         b. is the primary form of selective inattention.
         c. is a conjunctive dynamism.
         d. leads to the maintenance of interpersonal security.

e   41. Sullivan called the control of focal awareness that involves a refusal to see
         those things one does not wish to see
         a. dissociation.
         b. eidetic cognition.
         c. personifications.
         d. satisfactions.
         e. selective inattention.

c   42. Mandy is married to an abusive husband, but she refuses to admit that he has a
         serious problem. Sullivan would refer to this process as
         a. dissociation.
         b. syntaxic distortion.
         c. selective inattention.
         d. masochism.

d   43. Sullivan called the image a person has of self or others a
         a. dynamism.
         b. syntaxic distortion.
         c. malevolent transformation.
         d. personification.
         e. projection.

c   44. In Sullivanian theory, an infant's experience of her mother's punishment and
         disapproval leads to the development of the _____ personification.
         a. not-me.
         b. good-me.
         c. bad-me.
         d. good-mother.
         e. bad-mother.

a   45. Sullivan believed that awe, horror, loathing, or a "chilly crawling" sensation are
         manifestations of
         a. uncanny emotion.
         b. lust.
         c. malevolence.
         d. loneliness.

a   46. Sullivan said that an infant's experiences with reward and approval lead to
         a. the good-me personification.
         b. uncanny emotion.
         c. the malevolent transformation.
         d. a pampered style of life.

c   47. According to Sullivan, the not-me personification is
         a. eidetic.
         b. the primary basis of syntaxic cognition.
         c. based on infantile experience of sudden severe anxiety.
         d. based on infantile experience of the bad-nipple.

d   *48. During childhood, a child may invent playmates. Sullivan called these
         imaginary playmates
         a. sublimations.
         b. juveniles.
         c. ghosts.
         d. eidetic.
         e. actors

b   49. Sullivan referred to ways of perceiving, imagining, and conceiving experience as
         a. uncanny emotions.
         b. levels or modes of cognition.
         c. security operations.
         d. selective attention.
         e. dynamisms.

c   50. The earliest experiences in life are undifferentiated, momentary states that are
         incommunicable. Sullivan called these primitive kinds of experiences
         a. syntaxic.
         b. parataxic.
         c. prototaxic.
         d. none of these.

a   51. The process of seeing a cause-and effect-relationship between two events in
        close temporal proximity is what Sullivan called a
        a. parataxic distortion.
        b. security operation.
        c. prototaxic event.
        d. syntaxic slip.
        e. consensual validation.

b   52. Sullivan called private perceptions that cannot be accurately communicated
        to others
        a. prototaxic thoughts.
        b. parataxic distortions.
        c. unconscious archetypes.
        d. syntaxic episodes.

c   *53. When words and concepts begin having the same meaning for a child that they
        do for others, the child's primary mode of cognition, according to Sullivan, is
        a. prototaxic.
        b. parataxic.
        c. syntaxic.
        d. none of the above.

d   54. During transitional periods between Sullivanian stages of development,
        previously dissociated or selectively inattended experiences
        a. are consensually validated with peers.
        b. lead to the malevolent transformation.
        c. result in completely new not-me or bad-me personifications.
        d. may be permitted into the self-system.

a   55. The Sullivanian period beginning at birth and continuing until the development
        of articulate speech is the _____ stage.
        a. infancy
        b. childhood
        c. basic trust.
        d. bonding.
        e. babbling.

c   56. Sullivan regarded apathy and somnolent detachment as
        a. disjunctive dynamisms.
        b. natural reactions to need fulfillment.
        c. protections against extreme anxiety or terror.
        d. mechanisms of escape from euphoria.

b   57. The Sullivanian stage characterized by the beginning of syntaxic language and
        the learning of dramatizations and preoccupations is called
        a. infancy.
        b. childhood.
        c. juvenile era.
        d. preadolescence.
        e. adulthood.

d   58.   Sullivan called personalized language at the parataxic level
          a. prototaxic distortions.
          b. syntaxic language.
          c. syntaxic distortions.
          d. autistic language.

a   59.   Sullivan labeled a child's attempts to act or sound like significant authority
          figures, especially the mother or father,
          a. dramatizations.
          b. imitation.
          c. modeling.
          d. identification.
          e. preoccupations.

b   60.   During the Sullivanian stage of childhood, the child
          a. develops a dual personifications of the mother.
          b. retains the previous personifications of the mother on a parataxic level.
          c. both of the above.
          d. neither a nor b.

d   61.   The beginning of Sullivan's juvenile era is marked by the
          a. origin of syntaxic language.
          b. development of the intimacy dynamism.
          c. development of the lust dynamism.
          d. appearance of the need for playmates of equal status.

d   62.   The end of Sullivan's juvenile era is marked by the
          a. development of a consensually validated language.
          b. onset of puberty.
          c. complete integration of the self-system.
          d. beginning of intimacy with a single chum.

c   63.   During Sullivan's juvenile stage, a child should learn
          a. consensus, compromise, and chumship.
          b. cooperation, communication, and chumship.
          c. competition, compromise, cooperation.
          d. conspiracy, competition, and chumship.

d   64.   According to Sullivan, the development of an orientation toward living
          a. decreases zonal needs.
          b. blocks the development of tenderness needs.
          c. results in the physical survival of the individual.
          d. readies an individual for deeper interpersonal relationships.

d   *65. The outstanding characteristic of Sullivan's _____ stage is the beginning of
          the capacity to love.
          a. infancy
          b. childhood
          c. juvenile era
          d. preadolescence
          e. late adolescence

e   66. According to Sullivan, _____ is the most critical epoch because errors made earlier can be corrected at this time.
         a. childhood
         b. late adolescence
       · c. juvenile
         d. early adolescence
         e. preadolescence

c   67. Sullivan believed that the critical turning point in personality development is
         a. childhood.
         b. the juvenile era.
         c. preadolescence.
         d. infancy.

c   *68. Sullivan's stages of development differ from Freud's in that Sullivan placed more emphasis on what Freud called
         a. infancy.
         b. the Oedipal stage.
         c. the latency period.
         d. the prenatal period.
         e. the sadistic-anal period.

b   69. According to Sullivan, what is the relationship between lust and intimacy in normal, healthy development?
         a. Lust and intimacy are combined during early adolescence.
         b. Lust follows the development of intimacy.
         c. Lust develops during preadolescence, intimacy during the juvenile era.
         d. Lust and intimacy are separate during late adolescence and adulthood.

c   *70. The Sullivanian stage of early adolescence is marked by
         a. sexual maturation and mature love.
         b. development of same-sex chumships.
         c. the need for satisfaction of lust.
         d. the learning of cooperation and compromise.

d   71. According to Sullivan, lust interferes with security because
         a. lust can be successfully dissociated.
         b. one cannot selectively inattend to zonal needs.
         c. the energy of lust is directly transformed into anxiety.
         d. genital activity is associated with guilt, shame, and anxiety.

c   72. When lust and intimacy are directed toward the same person, which of Sullivan's stages has been reached?
         a. preadolescence
         b. early adolescence
         c. late adolescence
         d. the juvenile stage

a   73. Sullivan claimed that late adolescence ends with the
         a. establishment of a lasting love relationship.
         b. suppression of lust and elevation of tenderness.
         c. enhancement of security through decreases in intimacy.
         d. finding of a permanent occupation or profession.
         e. graduation from high school.

d 74. Sullivan had little to say about adulthood because he believed that
    a. personality development ends by late adolescence.
    b. psychotherapy with adults is useless.
    c. adults outgrow the need for same-sex peers.
    d. this stage is beyond the scope of interpersonal psychiatry.

a 75. Sullivan believed that most psychological disorders stem from
    a. interpersonal relationships.
    b. a bad-mother personification.
    c. lack of security operations.
    d. brain damage.
    e. toxic chemicals.

c 76. Sullivan's early therapeutic work was largely with
    a. psychopathic deviates.
    b. manic-depressive patients.
    c. schizophrenic patients.
    d. college students.
    e. delinquent preadolescents.

a 77. While doing therapy, Sullivan saw his role as that of a
    a. participant observer.
    b. best friend.
    c. detached adviser.
    d. father surrogate.

c 78. Research by Henry, Schacht, and Strupp suggests that in therapeutic relationships,
    a. therapists tend to adopt a superior attitude.
    b. patients tend to resist advice by therapists.
    c. patients tend to adopt behaviors that are consistent with the way their therapists treat them.
    d. therapists tend to demand that patients adopt a specific philosophy of life.

a 79. Research by Hilliard, Henry, and Strupp (2000) found that
    a. the early childhood experiences of therapists contributed to therapeutic outcome.
    b. the early childhood experiences of patients, but not of therapists, contributed to therapeutic outcome.
    c. successful patients, compared with unsuccessful patients, were more likely than unsuccessful patients to have had an imaginary playmate during childhood.
    d. successful patients, compared with unsuccessful patients, were less likely to have had an imaginary playmate during childhood.

c 80. Research suggests that children with imaginary playmates, compared with those who report not having imaginary playmates, were more likely to
    a. develop schizophrenic tendencies.
    b. be boys.
    c. have high levels of imagination.
    d. be lonely.

b   81.   Which of these statements represents the most valid criticism of current
          Sullivanian theory?
          a.   It is too narrow.
          b.   It is not currently generating much research.
          c.   It lacks internal consistency.
          d.   Its stages of development defy common sense.

d   82.   Sullivan's one-genus hypothesis states:
          a.   "Once upon a time, everything was lovely, but that was before I had to deal
               with people."
          b.   "Differences among people are more important than their similarities."
          c.   "To be human is to love; to love is to be human."
          d.   "Everyone is much more simply human than otherwise."

a   83.   Sullivan's concept of humanity includes the notion that
          a.   people become humans through their interpersonal relations.
          b.   people are driven by animal instincts from which they cannot escape.
          c.   differences among humans are more important than their similarities.
          d.   people are doomed to develop malevolent transformations to feel as though
               they were living among their enemies.

CHAPTER 9
ERIKSON: POST-FREUDIAN THEORY

ESSAY QUESTIONS

1. Compare and contrast Erikson's concept of ego psychology with Freud's psychoanalytic theory.

    A. In general terms, Erikson made three additions to Freudian theory: (1) he added four later stages to Freud's oral, anal, phallic, and latency stages; (2) he gathered data from historical and cultural sources, thus relying more on social factors than on biological factors; and (3) he emphasized the ego over the id.
    B. Erikson saw the ego as being capable of adapting to changes throughout the life cycle. He also identified three aspects of the ego: (1) the body ego, (2) the ego ideal, and (3) ego identity.
    C. An individual's cultural background has a strong influence on how the ego will develop. Some societies tend to produce generous people (the Sioux nation) and others produce hoarders (the Yurok tribe).
    D. The ego grows in stages according to the epigenetic principle; that is, each step of ego growth implies future growth and rests on previous development.

2. Discuss Erikson's basic assumptions that underlie his theory of developmental stages.

    A. Psychological growth takes place according to the epigenetic principle, meaning that one component arises out of another, has its own time of ascendancy, but does not entirely replace earlier components.
    B. Each stage has both a syntonic, or harmonious element, as well as a dystonic, or disruptive element. Both components are necessary for future growth.
    C. The conflict between the dystonic and syntonic elements produces an ego quality, or ego strength, called a basic strength.
    D. Each of the eight Eriksonian stages has a psychosexual mode, a psychosocial crisis, a basic strength, and a core pathology.
    E. Events in earlier stages do not cause later personality development. Ego identity is shaped by a multiplicity of conflicts and events.
    F. Each stage from adolescence on is marked by an identity crisis, or turning point filled with potential for catastrophe or for growth.

3. List the key concepts in Erikson's infancy stage.

    A. Erikson's infancy stage goes beyond Freud's oral stage to include an oral-sensory psychosexual mode of incorporating or taking in objects through all the sense organs.
    B. The two modes of incorporation are receiving and accepting.
    C. The psychosocial crisis of infancy is basic trust versus basic mistrust. Although trust is syntonic and mistrust is dystonic, both must be experienced during infancy.
    D. From the conflict between basic trust and basic mistrust emerges the basic strength of infancy—hope.
    E. The antithesis of hope is withdrawal, which is the core pathology of infancy.

MULTIPLE CHOICE QUESTIONS

c   *4.   In contrast to Freud, Erikson
     a.   placed greater emphasis on the id.
     b.   placed less emphasis on social and historical influences.
     c.   was not trained as a physician.
     d.   was trained as a physician.

a   5.   Erikson, unlike Jung and Adler,
     a.   never repudiated Freud's ideas.
     b.   rejected Freud's idea of unconscious motivation.
     c.   was personally psychoanalyzed by Sigmund Freud.
     d.   married Freud's daughter, Anna.

c   6.   Erikson's theory may be called "post-Freudian" because
     a.   he rejected Freud's psychoanalytic theory of personality.
     b.   Freud personally approved of Erikson's personality theory.
     c.   he built his theory on foundations that Freud laid.
     d.   he only accepted the theories of post-Freudian psychoanalysts.

c   7.   Erikson's life was marked by several
     a.   marriages.
     b.   personal analyses with Jung.
     c.   identity crises.
     d.   episodes of schizophrenia.

b   8.   Erikson's biological father
     a.   suffered from severe alcoholism.
     b.   was unknown to Erikson.
     c.   served as Freud's personal physician.
     d.   died when Erikson was an adolescent.
     e.   discovered Newfoundland.

d   9.   For Erikson, the years immediately after graduation from the gymnasium were marked by
     a.   studying to become a physician.
     b.   developing a bourgeois lifestyle.
     c.   being psychoanalyzed by Sigmund Freud.
     d.   feeling discontented and confused.

c   10.   Erikson was rescued from the life of a wandering artist by
     a.   fatherly advice from Sigmund Freud.
     b.   marriage to Joan Serson.
     c.   a letter from his friend Peter Blos.
     d.   a personal analysis by Anna Freud.

d   11.   Erikson's additions to Freudian theory included
     a.   elevating social factors above biological factors.
     b.   emphasizing the ego as the key to personality development.
     c.   accepting Jung's idea of the collective unconscious.
     d.   both a and b.
     e.   both b and c.

d   12.   Erikson believed that the ego is
        a.   the sense of "I."
        b.   the self-identity.
        c.   the center of personality.
        d.   all of the above.

c   *13.   According to Erikson, during childhood, the ego
        a.   is dormant.
        b.   develops from the superego.
        c.   is weak and pliable.
        d.   has greater strength than it does during adolescence.

a   14.   A person's capacity to unify experiences and actions in an adaptive manner defines Erikson's
        a.   ego.
        b.   identity crisis.
        c.   psychic imperative.
        d.   adolescent ideal.

d   *15.   Which of the following is NOT an aspect of the ego, according to Erikson?
        a.   body ego
        b.   ego identity
        c.   ego ideal
        d.   self-conscious ego

b   *16.   Erikson saw the ego as developing
        a.   only during adolescence.
        b.   within a social structure.
        c.   under the power of the id.
        d.   independent of social or historical factors.

a   17.   Erikson found that the prolonged and permissive nursing of Sioux infants resulted in _____ character traits.
        a.   oral
        b.   anal
        c.   phallic
        d.   infantile
        e.   latency

e   *18.   The belief of many Nazis that Germans represented the "master race" illustrates Erikson's concept of
        a.   group ego.
        b.   epigenetic unfolding.
        c.   identity crisis.
        d.   inflated ego.
        e.   pseudospecies.

c   *19.   Erikson's belief that the ego develops in a sequence, with each stage emerging from and being built upon a previous stage, illustrates the concept of
        a.   pseudospecies.
        b.   embryological imperative.
        c.   epigenetic principle.
        d.   psychic energy.

a   20. According to Erikson, each stage of life is characterized by
          a. an interaction of opposites.
          b. a multiplication of similarities.
          c. an increase in syntonic elements.
          d. a decrease in dystonic elements.

c   *21. According to Erikson, what is necessary for proper adaptation?
          a. syntonic elements only
          b. dystonic elements only
          c. both syntonic and dystonic elements
          d. neither syntonic nor dystonic elements

c   22. Erikson, believed that ego identity is shaped
          a. by past events.
          b. by future events.
          c. by the past, present, and anticipated events.
          d. mostly by biology.

a   23. "A crucial period of increased vulnerability and heightened potential" is
          Erikson's definition of a
          a   crisis.
          b. commitment.
          c. basic strength.
          d. core pathology.

c   24. For Erikson, infancy is a time of
          a. exclusion.
          b. active exploration.
          c. incorporation.
          d. exclusivity.

d   25. Erikson characterized the oral-sensory phase as a _____ mode of adaptation.
          a. dystonic
          b. syntonic
          c. psychosocial
          d. psychosexual
          e. functional

e   26. Tyler is sensitive to his infant daughter's needs. According to Erikson, because
          he meets those needs in a reliable and consistent manner, he is helping his
          daughter learn
          a. dependence.
          b. basic mistrust.
          c. sensory trust.
          d. hope.
          e. basic trust.

d   27. Erikson believed that one's ability to adapt is dependent on
          a. minimizing mistrust.
          b. maximizing trust.
          c. increasing dystonic tendencies and decreasing syntonic tendencies.
          d. a maximum ratio of trust to mistrust.

c   28.   Erikson believed that a sense of a readiness for danger and an anticipation of
          discomfort are adaptive aspects of
          a.   trust.
          b.   withdrawal.
          c.   mistrust.
          d.   syntonic tendencies.
          e.   hope.

a   *29. Erikson believed that the basic strength of infancy is
          a.   hope.
          b.   pleasure.
          c.   satisfaction.
          d.   dependence.
          e.   joy.

e   30.   According to Erikson, the core pathology of infancy is
          a.   disappointment.
          b.   indifference.
          c.   selfishness.
          d.   rage.
          e.   withdrawal.

c   *31. Freud's anal stage of development has a parallel in Erikson's _____ stage.
          a.   infancy
          b.   toddler
          c.   early childhood
          d.   phallic
          e.   mastery

b   32.   Self-control and interpersonal control are the tasks of the _____ stage of
          psychosocial development, according to Erikson.
          a.   infancy
          b.   early childhood
          c.   latter childhood
          d.   play age
          e.   school age

b   33.   The anal-urethral-muscular mode of psychosexual adjustment characterizes
          Erikson's _____stage.
          a.   infancy
          b.   early childhood
          c.   middle childhood
          d.   play age
          e.   phallic

a   34.   According to Erikson, _____ is a feeling of self-consciousness, of being looked
          at and exposed.
          a.   shame
          b.   doubt
          c.   guilt
          d.   autonomy

b   35. A feeling of not being certain, and that something remains hidden, characterizes
          Erikson's notion of
          a. guilt.
          b. doubt.
          c. willfulness.
          d. autonomy.
          e. shame.

c   *36. The resolution of the crisis of early childhood results in Erikson's basic
          strength of
          a. trust.
          b. love.
          c. will.
          d. purposefulness.
          e. competence.

c   37. Inadequate will, according to Erikson, is expressed as
          a. stubbornness.
          b. inhibition.
          c. compulsion.
          d. shame.
          e. autonomy.

a   38. Freud's phallic stage of psychosexual development parallels Erikson's
          _____ stage.
          a. play age
          b. early childhood
          c. adolescence
          d. infancy

d   *39. Erikson's genital-locomotor psychosexual mode accompanies the _____ stage.
          a. infancy
          b. adolescence
          c. school age
          d. play age

b   40. Erikson believed that the Oedipus and castration complexes are
          a. successfully resolved during adolescence.
          b. not always to be taken literally.
          c. a result of the phylogenetically inherited endowment.
          d. the same for males and females.

b   *41. Erikson saw the Oedipal situation as the prototype of
          a. psychopathology within the family setting.
          b. the lifelong power of human playfulness.
          c. conflict between males and females.
          d. competition between children and authority figures.

c   42. According to Erikson, the core conflict of the play age is
          a. trust versus mistrust.
          b. autonomy versus shame and doubt.
          c. initiative versus guilt.
          d. industry versus inferiority.

d   43. Erikson's core pathology of the play age is
            a. inferiority.
            b. shame.
            c. doubt.
            d. inhibition.
            e. aimlessness.

d   *44. Erikson suggested that the basic strength of the play age is
            a. trust.
            b. autonomy.
            c. initiative.
            d. purpose.

c   45. According to Erikson, the development of a conscience begins during
            a. infancy.
            b. early childhood.
            c. play age.
            d. latency.

e   46. Erikson's school age stage of psychosocial development parallels which of
            Freud's stages of psychosexual development?
            a. oral
            b. phallic
            c. anal
            d. genital
            e. latency

e   *47. According to Erikson, the major expansion of the child's social world beyond
            family members, to include peers and other adults, occurs during
            a. early childhood.
            b. adolescence.
            c. infancy.
            d. the play age.
            e. the school age.

b   48. According to Erikson, teaching and instructing in the ways of a society or
            culture typically occur during
            a. the play age.
            b. the school age.
            c. adolescence.
            d. early adulthood.
            e. late adulthood.

a   49. Erikson believed that sexual latency is important because it
            a. allows the child to divert energy to learning and social relations.
            b. fosters the development of will.
            c. signals a resolution of the Oedipus complex.
            d. allows the child to integrate the body ego.

c   *50. Industry versus inferiority is Erikson's psychosocial crisis of
            a. early childhood.
            b. the play age.
            c. the school age.
            d. adolescence.

d 51. Erikson believed that a child's maximum desire and readiness to learn occurs during
    a. infancy.
    b. early childhood.
    c. the play age.
    d. the school age.
    e. adolescence.

d 52. Erikson claimed that a child who learns to do a job well during the school age will develop a sense of
    a. will.
    b. purpose.
    c. inferiority.
    d. industry.
    e. autonomy.

e 53. According to Erikson, the foundation for "cooperative participation in productive adult life" is
    a. trust.
    b. purpose.
    c. will.
    d. initiative.
    e. competence.

a 54. A preoccupation with the Oedipal fantasy and the wasting of time with nonproductive play reflect Erikson's core pathology of
    a. inertia.
    b. inhibition.
    c. compulsion.
    d. withdrawal.
    e. guilt.

c 55. By the end of which of Erikson's psychosocial stages should a person develop a firm sense of ego identity?
    a. the play age
    b. the school age
    c. adolescence
    d. early childhood
    e. young adulthood

b *56. Erikson saw which stage as a time of psychosocial latency?
    a. infancy
    b. adolescence
    c. play age
    d. school age
    e. old age

a   57.   According to Erikson, during adolescence, a person is permitted to experiment
          with a variety of roles, values, and goals without making a lasting commitment.
          This reflects what aspect of adolescence?
          a. psychosocial latency
          b. stagnation
          c. incompetence
          d. purposelessness
          e. lack of will

d   58.   For Erikson, puberty is psychologically important because it
          a. is the beginning of both psychosocial and psychosexual latency.
          b. signals physical changes in the body.
          c. resolves the Oedipal situation.
          d. triggers expectations of future adult roles.

d   59.   According to Erikson, an identity crisis
          a. has no effect on ego strength.
          b. increases ego strength.
          c. decreases ego strength.
          d. may increase or decrease ego strength.

c   60.   Erikson defines identity both positively and negatively. Therefore, adolescents
          a. reject parental values and embrace peer group values.
          b. see identity only in terms of absolute right or wrong.
          c. affirm some values and reject others.
          d. accept positive aspects of their personality but reject negative aspects of
              ego identity.

a   61.   Rejection of family or community standards, inability to establish intimacy,
          and inability to concentrate on required tasks are symptomatic of what
          Erikson called
          a. identity confusion.
          b. an unresolved Oedipal situation.
          c. ideological inertia.
          d. ego idealism.
          e. identity stagnation.

a   62.   Erikson's psychosocial moratorium is characterized by
          a. crisis without commitment.
          b. commitment without crisis.
          c. both crisis and commitment.
          d. neither crisis nor commitment.

d   63.   People who have accepted the goals and values of their parents, but who have
          never seriously questioned their own identity, are considered to be at which of
          Erikson's identity states?
          a. identity diffusion
          b. identity achievement
          c. psychological moratorium
          d. identity foreclosure
          e. identity commitment

e   64.   The core pathology of adolescence, according to Erikson, is
            a.   withdrawal.
            b.   isolation.
            c.   inferiority.
            d.   incompetence.
            e.   role repudiation.

d   65.   The inability to synthesize various self-images and values into a workable
            identity is what Erikson called
            a.   stagnation.
            b.   identity foreclosure.
            c.   ego idealism.
            d.   role repudiation.
            e   psychological moratorium.

e   66.   Erikson believed that some degree of role repudiation is necessary for the
            a.   formation of personal identity.
            b.   injection of new ideas into society.
            c.   injection of new vitality into the social structure.
            d.   only a and c.
            e.   a, b, and c are all correct.

e   67.   The chief psychosexual accomplishment of young adulthood, according to
            Erikson, is
            a.   intimacy.
            b.   basic trust.
            c.   marriage.
            d.   reproduction.
            e.   none of the above.

c   68.   The ability to fuse one's identity with that of another without fear of losing it
            characterizes what Erikson called
            a.   identity achievement.
            b.   psychological moratorium.
            c.   intimacy.
            d.   sensuality.
            e.   cooperation.

c   69.   The psychosocial crisis of young adulthood, according to Erikson, is
            a.   identity versus identity confusion.
            b.   competence versus incompetence.
            c.   intimacy versus isolation.
            d.   generativity versus stagnation.

d   70.   According to Erikson, true intimacy can only be achieved
            a.   after the satisfaction of sexual desires.
            b.   through marriage.
            c.   during psychological moratorium.
            d.   after identity is established.

a   71. "The incapacity to take chances with one's identity by sharing true intimacy"
         defines Erikson's concept of
         a. isolation.
         b. stagnation.
         c. mistrust.
         d. psychological moratorium.

b   72. Erikson's basic strength of young adulthood is
         a. caring.
         b. love.
         c. trust.
         d. confidence.
         e. competence.

a *73. The core pathology of young adulthood, according to Erikson, is
         a. exclusivity.
         b. isolation.
         c. stagnation.
         d. selfishness.

c *74. Erikson claimed that for most people, the longest stage of psychosocial
         development is
         a. adolescence.
         b. young adulthood.
         c. adulthood.
         d. later adulthood.

d   75. Erikson claimed that procreativity encompasses
         a. caring for one's offspring.
         b. productive work.
         c. perpetuation of society.
         d. all of the above.

a   76. A willingness and readiness to be a part of society and to transmit cultural
         values to the next generation best describes Erikson's notion of
         a. procreativity.
         b. intimacy.
         c. competence.
         d. wisdom.

a   77. The antithesis of Erikson's generativity is
         a. stagnation.
         b. isolation.
         c. intimacy.
         d. wisdom.
         e. identity.

b   78. "A widening commitment to take care of the persons, the products, and the
         ideas one has learned to *care for*" is what Erikson called
         a. intimacy.
         b. care.
         c. procreativity.
         d. generativity.
         e. generalized sensuality.

d   79. According to Erikson, self-centeredness, provincialism, and pseudospeciation are all manifestations of
a. mistrust.
b. identity confusion.
c. isolation.
d. rejectivity.
e. despair.

d   *80. Erikson's final psychosexual stage is
a. generativity.
b. menopause.
c. impotency.
d. generalized sensuality.
e. neo-latency.

b   81. Erikson contended that an elderly person's delight in a variety of different physical sensations reflects
a. wisdom.
b. generalized sensuality.
c. intimacy with nature.
d. sexual sublimation.
e. procreativity.

a   82. For Erikson, integrity involves
a. feeling whole and coherent.
b. being physically and intellectually strong.
c. being honest and truthful.
d. never despairing.

c   83. The "informed and detached concern with life itself in the face of death itself" is how Erikson defined
a. mistrust.
b. detachment.
c. wisdom.
d. despair.
e. isolation.

a   84. Erikson's core pathology of old age is
a. disdain.
b. rejection.
c. rage.
d. impotence.

a   85. The discipline that combines psychoanalytic concepts with historical method is
a. psychohistory.
b. psychoanalytic history.
c. historical psychoanalysis.
d. analytical historiography.

b 86. Erikson's anthropological studies demonstrated
- a. the limitations of his theories with different cultures and societies.
- b. the influence of history and culture on personality development.
- c. how the development of primitive people's psychological development differs from contemporary Americans' development.
- d. a lack of support for his theory of psychosocial stages.

d 87. Erikson believed that an author of psychohistory should
- a. be totally objective and dispassionate.
- b. reject countertransference towards one's subject.
- c. objectively analyze and eliminate one's bias toward one's subject.
- d. be emotionally involved in one's subject.

a 88. One of Erikson's most controversial uses of play construction involved the
- a. investigation of sex differences in play construction.
- b. investigation of racial differences in play construction.
- c. investigation of adult–child differences in play construction.
- d. use of fantasy constructions in psychohistory.

a 89. Erikson suggested that differences between boys and girls in play construction themes are primarily due to
- a. anatomical differences between the genders.
- b. social training.
- c. differences in artistic abilities between the genders.
- d. unconscious biases on the part of researchers.
- e. chance.

c 90. Helson and Pals (2000) studied identity among women for more than 30 years and found that those who had a solid identity at age 21 were
- a. likely to be satisfied with a traditional domestic role.
- b. likely to be dissatisfied with a traditional domestic role.
- c. more creative at age 52 than were women with confused identity at age 21.
- d. less creative at age 52 than were women with confused identity at age 21.

b *91. Research by Michael Pratt and colleagues (1999) found that
- a. adults high in generativity scored low on moral reasoning.
- b. women scored higher in generativity than did men.
- c. generative adults were less likely than nongenerative adults to learn lessons from life experiences.
- d. generativity reaches its peak during late adolescence and early adulthood.

c. 92. In his concept of humanity, Erikson
- a. emphasized free choice.
- b. favored determinism.
- c. adopted a moderate view regarding free choice and determinism.
- d. rejected both free choice and determinism.

CHAPTER 10
SKINNER: BEHAVIORAL ANALYSIS

ESSAY QUESTIONS

1. Discuss the contributions of E. L. Thorndike and J. B. Watson to Skinner's learning theory.

    A. Thorndike's original law of effect held that responses to stimuli followed by a satisfier tend to be "stamped in," or learned. A second part of the law stated that responses to stimuli followed by an annoyer tend to be "stamped our," or eliminated.
    B. Thorndike later changed the law of effect to include only the first part, namely that reinforcement or reward increases the chances of a behavior being learned. This concept is at the core of Skinner's operant conditioning.
    C. Watson had an even greater effect on Skinner, especially his notions of science and psychology. Watson's insistence that human behavior must be studied scientifically impressed Skinner even before he began graduate school.
    D. Watson criticized traditional psychology for studying consciousness, introspection, instincts, sensations, perception, motivation, and mental states. He also insisted that the goal of psychology must be prediction and control of behavior. Throughout his career, Skinner adhered closely to Watson's position.

2. Discuss Skinner's philosophy of science as it applies to the study of human behavior.

    A. Skinner insisted that the study of human behavior is essentially the same as the study of other natural phenomena. Physical and biological scientists do not attempt to attribute motivation, needs, or drives to the objects or biological processes they study. Skinner believed that psychologists who consider these inner states as instigators of action are wasting their time.
    B. Skinner's scientific behaviorism allows for an interpretation of behavior but not an explanation of its causes. Interpretation permits the psychologist to generalize from one situation to another, but explanation is no more than fabricating stories.
    C. Skinner believed that science has three main characteristics: (1) it is cumulative; (2) it is an attitude that values empirical observation; and (3) it is a search for lawful relationships.
    D. Science—in contrast to art, philosophy, and literature—advances in a cumulative manner. In other words, scientific knowledge continues to expand at ever-increasing speeds, while other areas of inquiry advance slowly, if at all.
    E. Science values empirical observation. It deals with facts rather than with what someone has said about the facts. It rejects authority—even its own authority. It also demands intellectual honesty and suspends judgment until clear trends emerge.
    F. Third, science searches for order and lawful relationships. Scientific observations are guided by theoretical assumptions and the results of tested hypotheses.

3.   Distinguish negative reinforcement from both positive reinforcement and punishment.

    A. Negative reinforcement, like positive reinforcement, strengthens the behavior it follows.

    B. Positive reinforcement takes place when a positively valued stimulus increases the probability that a given behavior will occur. In comparison, negative reinforcement takes place when a negatively valued stimulus or condition is removed from a situation. In both cases, the behavior immediately preceding the reinforcer tends to be learned or strengthened.

    C. Negative reinforcement must not be confused with punishment, which does not strengthen behavior. Punishment is the presentation of an aversive stimulus or the removal of a positive one. With either type of punishment, psychologists are not able to make accurate predictions of behavior. With negative reinforcement (and positive reinforcement), psychologists can both predict and control behavior to a much greater extent.

MULTIPLE CHOICE QUESTIONS

c   4.   The label that best fits Skinner's work is
    a. social learning theory.
    b. humanistic theory.
    c. radical behaviorism.
    d. interpersonal theory.

a   *5.   Which term is LEAST descriptive of B. F. Skinner?
    a. cognitive psychologist
    b. determinist
    c. environmentalist
    d. radical behaviorist

e   6.   For Skinner, observable behavior
    a. is beyond the realm of science.
    b. is limited to internal events.
    c. is motivated by hypothetical constructs.
    d. results from unconscious psychodynamic processes.
    e. none of the above.

d   7.   Skinner believed that the most useful data for predicting and controlling behavior are
    a. the psychological components of the organism.
    b. the constitutional components of the organism.
    c. people's conscious perceptions of themselves.
    d. people's personal histories.

d   *8.   As a young man, Skinner wanted to become a
    a. physician.
    b. lawyer.
    c. psychologist.
    d. writer.

a   9. Skinner's laboratory research at Harvard consisted exclusively of
        experiments with
        a. non-human animals.
        b. undergraduates he taught.
        c. fellow graduate students.
        d. psychotherapy patients.
        e. mentally retarded adults.

c   10. Elms believes that Skinner's midlife crisis ended with
        a. the death of his father.
        b. his marriage.
        c. his writing of *Walden Two.*
        d. his election to the U.S. Senate.

c   11. Skinner's scientific behaviorism assumes that
        a. the study of human behavior must be based on methods that are quite
            different from those of other natural sciences.
        b. the motives of the subjects being observed must be given special
            consideration.
        c. human behavior is subject to the laws of science.
        d. human behavior cannot be studied scientifically.

c   12. Thorndike's original law of effect stated that
        a. responses that are followed immediately by a satisfier tend to be
            stamped in.
        b. responses that are followed immediately by an annoyer tend to be
            stamped out.
        c. both of the above.
        d. neither a nor b.

a   13. John Watson argued that
        a. the goal of psychology should be the prediction and control of behavior.
        b. psychologists should be primarily concerned with why people act as
            they do.
        c. psychology should be limited to the study of consciousness.
        d. psychology is not and cannot be a science.

b   14. Skinner's work was MOST influenced by
        a. Ivan Pavlov.
        b. John Watson.
        c. Harry Stack Sullivan.
        d. Albert Bandura.
        e. Sigmund Freud.

b   15. What was Skinner's position on such internal mental states as thinking
        and feeling?
        a. They do not exist.
        b. They exist, but scientists should not attribute behavior to them.
        c. They are essential to an understanding of human behavior.
        d. both b and c

b   *16. Skinner believed that the most critical aspect of science is
         a. hypothesis testing.
         b. an attitude that values empirical observation.
         c. measurement of physiological responses.
         d. reliable formulation of hypothetical concepts.

d   17. In his philosophy of science, Skinner
         a. began with complex organisms and then deduced specific principles.
         b. held that science must be able to explain the causes of natural phenomena.
         c. attempted to predict behavior but not to control it.
         d. attempted to discover the conditions under which behavior can be described,
             predicted, and controlled.
         e. held behavior to be neither lawful nor determined.

a   18. Which of the following is NOT a principal characteristic of science, according
         to Skinner?
         a. Science explains behavior.
         b. Science values empirical observation.
         c. Science is cumulative.
         d. Science is a search for order and lawful relationships

b   19. According to Skinner, scientists seldom fabricate data mostly because
         a. they are inherently more intellectually honest than most people.
         b. the correct data will ultimately be discovered and thereby embarrass the
             fabricator.
         c. they must take an oath of honesty when they become scientists.
         d. they are unbiased and uninterested in the results of their studies.

b   20. Operant conditioning is distinguished from classical conditioning primarily in
         that operant conditioning involves
         a. instincts.
         b. immediate reinforcement of a response.
         c. the pairing of a conditioned stimulus with an unconditioned stimulus.
         d. elicited rather than emitted behavior.
         e. all of the above.

c   *21. The three conditions essential to operant conditioning are
         a. the situation, the behavior, and the conditioned stimulus.
         b. the unconditioned stimulus, the conditioned stimulus and the organism.
         c. the antecedent, the behavior, and the consequence.
         d. the unconditioned stimulus, the "Skinner box," and the experimenter.

e   22. For Skinner, an important distinction between classical conditioning and
         operant conditioning is that in classical conditioning behavior is _____,
         whereas in operant conditioning behavior is _____.
         a. generalized; discriminated
         b. emitted; elicited
         c. extinguished; generalized
         d. recovered; discriminated
         e. elicited; emitted

a   *23. When operant conditioning is used to shape complex behavior such as playing a
          piano, reinforcement is applied
          a. through successive approximations.
          b. by the process of punishment.
          c. through an intermediary agent.
          d. by waiting for the target behavior to appear, then rewarding it.

c   24.   Skinner called any stimulus within the environment that strengthens behavior a
          a. reward.
          b. punishment.
          c. reinforcer.
          d. respondent.

a   25.   A response to a similar environment in the absence of previous reinforcement
          was Skinner's definition of
          a. stimulus generalization.
          b. stimulus control.
          c. stimulus discrimination.
          d. shaping.

c   26.   Concerning reinforcement, Skinner would most likely say that
          a. money is an innate reinforcer.
          b. money is reinforcing because it has value.
          c. money has value because it is reinforcing.
          d. all of the above.

b   27.   Any behavior that tends to reduce or avoid conditions that are detrimental to
          the survival of the organism is
          a. positively reinforced.
          b. negatively reinforced.
          c. extinguished.
          d. punished.

b   28.   During World War II, Skinner
          a. served in the Naval Air Force as a fighter pilot.
          b. trained pigeons to pilot missiles into enemy targets.
          c. worked in a VA hospital as a psychotherapist.
          d. made an unsuccessful attempt to become a U.S. senator.

a   *29. Skinner defines negative reinforcement as any condition that,
          a. when removed from a situation, increases the probability that a given
              behavior will occur.
          b. when added to a situation, increases the probability that a given behavior
              will occur.
          c. when removed from a situation, decreases the probability that a given
              behavior will occur.
          d. when added to a situation, decreases the probability that a given behavior
              will occur.

d   *30. Skinner believed that the effects of punishment are
          a. the same as the effects of reward.
          b. the exact opposite to those of reward.
          c. more predictable than those of reward.
          d. less predictable than those of reward.

a   31.   Negative and positive reinforcement are alike in that they
         a.   strengthen the behavior they follow.
         b.   involve the presentation of a beneficial stimulus.
         c.   involve the removal of an aversive stimulus.
         d.   extinguish the behavior they follow.
         e.   are not affected by schedules of reinforcement.

c   32.   Negative reinforcement and punishment are similar in that they both
         a.   strengthen a response.
         b.   weaken a response.
         c.   involve aversive stimuli.
         d.   have unpredictable effects on behavior.

b   *33.   Heather has a painful headache. She takes some aspirin and the pain stops. In the future when she has a headache, she will also take aspirin. Skinner would say that the taking of aspirin to reduce headache pain is
         a.   positively reinforced.
         b.   negatively reinforced.
         c.   extinguished.
         d.   successively approximated.
         e.   spontaneously recovered.

c   34.   Which of these did Skinner NOT list as an effect of punishment?
         a.   suppression of the behavior punished
         b.   suppression of related behavior
         c.   shaping of the target behavior
         d.   conditioning of negative feelings

c   35.   Unlike punishment, reinforcement
         a.   cannot derive from natural consequences.
         b.   can derive from human intervention.
         c.   provides a person with information as to what behavior is desired.
         d.   involves adding a negative stimuli or removing a positive stimuli.
         e.   can be used to control behavior.

d   *36.   According to Skinner, a clear example of a conditioned reinforcer would be
         a.   sex.
         b.   physical comfort.
         c.   food.
         d.   money.
         e.   sleep.

e   37.   Which of these would NOT be considered by Skinner to be a generalized reinforcer?
         a.   affection
         b.   approval
         c.   money
         d.   attention
         e.   food

a   38. Fixed-ratio, variable-ratio, fixed-interval, and variable-interval are examples of
        a. intermittent schedules.
        b. continuous schedules.
        c. schedules of punishment.
        d. slot machine payoffs.

c *39. Payment by piece rate (for example, paying a bricklayer a set amount for each
        brick laid) most closely approximates which schedule of reinforcement?
        a. fixed-interval
        b. variable-interval
        c. fixed-ratio
        d. variable-ratio

e   40. Which of these schedules would cost the experimenter the most reinforcers for
        the least number of responses?
        a. variable-interval
        b. fixed-interval
        c. variable-ratio
        d. fixed-ratio
        e. continuous

c   41. For humans, playing slot machines best illustrates the influence of a _____
        schedule of reinforcement.
        a. continuous
        b. fixed-ratio
        c. variable-ratio
        d. fixed-interval

d   42. With what schedule of reinforcement is an organism reinforced for the first
        response following a designated period of time?
        a. continuous
        b. fixed-ratio
        c. variable-ratio
        d. fixed-interval
        e. variable-interval

d   43. Payment by salary or wage most closely approximates which schedule
        of reinforcement?
        a. continuous
        b. fixed-ratio
        c. variable-ratio
        d. fixed-interval

e   44. To stop her 2-year-old daughter from crying, Sandy consistently gives the child
        a piece of candy whenever she cries. Such behavior is
        a. positively reinforcing for the child.
        b. negatively reinforcing for the child.
        c. positively reinforcing for Sandy.
        d. negatively reinforcing for Sandy.
        e. both a and d.

b 45. When she was in the 7th grade, Dawn made 10 written book reports. Now, she can no longer recall the title of eight of those books. Skinner would say this loss is most likely due to
   a. repression.
   b. forgetting.
   c. respondent extinction.
   d. operant extinction.

c 46. Behavior reinforced on an intermittent schedule is
   a. learned very rapidly.
   b. extinguished very rapidly.
   c. resistant to extinction.
   d. extinguished rapidly through punishment.

c 47. The systematic withholding of reinforcement previously contingent upon a response until the probability of the response diminishes to zero is Skinner's definition of
   a. positive punishment.
   b. negative punishment.
   c. extinction.
   d. successive approximation.
   e. negative reinforcement.

c 48. According to Skinner, the rate of operant extinction depends largely upon the
   a. use of aversive stimuli.
   b. inhibition of respondent extinction.
   c. schedule of reinforcement.
   d. use of continuous punishment.

d 49. Young Tyler has learned that his mother always hides the cookies on the top shelf of the hall closet. After Tyler's mother noticed cookies missing, she decided to hide the cookie jar in a new place. Tyler, after several unrewarding trips to the top shelf of the hall closet, stops looking there. Skinner would say that the disappearance of this response is due to
   a. forgetting.
   b. repression.
   c. respondent extinction.
   d. operant extinction.

d 50. Skinner believed that human personality is shaped by all these factors EXCEPT
   a. the individual's personal history of reinforcement.
   b. natural selection.
   c. evolution of cultures.
   d. the individual's personal drive state.

c 51. According to Skinner, as a species, human behavior is shaped by
   a. learned drives.
   b. social living.
   c. the contingencies of survival.
   d. reproduction.
   e. unintentional injuries.

c   52.   To Skinner, human personality is shaped by
          a.   contingencies of reinforcement.
          b.   natural selection.
          c.   both a and b.
          d.   neither a nor b.

d   53.   For Skinner, natural selection
          a.   is irrelevant to operant conditioning.
          b.   explains some animal behavior but no human behavior.
          c.   accounts for most human behavior.
          d.   is probably responsible for some human behavior.

b   54.   Skinner would view warfare as an example of
          a.   an aggressive instinct.
          b.   a maladaptive remnant of cultural evolution.
          c.   a maladaptive negative reinforcer.
          d.   behavior independent of cultural evolution.

b   55.   With reference to inner states such as thoughts and drives, Skinner said
          that they
          a.   are fictional constructs with no real existence.
          b.   exist, but should not be used as explanations of behavior.
          c.   are the foundations for explanations of behavior.
          d.   motivate but do not explain behavior.

d   *56. From the view of radical behaviorism, drives are
          a.   objective, observable causes of behavior.
          b.   the result of natural selection.
          c.   internal needs.
          d.   explanatory fictions.

c   57.   Concerning emotions, Skinner believed all EXCEPT which of the following?
          a.   A person's emotions are not directly observable to others.
          b.   The physical concomitants of emotions can be measured.
          c.   A large percentage of human behaviors are the result of emotions.
          d.   Emotions are subjectively real to the person experiencing them.
          e.   Pleasant emotions tend to be reinforcing for an individual.

d   58.   Concerning drives, Skinner said that they
          a.   are the causes of most human behaviors.
          b.   have no subjective existence.
          c.   can be either innate or learned.
          d.   refer to the effects of deprivation and satiation.

a   59.   Skinner explained problem solving by
          a.   the reinforcement of covert or internal responses.
          b.   the existence of a storehouse of memory.
          c.   the fact that humans have creative minds.
          d.   cue-producing responses.
          e.   innate drives.

b   60.   Regarding human thoughts and cognitions, Skinner believed that
a.   they could be understood by applying the principles of operant and respondent conditioning.
b.   they are covert behaviors that take place within the skin.
c.   they cannot be changed by the contingencies of reinforcement.
d.   they do not exist.

b   *61.   Skinner saw creative behavior as being the result of
a.   imagination.
b   mutations.
c.   intelligence.
d.   sublimations.
e.   a creative power.

b   *62.   Skinner believed that some behavior is unconscious because the person does not think about the aversive stimuli connected with it. Not thinking about aversive stimuli is an example of
a.   positive reinforcement.
b.   negative reinforcement.
c.   punishment.
d.   a reaction formation.

d   63.   Skinner accepted the concept of unconscious
a.   mental processes.
b.   cognition.
c.   conflicts.
d.   behavior.
e.   motivation.

d   64.   On the subject of dreams, Skinner believed that
a.   many dreams spring from a collective unconscious.
b.   dreams are beyond the scope of radical behaviorism.
c.   dreams can be used to predict the future.
d.   many dreams serve a wish-fulfillment purpose.

d   65.   According to Skinner, abused children may choose to remain with their parents because
a.   one parent may be rewarding them while the other is abusive.
b.   they may lack the means of countercontrol.
c.   they may be receiving a powerful intermittent reward.
d.   any of these reasons.

a   66.   Grant has been planning a trip to Italy after he graduates with a degree in art. How would Skinner explain Grant's planning?
a.   Grant's covert planning behavior is positively reinforcing.
b.   Grant's personal history of insufficient planning has been negatively reinforced.
c.   Grant simply desires to view Italian art.
d.   Grant has obsessive thoughts of viewing Italian art.

a   67. People who make rewards or punishments contingent on the behavior of
         another are using which of Skinner's methods of social control?
         a. operant conditioning
         b. respondent conditioning
         c. extinction
         d. describing contingencies

b   *68. According to Skinner, advertising is a method of social control through
         a. operant conditioning.
         b. describing contingencies.
         c. deprivation.
         d. satiation.

e   69. Which of these, according to Skinner, would be a means of self-control?
         a. physical restraint
         b. physical aids
         c. satiation
         d. deprivation
         e. all of the above

a   70. Skinner's technique of "doing something else" is used
         a. solely with self-control.
         b. solely with social control.
         c. with either self-control or social control.
         d. with neither self-control nor social control.

d   71. Skinner believed that passive resistance is most likely to be used
         a. prior to the strategy of escape.
         b. prior to revolt.
         c. in conjunction with physical restraint.
         d. after escape and revolt have failed.
         e. as a form of negative reinforcement.

b   *72. Skinner viewed the unhealthy personality as
         a. being essentially genetic in origin.
         b. a means of coping with excessive social control.
         c. stemming from internal conflict.
         d. a lack of productive interpersonal relationships.

e   73. For Skinner, inappropriate behavior is shaped by
         a. contingencies of positive reinforcement.
         b. contingencies of negative reinforcement.
         c. the effects of punishments.
         d. both a and b.
         e. a, b, and c are all correct.

a   74. Skinner would label masochistic behavior as an example of
         a. aversive self-stimulation.
         b. defective self-knowledge.
         c. blocking out reality.
         d. excessively vigorous behavior.
         e. excessively restrained behavior.

a   75.   Skinner saw the psychotherapist as a
          a.   controlling agent.
          b.   punitive authority figure.
          c.   major source of knowledge about human behavior.
          d.   necessary component of scientific psychology.
          e.   medical specialist.

c   76.   What Freud saw as unconsciously motivated defense mechanisms, Skinner
          viewed as
          a.   consciously motivated defense mechanisms.
          b.   attempts to protect the self-concept against anxiety.
          c.   inappropriate behaviors shaped by environmental contingencies.
          d.   unsuccessful attempts to defend the ego against guilt.

a   77.   Skinner's principal contribution to psychotherapy was as
          a.   a writer whose ideas have influenced the behavior therapy movement.
          b.   a writer whose ideas have helped shape current psychoanalytic thinking.
          c.   a practicing psychotherapist.
          d.   the author of *Walden Two*.

b   78.   Research with Skinner's behavior management techniques has generally
          shown that
          a.   punishment tends to improve learning for people with high levels
               of anxiety.
          b.   differences in temperament affect the manner in which people respond
               to behavior management techniques.
          c.   behavior management techniques change behavior only if people are
               motivated to change.
          d.   behavior management techniques are typically less effective that hypnosis
               in treating drug addiction.

b   79.   In his approach to science, Skinner
          a.   opposed theories.
          b.   opposed hypothetico-deductive methods.
          c.   favored attempts to build fictional constructs.
          d.   favored the use of large groups of participants.

d   80.   Skinner's view of humanity can best be termed as
          a.   humanistic.
          b.   teleological.
          c.   pessimistic.
          d.   deterministic.

d   81.   Skinner believed that self-control depends ultimately upon
          a.   will power.
          b.   punishment.
          c.   physical restraints.
          d.   environmental variables.
          e.   aversive stimuli.

a   82.   What is Skinner's basic view of human freedom?
           a.   The idea of freedom is positively reinforcing for many people.
           b.   By nature, people desire freedom and reject control.
           c.   Societies can advance only if they value personal freedom.
           d.   People can never be free until they embrace responsibility.
           e.   Both b and c are correct.

a   83.   Skinner believed that people
           a.   can design a society that will produce psychologically healthy personalities.
           b.   are by nature good and self-directed.
           c.   are by nature bad and must be controlled to protect society from their criminal behavior.
           d.   will become loving, self-directed, and self-actualizing when all their basic needs are satisfied.

CHAPTER 11
BANDURA: SOCIAL COGNITIVE THEORY

ESSAY QUESTIONS

1. Discuss specific ways in which Bandura's social cognitive theory differs from Skinner's behavioral analysis.

    A. Bandura holds that personality is molded by an interaction of behavior, personal factors (especially cognition), and the environment. In contrast, Skinner believed that behavior is ultimately shaped by the environment.
    B. Bandura believes that responses can be learned even in the absence of their occurrence, whereas Skinner contended that responses must occur in order to be reinforced.
    C. A fundamental difference between Bandura and Skinner is Bandura's emphasis on cognition. Bandura believes that people have the capacity for symbolization, which allows them to understand their environment and to partially regulate it without having had direct experience with every important aspect of that environment.
    D. Similarly, Bandura places more emphasis on vicarious experiences and vicarious reinforcement.
    E. Bandura holds that, in order for an event to be reinforcing, people must be aware of the connection between actions and outcomes. In other words, conditioning is cognitively mediated and not an inevitable consequence of the environment, as Skinner contended.

2. List and describe the components of Bandura's theory of self-regulation.

    A. Bandura believes that people have limited capacity for self-regulation. By using reflective thought, people can alter their environment and produce consequences of their actions.
    B. People also have some capacity to monitor their behavior and evaluate it in terms of their goals.
    C. Both external and internal factors play a role in self-regulation. External factors provide people with a standard for evaluating their own behavior as well as with the means for receiving reinforcement.
    D. These external factors interact with internal, or personal, factors to produce self-regulation. Bandura identified three internal requirements for self-regulation: (1) self-observation, (2) judgmental processes, and (3) affective self-reaction.
    E. The first step in self-regulation is for people to observe their behavior and its consequences.
    F. Next, people must judge the worth of their actions. They do this by applying both personal standards and standards of reference. In addition, judgmental processes depend on the overall value people place on an activity and their ability to attribute success or failure to their own efforts.
    G. Finally, people use affective self-reaction to regulate their behavior. The consequences of people's behavior are not determined solely by the environment but by their positive or negative response to how their behavior measures up to their personal standards.

3.   Discuss Bandura's concept of collective efficacy.

A. Collective efficacy refers to the level of confidence people have that their combined effort will produce social change. It is the result of the personal efficacy of many individuals working together to bring about social, political, or environmental change.

B. People can have high personal efficacy but low collective efficacy. However, personal and collective efficacy can complement one another to change one's lifestyle.

C. Several factors can hamper collective efficacy. First, in our modern transnational world, events in one part of the globe can affect people in other parts of the world. Second, recent technology that we neither understand nor control can lower collective efficacy. Third, entrenched bureaucracies discourage social change and reduce collective efficacy. Fourth, the scope and magnitude of problems such as war, famine, overpopulation, crime, and natural disasters may leave one with a sense of helplessness.

MULTIPLE CHOICE QUESTIONS

c   4.   Unlike Skinner's behavioral analysis, Bandura's social cognitive theory
a.   rejects the notion of goal-directed behavior.
b.   discounts the importance of reinforcement.
c.   recognizes the influence of chance encounters.
d.   downplays the effects of higher mental processes.

b   5.   Skinner believed that there is no learning without reinforcement. Bandura
a.   agrees with Skinner's observation.
b.   believes there is no reinforcement without cognition.
c.   asserts that learning is a consequence of the environment.
d.   believes that cognition is unnecessary for learning.

a   6.   Compared to Skinner's approach, Bandura's theory is more
a.   cognitive.
b.   environmental.
c.   deterministic.
d.   psychoanalytic.

d   7.   Albert Bandura is a native of _____, but has lived most of his life in
_____.
a.   Austria; the United States
b.   Japan; Germany
c.   the United States; Great Britain
d.   Canada; the United States

c   8.   Bandura calls the capacity to exercise control over our lives
a.   internal locus of control.
b.   free will.
c.   human agency.
d.   external locus of control.

a   9.   According to Bandura, the four core features of human agency are
          intentionality, _____, self-reactiveness, and self-reflectiveness.
          a. forethought
          b. self-efficacy
          c. positive reinforcement
          d. locus of control

d *10.   Bandura's reciprocal determinism assumes that personal conduct is a function of
          a. the environment.
          b. the person.
          c. behavior.
          d. all of the above.

c   11.   Bandura believes that cognition
          a. is solely responsible for behavior.
          b. serves as an autonomous force within the person.
          c. is determined by behavior and environment.
          d. both a and b.
          e. a, b, and c are correct.

a   12.   The notion that behavior is a consequence of a mutual interaction of three
          forces is what Bandura calls
          a. reciprocal determinism.
          b. higher cognitive processes.
          c. radical behaviorism.
          d. coincidental conduct.
          e. balanced counteraction.

e *13.   Bandura's P, or person, factor includes
          a. thought.
          b. memory.
          c. physical characteristics, such as size and social role.
          d. a and b but not c.
          e. a, b, and c are all correct.

d *14.   In Bandura's theory, chance encounters enter at which point in the reciprocal
          determinism paradigm?
          a. person
          b. self system
          c. behavior
          d. environment

d   15.   Bandura calls situations in life beyond one's deliberate control
          a. chance encounters.
          b. fortuitous events.
          c. destiny.
          d. a and b.

d *16.   Bandura reasons that if behavior were completely a function of
          the environment,
          a. the capacity for self-consciousness would not exist.
          b. behavior would be totally consistent and unchanging.
          c. reciprocal determinism would control behavior.
          d. behavior would be more varied and less consistent.

b   *17. Bandura views the self system as
           a.   an autonomous agent in control of behavior.
           b.   a set of cognitive structures used to evaluate behaviors.
           c.   capable of rendering divergent stimuli functionally equivalent.
           d.   a means of reducing anxiety.

e   18.   Bandura believes that attributing different behaviors to single or dual motives is
           a.   the most effective way to understand human behavior.
           b.   valid for animal but not human behavior.
           c.   unnecessary because behavior is unconsciously motivated.
           d.   necessary to explain the consistency of human behavior.
           e.   not a useful way to understand human behavior.

c   19.   Which expectations refer to Bandura's notion of one's prediction of the likely
           consequences of a behavior or set of behaviors?
           a.   efficacy
           b.   reinforcement
           c.   outcome
           d.   personal attributions
           e.   self-regulatory

a   *20.   According to Bandura, _____ is a person's expectations that he or she can or
           cannot execute the behavior necessary to effect a successful change in a
           particular situation.
           a.   self-efficacy
           b.   self-regulation
           c.   locus of control
           d.   disengagement of internal control

b   21.   Self-efficacy enters Bandura's reciprocal determinism paradigm at the point of
           a.   behavior.
           b.   person.
           c.   environment.
           d.   self-system.

e   22.   To Bandura, self-efficacy is synonymous with
           a.   outcome expectancies.
           b.   locus of control.
           c.   absence of anxiety and tension.
           d.   levels of aspiration.
           e.   none of these.

d   *23.   Bandura claims that self-efficacy can be increased or decreased through
           a.   vicarious experiences.
           b.   emotional arousal.
           c.   performance accomplishments.
           d.   any or all of the above.

c   *24. Erick is confident that he has the skills and abilities to be an excellent professional baseball player. However, he is uncertain whether he will be offered a job as a player. Thus, according to Bandura, he has _____ efficacy expectations and _____ outcome expectations.
   a. high; high
   b. low; high
   c. high; low
   d. low; low

a   *25. Ordinarily, the strongest source of self-efficacy, according to Bandura, is
   a. performance.
   b. vicarious experience.
   c. verbal persuasion.
   d. physiological arousal.
   e. internal standards of conduct.

b   26. In Bandura's view, vicarious experiences are likely to have their strongest effect on self-efficacy when the observer
   a. has a high level of physiological arousal.
   b. sees a person of equal ability succeed.
   c. has a high level of locus of control
   d. has extensive experience with the activity.
   e. has maximized the use of disengagement techniques.

b   27. In Bandura's view, self-efficacy is most likely to be increased when
   a. failure strengthens one's determination to succeed on future projects.
   b. one successfully performs a difficult task.
   c. one's best efforts fall a little short of success.
   d. one observes others failing at a task.

b   28. According to Bandura, in general, intense physiological arousal
   a. raises efficacy expectations.
   b. lowers efficacy expectations.
   c. initially lowers efficacy expectations but later it rapidly increases efficacy.
   d. has no effect on self-efficacy.

a   29. Bandura hypothesizes that performance outcomes are most likely to be successful under conditions of
   a. high efficacy and a responsive environment.
   b. high efficacy and an unresponsive environment.
   c. low efficacy and a responsive environment.
   d. low efficacy and an unresponsive environment.

d   *30. According to Bandura, low self-efficacy combined with an unresponsive environment will lead to
   a. the development of low internal locus of control.
   b. selective activation of disengagement of internal control.
   c. vigorous and persistent efforts to change the environment.
   d. the development of apathy, resignation, and helplessness.
   e. a beneficial performance attribution.

c   31. Bandura believes that
          a. self-efficacy and self-concept are synonymous.
          b. self-efficacy is another term for locus of control.
          c. people have different levels of self-efficacy in different situations.
          d. high levels of self-efficacy generalize to widely different situations.

b   32. The confidence people have that their combined efforts will produce social
          change is what Bandura calls
          a. socialism.
          b. collective efficacy.
          c. personal efficacy.
          d. democracy.

a   *33. Like most people, Madison relies on other people such as the police, the fire
          department, and mechanics to exercise indirect control over her life. Bandura
          calls this situation
          a. proxy agency.
          b. external reliance.
          c. collective efficacy.
          d. personal efficacy.

b   34. According to Bandura, collective efficacy
          a. springs from a collective mind.
          b. stems from the personal efficacy of many people working together.
          c. is more likely than personal efficacy to help a person quit smoking.
          d. is opposed to personal efficacy in Bandura's theory.

d   35. According to Bandura, collective efficacy is lowered when
          a. people believe that events in another part of the world affect them.
          b. people feel overwhelmed by the Internet.
          c. ice storms cut power to people's homes for several days.
          d. any or all of the above.

b   *36. The first requirement for self-regulation, according to Bandura, is
          a. a specific plan of action
          b. self-observation
          c. free will
          d. a non-hostile environment
          e. accurate modeling

b   37. Megan compares her test grade with that of other class members to determine
          her test performance. She is using which of Bandura's judgmental processes?
          a. personal standards
          b. standards of reference
          c. performance attribution
          d. positive reinforcement

e   *38. According to Bandura, in self-regulation, we may judge the worth of our actions
          on the basis of
          a. personal standards.
          b. performance attribution.
          c. a standard of reference.
          d. the value we place on those actions.
          e. all of the above.

c   39. Harrison, a professional photographer, is dissatisfied with his latest work,
         judging several pictures to be substandard according to his own criteria. Bandura
         would say that Harrison will probably
         a. learn to live with substandard performance.
         b. reward himself for substandard performance.
         c. withhold reward for substandard performance.
         d. become psychologically disturbed.

a   40. The concept that individuals respond positively or negatively to their behavior
         depending upon how it measures up to their personal standards is a process
         Bandura calls
         a. self-reaction.
         b. disinhibition.
         c. self-monitoring.
         d. self-efficacy.

a   41. Bandura believes that both external and internal factors play a role in self-
         regulation. An example of an internal factor would be
         a. performance attribution.
         b. money.
         c. praise.
         d. punishment.

c *42. Selective activation refers to Bandura's belief that self-regulatory influences
         a. are activated by an automatic controlling agent.
         b. narrow a person's field of perception.
         c. operate only if they are activated.
         d. are activated by environmental factors.

a   43. Which of these is NOT listed by Bandura as a mechanism through which
         behavior is disengaged from self-evaluative consequences?
         a. physical flight or running away
         b. displacement or diffusion of responsibility
         c. dehumanization of the victim
         d. minimizing or ignoring consequences

b *44. According to Bandura, disengagement of internal control is most likely to occur
         when
         a. a lawbreaker on trial attempts to convince the judge or jury of
             her innocence.
         b. an otherwise law-abiding citizen attempts to convince himself that his
             criminal acts are justified.
         c. the unconscious mind gains control of the conscious mind.
         d. the conscious mind gains control of the unconscious mind.

a *45. In Bandura's framework, selective activation and disengagement of
         internal control
         a. permit a person to minimize responsibility in an ambiguous situation.
         b. are nearly identical to Freud's concept of defense mechanisms.
         c. operate unconsciously and automatically.
         d. are attempts to justify to others one's own reprehensible behavior.

a 46. A government official who sanctions spying on and brutal physical harassment
       of legitimate, nonviolent demonstrators because "they are a threat to national
       security" is using Bandura's disengagement technique of
       a. moral justification.
       b. palliative comparison.
       c. rationalization.
       d. personal attribution.

e 47. A terrorist dismisses the death of one hostage as unimportant in comparison to
       the hundreds of his comrades killed by government security forces. This
       illustrates Bandura's disengagement technique of
       a. displacement.
       b. euphemistic labeling.
       c. personal attribution.
       d. diffusing responsibility.
       e. palliative comparison.

c 48. A hired killer refers to murdering another person as a "contract" or a "hit."
       This is an example of Bandura's disengagement technique of
       a. palliative comparison.
       b. moral justification.
       c. euphemistic labels.
       d. diffusing responsibility.

d 49. In Bandura's disengagement technique of displacement of responsibility, the
       consequences of one's actions are minimized by
       a. creating moral justifications for others' behavior.
       b. euphemistically labeling one's actions as harmless and beneficial.
       c. dehumanizing the victims of one's actions.
       d. placing responsibility on an outside source.

c 50. The bureaucrat who answers criticism by responding "That's the way things are
       done around here" is using Bandura's disengagement technique of
       a. palliative comparison.
       b. displacement of responsibility.
       c. diffusing responsibility.
       d. euphemistic labeling.
       e. moral justification.

c 51. A parent injures a child with a severe beating but explains that one should not
       spare the rod because that may spoil the child. This illustrates Bandura's
       disengagement technique of
       a. minimizing consequences.
       b. ignoring consequences.
       c. misconstruing consequences.
       d. dehumanization.
       e. euphemistic labeling.

e   52. A rapist excuses his violent assault on his victim by claiming the she provoked the attack by dressing provocatively. According to Bandura, this technique of disengagement is
    a. minimizing consequences.
    b. ignoring consequences.
    c. moral justification.
    d. dehumanizing the victim.
    e. blaming the victim.

d   *53. With regard to learning, Bandura believes that
    a. reinforcement does not facilitate learning.
    b. reinforcement is essential to learning.
    c. performance is the basic datum of psychological science.
    d. learning can occur in the absence of a response.

c   54. Bandura sees modeling as
    a. a more specific concept than imitation.
    b. synonymous with mimicry.
    c. an important method of learning.
    d. being the most important type of learning for high status people.

a   *55. Bandura discusses which two major types of learning?
    a. observational and enactive
    b. engaged and disengaged
    c. instinctive and acquired
    d. conscious and unconscious
    e. skillful and unskillful

e   56. For Bandura, learning through modeling involves
    a. adding and subtracting from the observed behavior.
    b. generalizing from one observation to another.
    c. symbolically representing information.
    d. a and b but not c.
    e. a, b, and c are correct.

d   57. Bandura recognizes all of these as processes that govern observational learning EXCEPT
    a. attention.
    b. representation.
    c. motivation.
    d. reinforcement.
    e. behavioral production.

b   *58. In modeling, Bandura claims people are most likely to attend to
    a. children.
    b. attractive models.
    c. people of lower social status.
    d. all of the above.

a   59. In order for observational learning to lead to new response patterns, Bandura
          claims that those patterns must be
          a. symbolically represented in memory.
          b. physically enacted immediately.
          c. followed by reinforcement on a continuous schedule.
          d. attended to in an accurate and unbiased manner.

d   60. According to Bandura, observing a model being punished for performance will
          decrease one's likelihood of
          a. attending to the modeled behavior.
          b. cognitively representing the performance.
          c. acquiring the modeled behavior.
          d. performing the modeled behavior.

c   61. Bandura claims that learning through modeling is
          a. an inefficient means of acquiring behaviors.
          b. impossible before the acquisition of language.
          c. facilitated by self-monitoring during performance.
          d. most efficient under conditions of low motivation.

a   *62. Bandura holds that reinforcement is
          a. cognitively mediated.
          b. automatic.
          c. a function of the environment.
          d. a function of the individual's history.
          e. an unnecessary concept for learning theory.

d   63. Bandura sees dysfunctional behaviors as
          a. expressions of the frustrated drive toward dominance or power.
          b. character weaknesses.
          c. strivings for self-fulfillment.
          d. initiated and maintained on the basis of social learning principles.

a   64. Much of Bandura's theory and research on dysfunctional behaviors has centered
          around aggression and
          a. phobias.
          b. schizophrenia.
          c. sexual disorders.
          d. senility.

c   65. According to Bandura, depressed individuals are inclined to punish themselves
          severely for poor performance. This illustrates a distortion of
          a. self-observation.
          b. judgmental processes.
          c. self-reaction.
          d. self-consciousness.
          e. self-activation.

d   66. Bandura claims that phobias are difficult to extinguish because they
          a. are a result of mental illness.
          b. stem from imbalances of neurotransmitters in the brain.
          c. are not affected by reinforcement.
          d. are maintained by avoidant behavior.

e   67.   Bandura contends that aggressive behavior can result from
          a.   observational learning.
          b.   direct reinforcement.
          c.   training or instruction.
          d.   bizarre beliefs.
          e.   all of the above.

c   68.   The classical study where children were exposed to models acting aggressively
          was conducted by Bandura, Ross, and Ross. These authors found that, after mild
          frustration,
          a.   girls behaved more aggressively than boys.
          b.   children displayed no more aggression that a control group of children
               exposed to non-aggressive models.
          c.   children exposed to a cartoon model displayed as much aggression as those
               exposed to a live model.
          d.   children exposed to a film model were about twice as aggressive as those
               exposed to a live model.

d   69.   To Bandura, the ultimate goal of therapy is
          a.   self-actualization.
          b.   the recovery of repressed experiences.
          c.   the elimination of all major problems.
          d.   self-regulation.

b   70.   In his approach to therapy, Bandura sees three levels of treatment: induction of
          change, generalization, and
          a.   extinction of old dysfunctional behaviors.
          b.   maintenance of newly acquired functional behaviors.
          c.   discrimination between functional and dysfunctional behaviors.
          d.   spontaneous recovery of old functional behaviors.

a   71.   Bandura's approach to therapy emphasizes
          a.   behavioral change.
          b.   minimizing disengagement.
          c.   exploration of dreams and fantasies.
          d.   the use of continuous positive reinforcement.
          e.   the discrimination of the effects of punishment.

b   72.   Bandura's treatment mode in which clients are trained to visualize models
          performing fearful behaviors is
          a.   overt modeling.
          b.   covert modeling.
          c.   vicarious modeling.
          d.   active imagination.
          e.   enactive mastery.

c   73.   Bandura's treatment technique that involves the extinction of anxiety or fear
          through self- or therapist-induced relaxation is
          a.   overt modeling.
          b.   vicarious modeling.
          c.   systematic desensitization.
          d.   enactive mastery.

a   74. Bandura believes that _____ is a mechanism common to all successful therapy
         techniques.
         a. cognitive mediation
         b. unconscious motivation
         c. increased arousal
         d. enhanced disengagement
         e. external reinforcement

d   75. Bandura believes that motivation to change dysfunctional behavior is
         enhanced by
         a. setting realistic goals.
         b. receiving feedback on performance.
         c. a continuous schedule of positive reinforcements.
         d. a and b.
         e. b and c.

c   *76. When Saul Shiffman and colleagues studied the effects of daily fluctuations in
         self-efficacy on smoking lapses and relapses, they found that
         a. women had higher quit rates than did men.
         b. daily ratings of self-efficacy predicted smokers' likelihood of lapsing.
         c. smokers who lapsed had greater fluctuations in their daily ratings of
             self-efficacy.
         d. a single lapse led invariably to a complete relapse.

e   77. Research by Zimmerman and colleagues found that grades of high-school
         students could be predicted by
         a. self-efficacy for academic achievement.
         b. student grade goals.
         c. prior grades.
         d. all of the above.
         e. only a and b.

b   78. Jerry Trusty (2000) found that
         a. middle-school students with high expectations for good grades were usually
             disappointed with their actual grades.
         b. boys were more likely than girls to profit from having a computer at home.
         c. girls were more likely than boys to seek and receive help from counselors.
         d. girls were more likely than boys to seek help from teachers.
         e. both a and b.

c   79. A notable feature of Bandura's theory is
         a. the lack of research generated.
         b. its reliance on speculation in the absence of empirical data.
         c. its internal consistency.
         d. its reliance on hypothetical concepts.

d   *80. In his concept of humanity, Bandura assumes that
         a. people are motivated more by genetics than by social influences.
         b. unconscious factors are more influential than conscious ones.
         c. people automatically strive for self-actualization.
         d. people are goal directed.

c   81.   On the issue of determinism versus free will, Bandura favors a position
that emphasizes
a.   freedom.
b.   determinism.
c.   partial determinism.
d.   none of the above.

c   82.   Basically, Bandura views humans as
a.   aggressive animals.
b.   driven by the master motive of self-actualization.
c.   cognitive animals.
d.   completely free to choose their own actions.

a   83.   Which two terms best fit Bandura's concept of personality?
a.   plastic and flexible
b.   consistent and stable
c.   reactive and proactive
d.   choice and responsibility

CHAPTER 12
ROTTER AND MISCHEL:
COGNITIVE SOCIAL LEARNING THEORY

ESSAY QUESTIONS

1. List Rotter's four variables of prediction and briefly define each of them.

   A. Rotter's variables of prediction are (1) behavior potential, (2) expectancy, (3) reinforcement value, and (4) the psychological situation.
   B. Behavior is the possibility that a particular response will occur at a given time and place.
   C. Expectancy is a person's perceived probability that a particular reinforcement will occur as the result of that person's behavior in a specific situation or situations.
   D. Reinforcement value is simply the value a person places on a particular reinforcement when the possibility of a number of reinforcements occurring is equal.
   E. The psychological situation is that part of the external and internal world to which a person is responding.

2. Explain Rotter's concepts of internal and external control of reinforcement.

   A. Internal and external control of reinforcement refers to Rotter's theory that people strive to reach goals because they have a generalized expectancy that such strivings will be successful.
   B. Rotter developed the Internal-External Control Scale to assess the general tendency for people to see a causal relationship between their own efforts and environmental consequences. This scale is often called the locus of control scale.
   C. People who score high on the scale (in an external direction) tend to explain away their successes as due to luck or chance, or conditions beyond their personal control.
   D. People who score in an internal direction tend to have generalized expectancies for success that are based on their own performance. That is, people high on internal locus of control believe that their own actions are important contributors to success. They are able to retain a high sense of personal control even after several failures.
   E. Scores on the scale are not causes of behavior but must be considered along with reinforcement value when predicting behavior potential.
   F. Locus of control is a global rather than a specific concept. It does not predict achievement in a specific situation.
   G. The scale should not be used to divide people into two distinct groups. People range from very high internal control to very high external control, but most people score along that continuum.
   H. Although internal control is generally valued over external control, people with very high internal locus of control may assume personal responsibility for events beyond their power.

3.   Discuss Mischel's person-situation interaction, or conditional view of personal dispositions.

   A.   Mischel believes that personal traits, or dispositions, are insufficient to initiate or guide a person's behavior. Conversely, he holds that the situation alone cannot determine and direct behavior. Instead, his person-situation model of dispositions hypothesizes that behavior is shaped by people's perceptions of themselves in a particular situation.
   B.   Mischel's model emphasizes the importance of specific goals in predicting behavior.
   C.   Mischel would say that miserly people will not always behave in a miserly manner. People inclined toward miserliness will use this trait along with other cognitive-affective processes to achieve a specific goal (for example, allowing a dining companion to leave the tip).
   D.   Most people are able to predict, or at least guess, another person's behavior by considering both the situation and that person's individual traits. Therefore, they are able to say that, for example, a certain person will tell a lie in one situation but not in another.

4.   List and briefly explain Mischel and Shoda's five cognitive-affective units.

   A.   Cognitive-affective units include a variety of psychological, social, and physiological aspects of personality and influence people to interact with their environment with a relatively stable pattern of variation. These units include people's (1) encoding strategies, (2) competencies and self-regulatory strategies, (3) expectancies and beliefs, (4) goals and values, and (5) affective responses.
   B.   Encoding strategies refer to people's ways of categorizing information from external stimuli. People process such external stimuli into personal constructs, including their self-concept, their view of other people, and their way of looking at the world.
   C.   Competencies refer to people's belief in what they can do in a given situation. Self-regulatory strategies permit people to control their own behavior through self-imposed goals and self-produced consequences.
   D.   People's expectancies and beliefs in any situation greatly influence how they will behave.
   E.   Self-formulated goals and subjective values help predict behavior in a specific situation. Two people with equal abilities and similar expectancies will behave differently depending on the value they place on success in a particular situation.
   F.   Affective responses include emotions, feelings, and physiological reactions. They combine with cognitions to form an interlocking cognitive-affective unit. In addition, they interact with each other to form the core of personality.

MULTIPLE CHOICE QUESTIONS

d   *5.   Unlike Skinner, Julian Rotter contended that an adequate theory of
         human behavior
         a.   is not possible at this stage in the development of psychology as a science.
         b.   should reject hypothetical constructs as explanations of behavior.
         c.   can be extrapolated from the study of animal behavior.
         d.   must be built on people's expectations of the future.

d   6.   By his own admission, Rotter was MOST influenced by
         a.   Freud.
         b.   Thorndike.
         c.   Jung.
         d.   Adler.

a   7.   At the core of Rotter's personality theory is his emphasis on
         a.   goals and expectancies.
         b.   the consistency of behavior.
         a.   the study of rats rather than pigeons.
         d.   the role of evolution in shaping personality.

d   8.   Which term describes Rotter's approach to personality?
         a.   interactionist
         b.   social-learning theory
         c.   cognitive theory
         d.   all of the above

a   *9.   Rotter assumed that
         a.   motivation is directed toward a goal.
         b.   people are primarily motivated to reduce tension.
         c.   motivation stems from the environment.
         d.   people are motivated only by internal needs.

b   *10. Rotter's empirical law of effect states that motivation is any condition or
         event that
         a.   allows one to escape from conflict.
         b.   moves one in the direction of a goal.
         c.   reduces tension or returns one to a state of homeostasis.
         d.   enacts laws in a nation ruled by an emperor.

a   11.   Rotter insisted that an adequate theory of personality must take into
         consideration the assumption that people
         a.   are capable of anticipating events.
         b.   are motivated primarily by drive reduction.
         c.   are controlled in the same manner as animals.
         d.   are only motivated by unconscious mental processes.

e *12. According to Rotter, four variables and their interactions must be analyzed to ensure accurate predictions. They include all the following EXCEPT
   a. behavioral potential.
   b. expectancy.
   c. psychological situation.
   d reinforcement value.
   e. law of effect.

c 13. "The potential for any given behavior to occur in a particular situation or set of situations as calculated in relation to any single reinforcement or set of reinforcements," is Rotter's definition of
   a. empirical law of effect.
   b. the psychological situation.
   c. behavior potential.
   d. expectancy.
   e. reinforcement value.

c *14. According to Rotter, the behavior potential in any situation is a function of
   a. expectancy.
   b. reinforcement value.
   c. both a and b.
   d. neither a nor b.

d 15. In Rotter's theory, the probability that a person will behave in a given manner depends basically on his or her
   a. expectation of receiving reinforcement.
   b. perceived value of the expected reinforcement.
   c. genetic endowment.
   d. both a and b.

c 16. According to Rotter, if expectancy is held constant and reinforcement value varies, then it becomes possible to predict
   a. the psychological situation.
   b. interpersonal trust.
   c. behavior potential.
   d. need value.
   e. all of the above.

d *17. When reinforcement value is held constant and expectancy varies, what factor in Rotter's theory can be predicted?
   a. reinforcement value
   b. expectancy
   c. empirical law of effect
   d. behavior potential
   e. drive strength

d 18. "The probability held by the individual that a particular reinforcement will occur as a function of a specific behavior on his [or her] part in a specific situation or situations" is Rotter's definition of
   a. empirical law of effect.
   b. need.
   c. reinforcement value.
   d. expectancy.
   e. behavior potential.

c   19. According to Rotter, overall expectancy of success in any given situation
        depends on a person's
        a. generalized expectancy.
        b. needs.
        c. both a and b.
        d. neither a nor b.

a   20. Rotter stated that when expectancies and situational variables are held constant,
        behavior is shaped by
        a. reinforcement value.
        b. freedom of movement.
        c. the specific expectancies.
        d. both b and c.

c *21. Rotter distinguished between internal reinforcement and external
        reinforcement. Internal reinforcement is determined by
        a. biological needs.
        b. the values of society.
        c. the person's subjective perceptions of the value of an event.
        d. one's history of rewards and punishments.

a   22. According to Rotter, reinforcement that satisfies a strong need generally
        a. is more highly valued than one that satisfies a weak need.
        b. tends to be negatively valued by the individual.
        c. is less likely to be valued than one that satisfies a weak need.
        d. tends to be negatively valued by society.

c *23. Rotter's basic prediction formula states that behavior potential is a function of
        a. heredity and environment.
        b. cognition and goals.
        c. expectancies and reinforcement value in a particular situation.
        d. interpersonal trust and locus of control.

e *24. Rotter's basic prediction formula is most useful when
        a. predicting novel behaviors.
        b. pertinent variables are rigorously controlled.
        c. making generalized predictions.
        d. need value is unknown.
        e. making specific predictions.

a *25. Rotter's concept of _____ allows for more generalized predictions than those
        permitted by the basic prediction formula.
        a. needs
        b. reinforcement value
        c. expectancy
        d. external reinforcement
        e. reinforcement-reinforcement sequence

b   26. Rotter saw needs as
        a. a state of deprivation.
        b. an indicator of the direction of behavior.
        c. a condition of arousal.
        d. basically comprising two categories: social and physiological.

d   27. Rotter's general prediction formula includes the concept of
        a. conditioned stimuli.
        b. learned response.
        c. reinforcement value.
        d. needs.
        e. interpersonal trust.

c *28. Rotter's most basic category of needs, in the sense that other needs are learned in relationship to it, is
        a. recognition-status.
        b. dominance.
        c. physical comfort.
        d. independence.
        e. love and affection.

e *29. For Rotter, the component "freedom of movement" is analogous to the more specific concept of
        a. behavioral potential.
        b. needs.
        c. reinforcement value.
        d. need potential.
        e. expectancy.

a *30. For Rotter, the degree to which a person prefers one set of reinforcements to another is called
        a. need value.
        b. need preference.
        c. need potential.
        d. freedom of movement.

b 31. According to Rotter, freedom of movement can be determined by
        a. holding need potential constant and observing one's need value.
        b. holding need value constant and observing one's need potential.
        c. varying need potential and need value together.
        d. minimizing need values and maximizing need potential.

b 32. In Rotter's theory of personality, what is the relationship between need potential and behavior potential?
        a. Need potential is a hypothetical concept whereas behavior potential refers to actual behavior.
        b. Need potential refers to a group of functionally related behaviors whereas behavior potential refers to a particular behavior.
        c. Need potential can be measured solely through the observation of behavior whereas behavior potential is inferred from test scores.
        d. There is no relationship between the two concepts.

a *33. In Rotter's general prediction formula, need potential is a function of
        a. freedom of movement and need value.
        b. behavior potential and the psychological situation.
        c. interpersonal trust and internal locus of control.
        d. heredity and environment.

c   34. According to Rotter, need potential is highest under conditions of
      a. low freedom of movement and high need value.
      b. high freedom of movement and low need value.
      c. high freedom of movement and high need value.
      d. low freedom of movement and low need value.

a *35. Rotter's Internal-External Control Scale is an attempt to
      a. measure generalized expectancies.
      b. place people into internal and external controlled categories.
      c. determine the causes of human behavior.
      d. predict behavior in a specific situation.
      e. measure psychological health.

d   36. According to Rotter, people with high internal locus of control believe that
      a. they can do well in nearly everything.
      b. luck is the principal determiner of success.
      c. there will always be wars, no matter how hard people try to prevent them.
      d. the source of control is generally within themselves.

b   37. Scores on Rotter's Internal-External Control Scale
      a. determine behavior.
      b. cannot be used to predict behavior in a specific situation.
      c. divide people into two distinct groups.
      d. can be used to predict psychopathology.

b   38. Rotter sees interpersonal trust as a
      a. specific expectancy.
      b. generalized expectancy.
      c. belief that people are basically good.
      d. tendency to believe anything anyone says.

b *39. "A generalized expectancy held by an individual that the word, promise, oral or
      written statement of another individual or group can be relied on" is Rotter's
      definition of
      a. social interest.
      b. interpersonal trust.
      c. external control of reinforcement.
      d. gullibility.

d   40. Rotter found that people who score high on the Interpersonal Trust Scale are
      generally more likely to _____ than are people who score low on this scale.
      a. be psychologically disturbed
      b. lie to others
      c. lie to themselves
      d. respect the rights of others

d   41. According to Rotter, people who are likely to give others a second chance tend
      to score
      a. high on internal control of reinforcement.
      b. low on interpersonal trust.
      c. high on external control of reinforcement.
      d. high on interpersonal trust.

a *42. According to Rotter, conflict is most likely to arise when freedom of movement is
   a. low and need value is high.
   b. high and need value is low.
   c. high and need value is high.
   d. low and need value is low.

e 43. Rotter defined maladaptive behavior as behavior that
   a. satisfies a neurotic need.
   b. has low need value and high freedom of movement.
   c. moves a person closer to a desired goal.
   d. stems from repression of sexual drives.
   e. fails to move a person closer to a desired goal.

c 44. The goal of Rotter's approach to psychotherapy was the
   a. extinction of maladaptive behaviors.
   b. acquisition of a unifying philosophy of life.
   c. changing of the patient's orientation toward life.
   d. elimination of all problems.
   e. uncovering of unconscious material.

d 45. According to Rotter, individuals who set their goals too high
   a. develop correspondingly high expectancies of success.
   b. score high on internal control of reinforcement.
   c. quickly change to lower level goals when they fail.
   d. engage in avoidant behavior due to frustration.

b 46. Although Mischel has much in common with Bandura and Rotter, his unique contribution to social learning theory is his research on
   a. sexual dysfunction.
   b. delay of gratification.
   c. interpersonal trust.
   d. self-efficacy.
   e. the frustration-aggression hypothesis.

a 47. Mischel's chief argument with trait theory is that it
   a. assumes that behavior is quite consistent.
   b. is based on factor analysis.
   c. overlooks the subjective judgments of individuals.
   d. has an unscientific genetic component.
   e. rejects individual freedom and responsibility.

a 48. Mischel is most likely to say that
   a. an individual's behaviors can be quite inconsistent from one situation to another.
   b. an individual's personality traits are not likely to endure over a period of time.
   c. human behavior is completely shaped by the laws of reinforcement.
   d. human personality is shaped mostly by chance encounters and fortuitous events.

d   49.   Walter Mischel was born in the same city where _____ lived most of his life.
          a.   Albert Bandura
          b.   Carl Jung
          c.   Al Capone
          d.   Sigmund Freud.

a   50.   While still a graduate student, Mischel was influenced by which two teachers?
          a.   Rotter and Kelly
          b.   Bandura and Skinner
          c.   Klein and Anna Freud
          d.   Adler and Fromm

b   51.   Mischel's early research led him to believe that behavior is mostly a function of
          a.   chance and fortuitous events.
          b.   the situation.
          c.   relatively stable personal traits.
          d.   a person's motivation
          e.   none of the above.

d   52.   To Mischel, behavior is mostly likely to be caused by
          a.   global personal dispositions.
          b.   genetic factors.
          c.   personality traits.
          d.   people's perception of themselves in a particular situation.

c   53.   In Mischel and Shoda's model, behavior is shaped by people's specific cognitive
          and affective processes plus
          a.   their previous experiences with reinforcement.
          b.   the unique situation.
          c.   their personal dispositions.
          d.   their motivation.

d   54.   A study by Wright and Mischel asked children and adults to report everything
          they knew about certain groups of children. Findings from this research
          suggested that
          a.   children were more likely than adults to give specific predictions of
               behavior of the target group of children.
          b.   adults were more likely than children to hedge their descriptions of behavior
               of the target group of children.
          c.   neither children nor adults were able to predict the behavior of the target
               group of children.
          d.   both children and adults recognized the interrelationship between situations
               and behavior.

c   55.   Mischel's consistency paradox is based on his notion that
          a.   laypeople believe that behavior is consistent, but professional psychologists
               see it as inconsistent.
          b.   laypeople believe that behavior is inconsistent, but professional
               psychologists see it as consistent.
          c.   both laypeople and professional psychologists see behavior as consistent,
               whereas research suggests that it is inconsistent.
          d.   both laypeople and professional psychologists see behavior as inconsistent,
               whereas research suggests that it is consistent.

d   56.   Mischel and Shoda's cognitive-affective personality system is an attempt to
           account for
           a.   variability across situations.
           b.   people's inconsistent behaviors.
           c.   people's stability of behavior.
           d.   both a and c.
           e.   all of the above.

b   57.   Mischel and Shoda's cognitive-affective personality system predicts that a
           person's behavior will
           a.   be stable from one situation to another.
           b.   change from one situation to another but in a meaningful manner.
           c.   change from one situation to another depending solely on differences
                in the situation.
           d.   change as personal dispositions change.

a   *58.   According to Mischel, behavior is determined by
           a.   the interaction of person variables with situational variables.
           b.   environmental contingencies.
           c.   relatively permanent personal dispositions.
           d.   the interaction between need potential and freedom of movement.

b   59.   Mischel and Shoda's cognitive-affective personality system holds that
           a.   thoughts and emotions act independently to produce behavior.
           b.   apparent inconsistencies in people's behavior reflect stable patterns of
                variation and can be used to predict behavior.
           c.   apparent inconsistencies in people's behavior are due to random error that
                invalidates any predictions of behavior.
           d.   behaviors are an outgrowth of stable, global personality traits—both
                cognitive and affective.

a   60.   Mischel's conditional model suggests that behavior is caused by
           a.   people's view of themselves in a particular situation.
           b.   people's view of environmental reinforcers.
           c.   global personal traits acquired during infancy.
           d.   a unifying master motive acquired during early adolescence.

a   *61.   Mischel and Moore (1973) found that children who were encouraged to imagine
           real rewards while viewing pictures of rewards
           a.   could not wait as long for the rewards as could children who were merely
                exposed to pictures of the rewards.
           b.   were able to wait the entire test time for the rewards.
           c.   were able to wait longer for the rewards than children who were exposed to
                the actual rewards.
           d.   could not wait as long for the rewards as could children who were exposed to
                the actual rewards.

c   62.   Research by Mischel and Staub found that 8th-grade boys who believed that
           they had been successful on an earlier task
           a.   tended to choose immediate, but less valuable rewards.
           b.   chose immediate, more valuable rewards.
           c.   were able to wait for more valued, contingent rewards.
           d.   showed widely varied choices in a delay of gratification task.

a   63.   Which of the following is NOT one of Mischel and Shoda's
            cognitive-affective units?
            a.   self-efficacy
            b.   encoding strategies
            c.   goals and values
            d.   competencies and self-regulatory strategies
            e.   expectancies and beliefs

d   64.   Mischel believes that perhaps the most stable of all person variables is
            a.   self-efficacy.
            b.   interpersonal trust.
            c.   encoding strategies.
            d.   cognitive competencies.

b   65.   Mischel suggests that one reason why our behavior tends to be inconsistent is
            that we
            a.   have no unifying master motive.
            b.   have difficulty predicting the behavior of others.
            c.   lack a consistent philosophy of life.
            d.   all of the above.
            e.   none of the above.

d   66.   According to Mischel, behavior tends to be consistent in different situations to
            the extent that
            a.   we subjectively evaluate those situations.
            b.   we objectively evaluate those situations.
            c.   our expectancies are flexible.
            d.   our expectancies are unchanging.

c   67.   Mischel believes that people regulate their own behavior through
            a.   external rewards and punishments.
            b.   an internal locus of control.
            c.   self-imposed goals and self-produced consequences.
            d.   a self-created master motive.

d   68.   A study by Tiggermann and Rothblum found that people who were satisfied with
            their own weight and who had an internal weight locus of control tended to
            a.   demonstrate sympathy for overweight women.
            b.   experience empathy for overweight men but not women.
            c.   negatively stereotype overweight men but not women.
            d.   negatively stereotype overweight women but not men.

c   69.   When Mendoz-Denton and colleagues (1997) studied reactions to the O. J.
            Simpson verdict, they found that
            a.   participant's race was the primary factor in agreeing or disagreeing with the
            verdict.
            b.   European Americans who agreed with the verdict had very different
                 thoughts and feelings about than did African Americans who agreed with the
                 verdict.
            c.   European Americans who agreed with the verdict had thoughts and feels
                 that were quite similar to those of African Americans who agreed with the
                 verdict.
            d.   both a and b are correct.

b   70.   An important aspect of Rotter's concept of humanity is his belief that people
            a.   are motivated by the single drive of self-actualization.
            b.   are motivated more by their perceptions of events than by the events
            themselves.
            c.   can best be understood as extensions of laboratory animals.
            d.   are driven by their past experiences with reinforcement.

b   71.   In their concepts of humanity, both Rotter and Mischel
            a.   emphasize determinism over free choice.
            b.   have a more teleological than causal explanation of behavior.
            c.   are highly optimistic.
            d.   stress unconscious forces over conscious ones.
            e.   take a biological rather than a social view.

CHAPTER 13
CATTELL AND EYSENCK:
TRAIT AND FACTOR THEORIES

ESSAY QUESTIONS

1. Explain briefly how factor analysis is used to measure personality traits.

    A. Factor analysis is a mathematical technique for reducing a large number of variable to a few. Both Cattell and Eysenck use factor analysis to measure personality traits or factors.
    B. Factor analysts determine intercorrelations of a large variety of measures taken from many people. Some of these intercorrelations will reveal scores that tend to cluster together, suggesting a factor, or unit of personality.
    C. Next, analysts determine the extent to which each individual score contributes to the various factors. Correlations of scores with factors are called factor loadings.
    D. For mathematically derived factors to have psychological meaning, the axes on which the scores are plotted are rotated into a mathematical relationship with each other. When the rotation is oblique, many factors result; with orthogonal rotation, only a few factors emerge.
    E. Cattell's oblique rotation has resulted in 16 first-order traits, whereas Eysenck's orthogonal rotation has yielded only three general traits, or superfactors.

2. Describe Cattell's method of data collection and investigation.

    A. Cattell used an inductive method in building his theory of personality; that is, he had some hypothesis or theory in mind before he began gathering data.
    B. Cattell has attempted to assess both common traits (extracted from the study of many people) and unique traits (personal dispositions peculiar to one individual). To measure unique traits, Cattell used the P technique, which drew scores from only one person.
    C. To complement the P technique, Cattell devised the dR (differential R) technique, which correlates scores of many people on many variables obtained at two different occasions.
    D. Cattell has relied on three media of observations: L data, or observations by other people; Q data, or scores from personality questionnaires or other self-observations; and T data, or scores obtained from objective tests that assess ability or some other data and that cannot be faked.
    E. Ideally, if measurement were perfectly reliable and valid, all media of observations would yield the same set of factors.

3. Name and describe Eysenck's three general types, or superfactors.

    A. As opposed to Cattell, Eysenck has built his personality theory on measures of types, or superfactors. The superfactors are broader than traits, with a single trait forming a cluster of several traits. Eysenck's procedure has yielded only three general bipolar types: extraversion/introversion (E), neuroticism/stability (N), and psychoticism/superego functioning (P).
    B. Extraverts are sociable, impulsive, lively, quick-witted, and optimistic. They enjoy taking risks and seek other types of excitement, including stimulating social activities. Introverts are quiet, passive, unsociable, careful, reserved,

thoughtful, pessimistic, peaceful, and controlled; they have a congenitally low cortical arousal level that keeps them from exciting, dangerous activities.

C. High N scores are overreactive, frequently complain of vague physical symptoms, and have difficulty returning to a normal state after emotional arousal. Low N scores are emotionally stable, calm, even-tempered, and controlled.

D. People who score high on P are not necessarily suffering form a psychosis, but they do have a high predisposition to develop pathology under periods of high stress.

E. According to Eysenck, all three types have a strong genetic component.

MULTIPLE CHOICE QUESTIONS

a   4.   The descriptive and distinguishing qualities that characterize a person are what Cattell and Eysenck called
     a.   traits.
     b.   states.
     c.   factors.
     d.   superfactors.

c   *5.   Cattell and Eysenck relied mostly on which method of identifying traits?
     a.   intuition
     b.   psychoanalysis
     c.   factor analysis
     d.   twin studies

d   6.   Which trait theorist is a native of England but has lived most of his professional life in the United States at both the Universities of Illinois and Hawaii?
     a.   Rotter
     b.   Kelly
     c.   Eysenck
     d.   Cattell

e   *7.   According to Cattell and Eysenck, a relatively permanent disposition of an individual, inferred from that person's behavior, is a
     a.   state.
     b.   construct.
     c.   factor.
     d.   type.
     e.   trait.

c   *8.   In Cattell's inductive method of research,
     a.   data come from hypotheses generated from clinical research.
     b.   hypotheses guide the collection of relevant data.
     c.   no preexisting hypotheses determine the collection of data.
     d.   hypotheses are generated before data is factor analyzed.

b   9.   In general, the purpose of factor analysis is to
           a.   investigate differences between two groups of subjects.
           b.   reduce a large number of variables to a smaller number of basic factors.
           c.   construct inductive theories of personality.
           d.   construct deductive theories of personality.

a   10.   In factor analysis, correlations of scores with factors are called
           a.   factor loadings.
           b.   factor theories.
           c.   trait theories.
           d.   superfactors.

d   *11. An example of a unipolar trait would be
           a.   extraversion/introversion.
           b.   dominance versus submission.
           c.   Eysenck's P (psychoticism).
           d.   shoe size.

b   12.   The authors compare Cattell and Eysenck to two cartographers setting out to
           map the earth. Based on this hypothetical situation,
           a.   Cattell would limit his work to Europe and Africa.
           b.   Cattell would chart the entire globe.
           c.   Eysenck would map every river, hill, and stream.
           d.   Cattell would measure only the large features of the earth, such as the
                oceans and continents.

a   13.   Traits generated through factor analysis may be either _____ or _____.
           a.   unipolar; bipolar.
           b.   unidimensional; multidimensional.
           c.   conscious; unconscious.
           d.   loaded; unloaded.
           e.   static; rotated.

e   14.   Cattell extracted more traits from his data than Eysenck. This is partially
           explained by Cattell's
           a.   hypotheses prior to data collection.
           b.   vast quantity of data collected.
           c.   time frame for collection of data.
           d.   types of subjects used to generate data.
           e.   use of oblique rotation.

a   *15. Which correlation technique was used by Cattell to measure unique traits, or
           characteristics within the individual?
           a.   P technique
           b.   R technique
           c.   Q technique
           d.   both b and c

b   *16. Temporary changes in behavior due to immediate environmental changes are
           what Cattell called
           a.   traits.
           b.   states.
           c.   syndromes.
           d.   types.

c   17.   A correlational method that involves one person taking two or more tests on
           many occasions is what Cattell called the
           a.   R technique.
           b.   dR technique.
           c.   P technique.
           d.   Q technique.

e   18.   Cattell believed that fluctuations in behavioral and physiological states are most
           reliably calculated by the
           a.   R technique.
           b.   P technique.
           c.   dR technique.
           d.   both a and b.
           e.   both b. and c.

a   *19.   Cattell attempted to measure human personality from three directions, using L
           data, Q data, and T data. Which of the following is an example of T data?
           a.   aptitude test scores
           b.   an autobiography
           c.   a biography
           d.   supervisory ratings

b   20.   According to Cattell, grades recorded on a student's college transcript are
           _____ data.
           a.   L
           b.   L(T)
           c.   L(R)
           d.   Q
           e.   T

b   21.   Which of Cattell's media of observation could NOT be used with animals such
           as dogs or cats?
           a.   L data
           b.   Q data
           c.   T data
           d.   none of the above can be used to measure animal behavior

c   22.   According to Cattell, Q data
           a.   cannot be faked.
           b.   are a form of objective test.
           c.   should be corroborated by correlations with behavioral data.
           d.   reveal the uniqueness of each individual.

e   23.   For Cattell, personality inventories such as the Rorschach and other
           "projective" instruments yield _____ data.
           a.   L
           b.   L(T)
           c.   L(R)
           d.   Q
           e.   T

d   24. According to Cattell, if several surface traits are highly correlated with one
         another, then some _____ is holding them together.
         a. hypothetical trait
         b. superfactor
         c. temperament trait
         d. source trait

e *25. Cattell believed that surface traits
         a. are products of clusters of source traits.
         b. hold together several different source traits.
         c. are the primary traits underlying all behavior.
         d. are responsible for intercorrelations among source traits.
         e. can serve as indicators of underlying source traits.

b   26. Cattell called traits that result from clusters of other traits
         a. surface traits.
         b. source traits.
         c. hexitic traits.
         d. temperament.

c   27. If factor analytic measurement techniques were perfectly reliable and valid,
         a. L, Q, and T data would each reveal separate sets of factors.
         b. L and T data would yield one set of factors with Q data yielding an
             independent set.
         c. all three media would yield the same set of factors.
         d. all three media would yield a single personality factor.

d   28. Cattell classified traits that refer to how far or how fast one can perform a
         given activity as _____ traits.
         a. temperament
         b. motivational
         c. dynamic
         d. ability

c   29. The total number of primary traits, both normal and pathological, that Cattell
         and his associates identified is about
         a. 2 or 3.
         b. 10.
         c. 35.
         d. 240.

a   30. According to Cattell, surface traits that cluster together do so because of
         an underlying
         a. source trait.
         b. temperament trait.
         c. master motive.
         d. ability trait.
         e. physiological need.

a   31. Most of Cattell's personality traits are also _____ traits.
         a. temperament
         b. ability
         c. surface
         d. common

e 32. When comparing Cattell's factor A to his factor P, we can say that factor P
   a. emerges most clearly from factor analysis.
   b. is more difficult to clearly extract from factor analysis.
   c. accounts for a smaller amount of variance.
   d. both a and c.
   e. both b and c .

c *33. Cattell believed that pathological personalities are marked by
   a. the presence of one or more abnormal traits.
   b. an extreme imbalance of normal traits.
   c. either a or b.
   d. neither a nor b.

c 34. Cattell identified second-order factors by
   a. inductive reasoning.
   b. deductive reasoning.
   c. factor analysis of first order traits.
   d. factor analysis of third order traits.

c 35. Of Cattell's 12 abnormal primary source traits, the first seven traits, symbolized by the letter D, are _____ traits.
   a. disordered
   b. disruptive
   c. depressive
   d. delusional
   e. dementia

c 36. Cattell's second-order source traits are _____ with the primary factors.
   a. positively correlated
   b. negatively correlated
   c. both positively and negatively correlated
   d. uncorrelated

b 37. For Cattell, a specific course of action or desire to act in response to a given situation characterizes
   a. an ability.
   b. an attitude.
   c. the dynamic lattice.
   d. a subsidiation chain.
   e. intelligence.

e 38. Cattell derived his list of human ergs from _____ data.
   a. L
   b. L(T)
   c. L(R)
   d. Q
   e. T

a   39. For Cattell, which term is most nearly equivalent to animal
         instinctual patterns?
         a. ergs
         b. sems
         c. sentiments
         d. superego strength
         e. ego strength

b   *40. Cattell called culturally acquired traits
         a. ergs.
         b. sems.
         c. attitudes.
         d. emotions.

d   41. In Cattell's dynamic lattice, sems are
         a. the outcome of attitudes.
         b. primary dynamisms responsible for primary factors.
         c. energy sources of ergs.
         d. intermediate goals between ergs and attitudes.
         e. socially acquired ergs.

d   *42. Cattell's dynamic lattice includes
         a. attitudes.
         b. ergs.
         c. sems.
         d. all of the above.

c   43. Which sem, according to Cattell, has a special importance because of its crucial
         position in integrating other sems?
         a. superego
         b. ego
         c. self-sentiment
         d. self-concept
         e. self-identity

b   44. The complex network of attitudes, ergs, and sems is illustrated by Cattell's
         a. T data.
         b. dynamic lattice.
         c. Multiple Abstract Variance Analysis.
         d. self-sentiment.

c   45. Which family constellation has NOT been included in Cattell's MAVA method
         of estimating heritability?
         a. identical twins reared together
         b. fraternal twins reared together
         c. identical twins reared apart
         d. siblings reared together
         e. half siblings reared apart

b   46. Based on his research, Cattell concluded that intelligence
         a. is due more to environmental than genetic influences.
         b. is due more to genetic than environmental factors.
         c. isn't a primary factor.
         d. is only of the "fluid" type.

b 47. Eysenck is a native of _____, but he has lived his adult life in _____.
a. the United States; England
b. Germany; England
c. Poland; the United States
d. England; the United States

a 48. The people who most influenced Eysenck were
a. Cyril Burt, Charles Spearman, and Ivan Pavlov.
b. R. B. Cattell, J. B. Watson, and B. F. Skinner.
c. Sigmund Freud and Alfred Adler.
d. E. L. Thorndike, A. H. Maslow, and Julian Rotter.

c 49. Which of the following is NOT listed by Eysenck as a criterion for identifying a factor?
a. It must possess social relevance.
b. There must be psychometric evidence for its existence.
c. The factor must be identified through the inductive method.
d. It must relate to some reasonable theory of personality.
e. The factor must possess heritability.

d 50. Which is the correct order of levels of behavioral organization from the simplest to the most complex, according to Eysenck?
a. habitual response, specific responses, traits, types
b. types, traits, habitual responses, specific responses
c. habitual responses, traits, specific responses, types
d. specific responses, habitual responses, traits, types

a 51. Eysenck's three general types or superfactors are
a. bipolar factors.
b. unique surface traits.
c. pathological factors.
d. surface traits.

c 52. Eysenck's psychoticism factor (P) is characteristic of
a. normal personalities only.
b. abnormal personalities only.
c. both normal and abnormal personalities.
d. neither normal nor abnormal personalities.

d *53. Eysenck believed that the primary difference between extraverts and introverts is one of
a. mother-infant relationships.
b. objectivity/subjectivity.
c. neuroticism/stability.
d. cortical arousal level.
e. gender.

e 54. Eysenck claimed that extraverted types are characterized by all the following traits EXCEPT
a. sociable.
b. impulsive.
c. lively.
d. playful.
e. thoughtful.

c   *55. According to Eysenck, introverted types are characterized by all the following
          traits EXCEPT
          a. quiet.
          b. passive.
          c. optimistic.
          d. sober.
          e. thoughtful.

e   56. Eysenck believed that introverts are characterized by
          a. lower levels of cortical arousal.
          b. higher levels of cortical arousal.
          c. low sensory threshold.
          d. both a and b.
          e. both b and c.

a   57. According to Eysenck, low levels of cortical arousal and high sensory thresholds
          characterize individuals who score high on the _____ scale.
          a. extraversion.
          b. introversion.
          c. psychoticism.
          d. neuroticism.

b   58. Eysenck's P type is a bipolar factor consisting of
          a. psychoticism and neuroticism.
          b. psychoticism and superego.
          c. proactivity and passivity.
          d. punctuality and procrastination.

d   59. According to Eysenck, high P scorers are
          a. punctual and precise.
          b. caring and cooperative.
          c. social and agreeable.
          d. impulsive and hostile.

d   60. Eysenck claimed that introverted neurotics are characterized by all of the
          following EXCEPT
          a. anxiety.
          b. depression.
          c. phobias.
          d. hysteria.
          e. obsessive-compulsive symptoms.

b   61. According to Eysenck, an individual characterized by hysteria, suggestibility,
          and somatic symptoms would score high on the _____ scale.
          a. extraversion
          b. neuroticism
          c. psychoticism
          d. superego

a   62. In Eysenck's theory of personality, the three basic factors of P, E, and N are
          a. unrelated to each other.
          b. primary traits.
          c. negatively related to each other.
          d. a single unified factor

d *63. According to Eysenck's findings, cold, nonconforming, and aggressive
      personalities tend to score high on
      a. extraversion.
      b. introversion.
      c. neuroticism.
      d. psychoticism.

c 64. In Eysenck's theory of personality, individuals who tend to be empathetic,
      caring, cooperative, and highly socialized score
      a. low on neuroticism.
      b. high on introversion.
      c. low on psychoticism.
      d. high on extraversion.

d 65. Some people are vulnerable to organic and psychiatric illness because they have
      a genetic or acquired weakness that predisposes them to the illness. This
      explanation for an illness is what Eysenck called the
      a. psychoticism factor.
      b. hardiness model.
      c. biological imperative.
      d. diathesis-stress model.

c 66. What evidence did Eysenck present on the biological bases of personality?
      a. People in different parts of the world have different types of personality.
      b. People tend to change their personality patterns as they age.
      c. Identical twins are more similar in personality than are fraternal twins
         reared together.
      d. Identical twins and fraternal twins reared together are equally similar.

b 67. Eysenck argued that many experimental studies on the same topic yield
      inconclusive or inconsistent results because the experimenters failed to
      a. match participants on gender and age.
      b. consider personality as a factor.
      c. use the proper statistical procedures.
      d. consider the motivation of participants.

a 68. Eysenck and Grossarth-Maticek found that
      a. people with a helpless, hopeless attitude tended to die more from cancer
         than from heart disease.
      b. people who reacted to frustration with anger and emotional arousal tended
         to die more from cancer than from heart disease.
      c. people who regarded their own autonomy as important had high death rates
         from both cancer and heart disease.
      d. no relationship between personality factors and disease.

a 69. Research on creative scientists has generally found that
      a. both male and female creative scientists score high on dominance,
         self-confidence, and adventurousness.
      b. male creative scientists are more withdrawn and anxious than people
         in general.
      c. male, but not female, creative scientists are more intelligent and
         self-confident than other people.
      d. all of the above.

c   70.   Research using the Eysenck Personality Questionnaire has found that creative
            scientists score higher than people in general on
            a.   introversion.
            b.   conformity.
            c.   psychoticism.
            d.   superego functioning.

b   71.   Research tends to support the hypothesis that both creative artists and creative
            scientists, compared with noncreative people, are more
            a.   extraverted and humble.
            b.   introverted and hostile.
            c.   psychotic and close-minded.
            d.   neurotic and submissive.

b   72.   Which of the following statements would NOT be generally acceptable to trait
            and factor theorists?
            a.   Personality traits can be identified by means of correlational studies.
            b.   Personality traits are mostly determined by environmental factors.
            c.   Personality traits and states can be measured by means of
                  questionnaire data.
            d.   Traits and states can be used to explain individual differences in behavior.

b   73.   Cattell and Eysenck
            a.   agree on the number of personality factors, but disagree on their names.
            b.   disagree on the number of personality factors to be extracted.
            c.   both rely primarily on hypothetical-deductive reasoning.
            d.   both began with the same test data, but they arrived at different factors
                  through different statistical methods.

c   74.   Although Cattell and Eysenck are difficult to rate on several dimensions for a
            concept of humanity, they clearly rate high on
            a.   the teleological dimension.
            b.   pessimism.
            c.   genetic influences.
            d.   free will.
            e.   unconscious influences.

CHAPTER 14
ALLPORT: PSYCHOLOGY OF THE INDIVIDUAL

ESSAY QUESTIONS

1. Discuss Allport's concept of personal dispositions and explain how personal dispositions differ from traits.

    A. Allport distinguished between common traits, which are shared by two or more people, and personal dispositions, which are peculiar to one person.
    B. Common traits allow for inter-individual comparisons, but personal dispositions are individual and do not permit inter-individual comparisons. One person's dominance is different from another person's dominance.
    C. Allport identified three overlapping levels of personal dispositions: (1) cardinal, (2) central, and (3) secondary.
    D. Cardinal dispositions are so obvious and dominating that they cannot be hidden from others. Not everyone has a cardinal disposition. Allport identified several historical and fictional people who possessed a cardinal disposition (for example, Don Juan, the Marquis de Sade, and Narcissus).
    E. Allport believed that everyone has 5 to 10 central dispositions around which their lives revolve. These central dispositions should characterize a person in a variety of different situations.
    F. Secondary dispositions may not be manifested in every situation, yet they occur with some regularity and are responsible for many of a person's behaviors.
    G. Allport also divided personal dispositions into motivational dispositions, which are strongly felt and derive from basic needs, and stylistic dispositions, which refer to the manner in which a person behaves. Stylistic dispositions do not motivate behavior; rather, they guide behavior.

2. Describe Allport's notion of functional autonomy and give examples of functionally autonomous behaviors.

    A. Allport's most distinctive and controversial concept is his concept of functional autonomy. Functional autonomy suggests that some human motives are functionally independent from the original motive responsible for a particular behavior.
    B. Motives that are not functionally autonomous include those that are responsible for reflex actions, basic drives and needs, and psychopathological behaviors.
    C. Allport described two levels of functional autonomy: perseverative and propriate.
    D. Perseverative functional autonomy is the tendency of certain basic behaviors to continue in the absence of reinforcement. Examples of perseverative functionally autonomous behaviors include addiction to drugs and rats running a maze "just for the fun of it."
    E. Propriate functionally autonomous behaviors are self-sustaining motives that are related to the proprium. Examples of propriate functionally autonomous behaviors include working at a hobby or pursuing an interest that one regards as dear and important.

3.   Discuss Allport's concept of the psychologically healthy personality.

A. Allport believed that psychologically healthy people are motivated by conscious processes and are more flexible and autonomous than unhealthy people. They are active, secure, and in charge of their lives.

B. Allport identified six criteria for the mature personality. The first criterion is an extension of the sense of self. Healthy people are not self-centered but are capable of identifying with their fellow humans.

C. They also possess a warm relating of self to others; that is, they have the capacity to love others in a non-self-centered way.

D. Third, these people have emotional security and self-acceptance. They are not overly troubled when things do not go their way.

E. They are realistic and do not live in a make-believe world. They are problem-centered rather than self-centered.

F. Psychologically healthy people possess both insight and humor. They understand themselves and have the capacity to laugh at themselves without belittling themselves.

G. These healthy individuals also have a unifying philosophy of life and a clear vision of the purpose of life. This philosophy of life may or may not be religious, yet it is usually characterized by a mature conscience and a strong desire to serve other people.

MULTIPLE CHOICE QUESTIONS

b   *4.   Allport's principal concern in personality theory was with
         a.   factor analysis.
         b.   the uniqueness of the individual.
         c.   the heritability of personality traits.
         d.   early childhood experiences.
         e.   unconscious motivation.

c   5.   Which concept best describes Allport's view of personality?
         a.   reactive
         b.   unconscious motivation
         c.   uniqueness
         d.   abnormal development

a   6.   For Allport, the most basic question underlying all personality theory is:
         a.   What is the proper balance between universal laws and individual uniqueness?
         b.   How can behavior be determined yet free?
         c.   What is the proper sequence of experience for optimum personality growth?
         d.   How can psychologists be sure of the validity and reliability of data?
         e.   How can the major influences on personality be studied?

c   *7.   Allport's approach to personality can best be termed
         a.   trait and factor.
         b.   psychoanalytic.
         c.   eclectic.
         d.   a behavioral analysis.

a   8.   Allport's statement, "I know in my bones that my opponents are partly right," reflects his
        a.   eclecticism.
        b.   particularism.
        c.   striving for superiority.
        d.   provincialism.

a   9.   When Allport was a young man, he spent a year teaching in Europe. On his return trip home, he visited with his brother Fayette and had a memorable meeting with
        a.   Freud.
        b.   Adler.
        c.   Hitler.
        d.   Jung.
        e.   Churchill.

e   10.   With regard to self-reports such as diaries and letters, Allport
        a.   rejected them as invalid and unreliable.
        b.   looked for their underlying unconscious meanings.
        c.   insisted that their latent content be examined.
        d.   accepted them if they agreed with his theory.
        e.   was inclined to accept them at face value.

c   *11.   Allport criticized older theories of personality for
        a.   using outmoded terms and concepts.
        b.   rejecting nomothetic methods of psychological research.
        c.   neglecting the normal, psychologically healthy individual.
        d.   neglecting investigations of the dynamics of personality.

a   *12.   Allport believed that psychoanalytic and learning theories
        a.   are basically homeostatic.
        b.   study the psychological healthy individual.
        c.   are basically proactive.
        d.   all of the above.
        e.   a and b only.

c   *13.   Allport called theories in which people are seen as being motivated primarily by needs to reduce tension and to return to a state of equilibrium as
        a.   proactive theories.
        b.   retroactive theories.
        c.   reactive theories.
        d.   eclectic theories.

a   14.   Allport's notion that people are capable of consciously acting upon their environment in new and innovative ways that permit psychological growth is illustrated by
        a.   proactive behavior.
        b.   reactive behavior.
        c.   causality.
        d.   determinism.
        e.   neurosis.

a   15. Allport favored a view of personality that regards behavior as
          a. proactive.
          b. reactive.
          c. homeostatic.
          d. learned.
          e. nonscientific.

e   16. Because Allport believed that a personality theory must be broad enough to
          encompass the growing, evolving individual as well as the static, adjustive
          person, he advocated the _____ approach to theory building.
          a. common sense
          b. intuitive
          c. subjective
          d. experimental
          e. eclectic

c   17. Allport's comment to therapists to not "forget what you have decided to
          neglect" is an expression of his
          a. optimistic attitude toward human personality.
          d. belief that personality theorists must expand their research base.
          c. eclectic attitude.
          d. existential beliefs.

e   *18. "The dynamic organization within the individual of those psychophysical
          systems that determine his characteristic behavior and thought" is Allport's
          definition of
          a. a system.
          b. temperament.
          c. traits.
          d. personal disposition.
          e. personality.

a   19. Allport's definition of personality included the notion of personality as
          a. both dynamic and organized.
          b. exclusively physiological.
          c. determined in early childhood.
          d. divided into two major types: introverts and extraverts.
          e. all of the above.

b   20. The term "character" originally meant
          a. an actor.
          b. a marking or engraving.
          c. an abnormal individual.
          d. determinism.

d   21. For Allport, the human personality implies
          a. both process and product.
          b. both substance and change.
          c. both order and diversification.
          d. all of the above.

a 22. To Allport, the two most important structures of personality are
    a. personal dispositions and the proprium.
    b. primary traits and secondary traits.
    c. cardinal traits and primary traits.
    d. common traits and superfactors.

a 23. Allport objected to the label "trait psychologist" because
    a. he believed that the concept of traits does not allow for individual uniqueness.
    b. he felt that traits had no proven existence.
    c. he believed that the concept of traits was too specific.
    d. he did not regard himself as a psychologist.
    e. none of the above.

a 24. For Allport, common traits
    a. are shared by several people.
    b. can be used for intraindividual comparisons.
    c. are more important than personal traits.
    d. a and b

b *25. With regard to traits, Allport held that they
    a. are of two kinds: primary (inherited) and secondary (learned).
    b. are of two kinds: common and individual (personal dispositions).
    c. have no psychological significance.
    d. must be extracted through factor analysis.

d 26. Allport and Odbert found about _____ personally descriptive words in a standard dictionary.
    a. 7
    b. 450
    c. 4,500
    d. 18,000

d *27. According to Allport's definition, personal dispositions
    a. render different stimuli functionally equivalent.
    b. both initiate and guide behavior.
    c. have both a neurological and a psychological component.
    d. all of the above.
    e. none of the above.

c 28. To Allport, personal dispositions differ from traits in that they
    a. have the capacity to render many stimuli functionally equivalent.
    b. initiate and guide behavior.
    c. are peculiar to the individual.
    d. are neuropsychic structures.

a 29. Allport placed personal dispositions on a continuum from
    a. central to peripheral.
    b. conscious to unconscious.
    c. reactive to proactive.
    d. determined to undetermined.
    e. developed to undeveloped.

b   *30. According to Allport, personal dispositions that are so dominating in one's life
           that they cannot be hidden are called
           a. central traits.
           b. cardinal traits.
           c. primary traits.
           d. learned traits.

e   31.   Allport hypothesized that the number of central dispositions for any one
           person would be about
           a. two or three.
           b. 30 to 50.
           c. 500 to 600.
           d. 4,500.
           e. none of the above.

b   32.   Most people who knew Allport described him as reserved, prim, and orderly.
           Allport would say that these descriptions are in terms of _____ dispositions.
           a. cardinal
           b. central
           c. secondary
           d. peripheral
           e. proactive

c   *33.   Personal dispositions that are not central to personality yet occur with some
           regularity and are responsible for much of one's specific behaviors Allport
           terms _____ dispositions.
           a. common
           b. cardinal
           c. secondary
           d. propriate
           e. reactive

e   34.   Allport objected to psychoanalysis chiefly because he felt that Freud
           a. placed too much emphasis on the uniqueness of the individual.
           b. placed too little emphasis on the uniqueness of the individual.
           c. did not adequately understand Americans.
           d. was too concerned with the superego function.
           e. placed too much emphasis on the unconscious motivation.

d   35.   Allport called strongly felt personal dispositions that initiate action
           a. dynamic traits.
           b. cardinal dispositions.
           c. central traits.
           d. motivational dispositions.
           e. stylistic traits.

e   *36.   Allport termed less intensely felt personal dispositions that guide action
           _____ dispositions.
           a. dynamic
           b. central
           c. cardinal
           d. motivational
           e. stylistic

c *37. Those behaviors and characteristics that one regards as central to one's life are said by Allport to belong to the
a. self.
b. ego.
c. proprium.
d. society.
e. superego.

e 38. Those aspects of a person that are regarded as important to a sense of self-identity and self-enhancement are what Allport called
a. cardinal traits.
b. the ego.
c. the self.
d. the self-concept.
e. the proprium.

c *39. Allport believed that people are motivated primarily by
a. the single need for self-actualization.
b. both sex and aggression.
c. both the need to adjust and the need to grow or change.
d. the need to gain superiority over others.

e 40. The capstone of Allport's theory of motivation is the concept of
a. the proprium.
b. the open system.
c. common traits.
d. propriate strivings.
e. functional autonomy.

a *41. Allport's concept that some human motives are independent from the original motive responsible for behavior was termed
a. functional autonomy.
b. functional fixedness.
c. propriate strivings.
d. propriate perseveration.
e. bimodal motivation.

b 42. Allport's theory of motivation emphasizes the
a. unchanging nature of drives.
b. contemporaneity of motives.
c. concept of hierarchy of needs.
d. drive-reduction hypothesis.
e. principle of equivalence.

d *43. Allport saw people as being motivated mostly by
a. the need to reduce tension.
b. cultural influences.
c. unconscious forces.
d. a variety of motives.

b   44. Allport contended that adult motives are
          a. totally unconscious.
          b. basically different from children's motives.
          c. a form of homeostatic regulation.
          d. tied to a single master drive or motive.

b   *45. Allport's criteria for an adequate theory of motivation included all EXCEPT
          the idea that the theory must
          a. allow for the cognitive processes of planning and intention.
          b. be based on the concept of a single master motive.
          c. acknowledge the fact that motives exist in the present.
          d. allow for concrete, unique motives.

c   46. "Any acquired system of motivation in which the tensions involved are not of
          the same kind as the antecedent tensions from which the acquired system
          developed" is Allport's definition of
          a. an open system.
          b. the proprium.
          c. functional autonomy.
          d. idiographic science.

d   47. Perseverative functional autonomy is
          a. the most complex form of functional autonomy.
          b. the capstone of Allport's theory of personal dispositions.
          c. found in both animals and humans.
          d. all of the above.

c   48. Which of these is most likely based on perseverative functionally
          autonomous motives?
          a. regression to an infantile stage of development
          b. contraction of the pupil of the eye
          c. addiction to nicotine
          d. watching one's favorite TV program

c   *49. Allport's master system of motivation that confers unity on personality
          is called
          a. the ego.
          b. perseverative functional autonomy.
          c. propriate functional autonomy.
          d. the self-concept.

d   50. According to Allport, present motives are functionally autonomous to the
          extent that they
          a. stem from early childhood experiences.
          b. are reinforced by physiological drives.
          c. are reinforced by significant others.
          d. seek new goals.
          e. represent pathological behavior.

d 51. According to Allport, any symptom that cannot be extinguished through psychotherapy or does not change as self-concept changes is
    a. homeostatic.
    b. reactive.
    c. a propriate striving.
    d. functionally autonomous.

a 52. Unconscious processes, said Allport, play an important role in
    a. motivating pathological behavior.
    b. the lives of all people.
    c. motivating healthy adults.
    d. no situations.

c 53. The motives of the mature individual, Allport said, would be
    a. to seek self-actualization.
    b. self-centered.
    c. functionally autonomous.
    d. based on early childhood experiences.
    e. to maintain the status quo.

e *54. Which of these would NOT be characteristic of the mature, healthy personality, according to Allport?
    a. warm relating of self to others
    b. insight and humor
    c. unifying philosophy of life
    d. extension of the sense of self
    e. self-centeredness

b 55. For Allport, the earmark of maturity is
    a. self-love.
    b. self-extension.
    c. self-acceptance.
    d. realistic perceptions.
    e. insight and humor.

a 56. Allport believed that insight and humor may be aspects of
    a. self-objectification.
    b. emotional maturity.
    c, reactive behavior.
    d. the self as knower.
    e. extrinsic religious orientation.

a 57. Allport's approach to science emphasizes which methods?
    a. morphogenic
    b. statistical
    c. nomothetic
    d. longitudinal
    e. cross-cultural

a 58. For Allport, the term "morphogenic" refers to
    a. patterned properties of the whole organism.
    b. propriate strivings common to all people.
    c. the organization aspect of the proprium.
    d. motivation aspects of proactive behavior.

e   59.   Examples of Allport's completely morphogenic methods include all the
          following EXCEPT
          a. autobiographies.
          b. self-anchoring scales.
          c. body gestures.
          d. voice patterns.
          e. self-rating scales.

a   60.   The case of Marion Taylor was interesting to Allport because he studied her
          personality through which morphogenic method?
          a. diaries
          b. dreams
          c. doodles
          d. voice patterns

e   61.   Allport used Jenny's letters to support his view that personality
          a. is a result of unconscious psychodynamic conflicts.
          b. can be determined through handwriting analysis.
          c. is best understood through nomothetic laws.
          d. is limited to directly observable behavior.
          e. should be studied from the individual's point of view.

d   62.   The technique that Baldwin developed to analyze the structure of Jenny's
          personality from her letters was called
          a. factor analysis.
          b. the nomothetic procedure.
          c. content analysis.
          d. personal structure analysis.
          e. the analysis of functional autonomy.

b   63.   Page's factor analysis of the letters from Jenny revealed
          a. a classical paranoid schizophrenic woman.
          b. eight to ten central traits.
          c. three secondary traits.
          d. traits quite different from those derived by Allport through
              commonsense analysis.

e   64.   The Religious Orientation Scale (ROS) assumes both _____ and _____
          orientation toward religion.
          a. a theistic; an atheistic
          b. a group; an individual
          c. a historical; a function
          d. a trait; a personal disposition
          e. an intrinsic; an extrinsic

a   65.   Research has found that highly prejudiced churchgoers scored
          a. high on extrinsic religious orientation.
          b. high on intrinsic religious orientation.
          c. high on both the extrinsic and intrinsic religious orientation.
          d. low on both the extrinsic and intrinsic religious orientation.

c 66. Research indicates that people who score high on the Intrinsic scale of the Religious Orientation Scale tend to
    a. be highly anxious.
    b. be highly prejudiced.
    c. have good psychological health.
    d. both a and b.
    e. none of the above.

d 67. When Robert Kosek (1999) gave a version of the Religious Orientation Scale to middle school students in Poland, he found that students with an intrinsic religious orientation, compared with those with an extrinsic orientation,
    a. were more prejudiced.
    b. scored lower on tests of quantitative ability.
    c. were more likely to be only children.
    d. were more agreeable and conscientious.

a 68. Research suggests that people who score high on the Extrinsic scale of the Religious Orientation Scale tend to
    a. have more than their share of personal problems.
    b. not to go to church on a regular basis.
    c. have greater self-control than those who score high on the Intrinsic Scale.
    d. have good emotional health.

d 69. Research by Ralph Hood and colleagues found that people with an intrinsic religious orientation
    a also scored high on internal locus of control.
    b. also scored high on external locus of control.
    c. also scored high on the extrinsic religious orientation scale.
    d. had better mental health and fewer problems than people with an extrinsic religious orientation.

d 70. Allport's theory of personality is based mostly on
    a. clinical experience.
    b. factor analytical studies.
    c. experimental investigation.
    d. philosophical speculation and common sense.

a 71. A weakness of Allport's theory of personality is that it
    a. is difficult to falsify.
    b. is too optimistic.
    c. is too pessimistic.
    d. is not internally consistent.
    e. contains many terms not carefully defined.

c 72. Allport's view of humanity includes the idea that
    a. people are motivated primarily to reduce tension.
    b. personality is determined by cultural factors.
    c. people not only seek to reduce tensions but to establish new ones.
    d. people are essentially reactive.

c   73. With regard to freedom and determinism, Allport held
          a.   a deterministic view.
          b.   that people are completely free.
          c.   that freedom could be expanded.
          d.   an existential view.

a   74. According to Allport, which people have the highest level of free will?
          a.   psychologically healthy, reflective, and intelligent people
          b.   infants who have not yet learned self-control
          c.   old people near death who have no fear of the future
          d.   preadolescents who have not yet become involved in sexual relationships

CHAPTER 15
KELLY: PSYCHOLOGY OF PERSONAL CONSTRUCTS

ESSAY QUESTIONS

1.　Discuss Kelly's philosophical position.
   - A. Kelly believed that human behavior is shaped both by reality and by an individual's perception of reality.
   - B. Although the universe is real, Kelly insisted that different people construe it in different ways. Thus, personal constructs, or a person's way of interpreting and explaining events, are the basic units of prediction.
   - C. Kelly believed that people, in their daily decision making, behave much like scientists. That is, they observe, ask questions, anticipate answers to those questions, perceive relationships between events, hypothesize about possible solutions, and predict potential outcomes.
   - D. Kelly also held that we should perceive scientists and scientific theories with the same level of skepticism that we hold for other individuals and ideas. Each theory is but a set of half-truths and should be open to future restructuring.
   - E. Because people continually strive to make sense out of their continuously changing world, they potentially have alternative ways of looking at things. Kelly coined the term "constructive alternativism" to refer to his contention that our present interpretations of the world are subject to revision or replacement.

2.　Discuss the fundamental postulate of Kelly's theory.

   - A. Kelly's fundamental postulate is that people's processes are psychologically channelized by the ways in which they anticipate events. That is, people's behavior (thoughts and actions) is shaped by the way they see the future.
   - B. Kelly's theory was solely concerned with each individual person functioning as a total being. Drives, needs, and motives play no part in his theory.
   - C. People move with a direction through a network of flexible pathways and are capable of directing their movement toward some end or purpose.
   - D. People guide their actions according to the ways they predict the future. Their present view of the future—not past experiences or the future itself—determines their present behavior.

3.　Define Kelly's concept of role, including core role.

   - A. Kelly's notion of role is embedded in his sociality corollary, which holds that to the extent that we construe the construction processes of another person, we may play a role in the social processes of that person.
   - B. Role refers to a pattern of behavior that results from our understanding of the constructs of other people with whom we are interacting. Our construction of our role in relation to another person need not be accurate, yet it shapes our behaviors and thoughts toward that person.
   - C. People have both peripheral roles and core roles. With our core role, we define our self in terms of who we really are. Our core role gives us a sense of identity and provides us with a set of directions for daily living. Our numerous peripheral roles are less central to our self-concept and allow us to appear different to different people.

MULTIPLE CHOICE QUESTIONS

b   *4.   Kelly's theory of personal constructs can MOST accurately be called
        a.   a behavioral theory.
        b   a metatheory.
        c.   an existential theory.
        d.   a cognitive theory.

a   5.   Kelly called the interpretations people place on events
        a.   constructs.
        b.   alternatives.
        c.   postulates.
        d.   corollaries.

e   6.   Kelly's belief that alternative constructions are always possible reflects the
          philosophical position of
        a.   the plasticity corollary.
        b.   Rep test revisionism.
        c.   the phenomenological postulate.
        d.   radical behaviorism.
        e.   none of the above.

a   7.   Kelly's early background reveals a
        a.   spotty formal education.
        b.   close relationship with an older sister.
        c.   close relationship with an older brother.
        d.   strong dependence on his parents until he was 30 years old.

c   8.   Kelly became a psychotherapist
        a.   when he learned that the University of Edinburg had no other openings.
        b.   as a result of a chance encounter with Freud.
        c.   when he saw a need for students in Kansas to cope with the dust bowl and
             the Great Depression.
        d.   to supplement his meager pay as a college professor.

e   9.   Which set of terms is most consistent with Kelly's concept of personal
          constructs?
        a.   early childhood experiences
        b.   archetypes, complexes, and instincts
        c.   individualized rewards and punishments
        d.   adolescent development
        e.   interpretation and explanation of events

c   10.   The notion that the ONLY reality is our perception reflects the
        a.   psychoanalytic approach.
        b.   behavioral view.
        c.   phenomenological system.
        d.   personal construct approach.
        e.   dichotomous view.

d   *11. Kelly believed that people's attempts to interpret and explain events is similar to that of
    a. teachers.
    b. psychologists.
    c. artists.
    d. scientists.
    e. therapists.

b   12. Kelly held that
    a. scientific inquiry should be limited to trained scientists.
    b. nonscientists make observations and draw conclusions in much the same manner as trained scientists.
    c. an overemphasis on scientific method has restricted the growth of psychology.
    d. an underemphasis on scientific method has restricted the growth of psychology.

b   13. Kelly believed that the conclusions of scientists should be regarded
    a. as truth.
    b. with skepticism.
    c. as folly.
    d. as guidelines by which to live a self-fulfilling life.
    e. as theories.

d   *14. Like Carl Rogers, Kelly believed that his theory of personality
    a. emphasizes the importance of unconscious motivation.
    b. explains both human and animal behavior.
    c. is not subject to change or revision.
    d. is tentative and subject to restructuring.
    e. does not account for abnormal personality development.

c   *15. Kelly's constructive alternativism assumes that
    a. people use past events to construct a philosophy of life.
    b. people build obstacles in the path toward success.
    c. present interpretations of events are subject to revision and change.
    d. truth is acquired by a piecemeal accumulation of facts.
    e. truth is acquired in large pieces by rapid breakthroughs.

a   16. Kelly would agree with Adler
    a. that one's interpretation of events is more important than the events themselves.
    b. on the importance of early childhood experiences.
    c. that personal superiority is the one dynamic force behind people's actions.
    d. that the value of a person's life should be judged from the view of social interest.

d   *17. Which statement is NOT an assumption Kelly accepted?
    a. The universe exists.
    b. The universe functions as an integral unit.
    c. The parts of the universe interact precisely with each other.
    d. The universe is beyond human knowledge and understanding.

e   18. Unlike Adler, Kelly pointed out that our interpretation of events receive
         meaning through
         a. social interest.
         b. self-perception.
         c. creative power.
         d. a causal view of the universe.
         e. a dimension of time.

d   *19. According to Kelly, facts
         a. determine a person's future.
         b. are determined by past events.
         c. dictate our view of the world.
         d. carry meaning for us to discover.
         e. are acquired solely through the scientific method.

d   *20. Kelly called the transparent templates or patterns that help us make sense out
         of the world
         a. paradoxical vision.
         b. facts.
         c. philosophies.
         d. personal constructs.
         e. principles of organization.

a   *21. According to Kelly, a construct is built on at least
         a. one comparison and one contrast.
         b. one comparison and two contrasts.
         c. two comparisons and one contrast.
         d. two comparisons and two contrasts.

c   22. Regan and Carter are tall; Jeff is fat. Kelly would say that these statements
         illustrate the incorrect use of a construct because constructs
         a. only point to similarities.
         b. only emphasize differences.
         c. must occur within the same context.
         d. must be multidimensional comparisons.

a   23. Kelly held that, generally speaking, people
         a. attempt to improve their constructs.
         b. are completely unaware of their personal constructs.
         c. rarely, if ever, attempt to change their constructs.
         d. are completely conscious of their personal constructs.

d   24. Kelly's theory of personal constructs assumes
         a. an ever-changing world.
         b. an unchanging world.
         c. a real world.
         d. both a and c.
         e. both b and c.

d   *25. Kelly's basic postulate assumes that behavior is guided by
         a. present memories of past experiences.
         b. past experiences.
         c. future events.
         d. present perceptions of future events.

c 26. Kelly's personal construct theory emphasizes the notion that
    a. people are motivated by basic needs or drives.
    b. humans are social animals.
    c. people are constantly changing the way they view events.
    d. the world has no objective existence.

d 27. According to Kelly, because individuals have a personal investment in their established constructs, they
    a. are motivated to perceive reality correctly.
    b. are willing to modify their constructs instantly.
    c. behave in an adaptive manner.
    d. are resistant to changing them.
    e. behave in a self-serving manner.

c 28. Kelly's fundamental postulate of personal construct theory
    a. states that personality is fictional.
    b. reflects objective, scientifically established facts.
    c. is a tentative assumption about personality.
    d. illustrates a phenomenological approach.
    e. points to the biological origins of personality.

a *29. The idea that people interpret future events according to recurrent themes reflects Kelly's _____ corollary.
    a. construction
    b. similarity
    c. individuality
    d. organization

d 30. Personal construct theory assumes that behavior is
    a. shaped by past experiences.
    b. lawful and predictable.
    c. molded by heredity.
    d. guided by the way people anticipate events.

a 31. Kelly's notion that a person construes similar events as if those events were identical is what Kelly called the _____ corollary.
    a. construction
    b. individuality
    c. dichotomy
    d. comprehensive
    e. organization

d 32. Which situation best illustrates Kelly's individuality corollary?
    a. Kevin and Ramona both describe rats as "filthy."
    b. Kevin observes that plants growing above ground are usually some shade of green.
    c. Ramona notices that dogs come in a wide variety of sizes, shapes, and colors.
    d. Kevin likes Miss Dawson, his first-grade teacher, but Ramona dislikes her.

b   33.   "Persons differ from each other in their construction of events." This is a
            statement of Kelly's _____ corollary.
            a. organization
            b. individuality
            c. dichotomy
            d. choice

a   34.   All women are humans: all humans are mammals: all mammals are animals.
            This statement expresses Kelly's _____ corollary.
            a. organization
            b. commonality
            c. sociality
            d. fragmentation
            e. individuality

e   35.   People arrange their constructs to avoid conflicts and transcend contradictions.
            This illustrates Kelly's _____ corollary.
            a. dichotomy
            b   construction
            c. choice
            d. individuality
            e. organization

a   *36.   Kelly's organization corollary assumes which type of relationship
            among constructs?
            a. ordinal
            b. nominal
            c. ratio
            d. proportional
            e. interval

e   37.   Kelly's insistence that a construct is an either/or proposition is reflected in
            which corollary?
            a. dualistic
            b. bimodal
            c. contrast
            d. symmetry
            e. dichotomy

b   38.   According to Kelly, a person's construct system
            a. is mostly inherited.
            b. is made up of a finite number of opposite constructs.
            c. prevents free choice.
            d. anticipates an infinite range of events.
            e. cannot tolerate incompatible subsystems.

c   39.   According to Kelly, the minimum number of events required to form a
            construct is
            a. one.
            b. two.
            c. three.
            d. four.
            e. five.

a 40. Kelly's choice corollary allows people to extend and define
    a. future constructs.
    b. past experiences.
    c. their physiological needs.
    d. their superegos.

a *41. Personal constructs, according to Kelly, are
    a. convenient for a limited range of events.
    b. directed primarily toward the reorganization of past experiences.
    c. unnecessary personal communication.
    d. made up of ambiguous rather than clear-cut events.

b 42. Which of these statements would Kelly say represents a construct as opposed to a concept?
    a. Roses are red.
    b. Chris is taller than Holly but not as heavy.
    c. Jupiter is a planet and a god.
    d. Trees lose their leaves in the autumn.

c 43. To Kelly, our actions are shaped by
    a. past experiences.
    b. events.
    c. our anticipation of events.
    d. positive and negative reinforcers.

a 44. According to Kelly, dichotomies _____ a construct's range of convenience.
    a. limit
    b. expand
    c. contrast
    d. energize

d 45. It is not what happens around us that make us experienced; it is successive construing and reconstruing that enriches our lives. This statement reflects Kelly's _____ corollary.
    a. range
    b. fragmentation
    c. commonality
    d. experience

b *46. According to Kelly, a permeable construct
    a. results in delusions and hallucinations.
    b. facilitates change and adaptation.
    c. leads to rigid, inflexible opinions.
    d. leads to rigid, inflexible actions.

d 47. Grant tends to see all his experiences with women as power struggles. Which of Kelly's corollaries is best illustrated by Grant's refusal to change his attitude toward women?
    a. dichotomy corollary
    b. choice corollary
    c. range corollary
    d. modulation corollary
    e. fragmentation corollary

d   *48. Kelly's fragmentation corollary
        a. assumes the rigidity of behavior.
        b. accounts for all behaviors not explained by his other corollaries.
        c. is his fundamental postulate.
        d. accounts for the fact that people can hold seemingly incompatible beliefs.

c   49. Kelly's fragmentation corollary allows for
        a. a lack of dichotomous constructs.
        b. blending of similar constructs.
        c. coexistence of incompatible constructs.
        d. the lack of permeable constructs.

e   50. The fact that two people may see two different events in a similar fashion is
        explained by Kelly's _____ corollary.
        a. fragmentation
        b. sociality
        c. modulation
        d. range
        e. commonality

c   51. Kelly stated that people belong to the same cultural group because they
        a. behave in a similar fashion.
        b. choose to do so.
        c. construe their experience in the same way.
        d. are bound by time and geography.

d   52. According to Kelly, people's processes will be psychologically similar if
        these people
        a. experience the same event.
        b. experience a similar but not identical event.
        c. construe similar events differently.
        d. construe events in a similar manner.

a   53. While talking with Connor, Matt anticipates what Connor will say next. This
        event is best accounted for by Kelly's _____ corollary.
        a. sociality
        b. modulation
        c. dichotomy
        d. range

b   *54. According to Kelly, our pattern of behavior that results from our understanding
        of the constructs of others is our
        a. personality.
        b. role.
        c. trait.
        d. socioeconomic status.

a   *55. Kelly believed that our definition of our self in terms of who we really are is
        a. our core role.
        b. our peripheral role.
        c. our subjective role.
        d. our objective role.

a   *56. Kelly called those roles that give us a sense of identity and provide guidelines for living _____ roles.
    a. core
    b. peripheral
    c. central
    d. personal
    e. cardinal

c   57. According to Kelly, psychologically unhealthy people
    a. have few if any personal constructs.
    b. have too many personal constructs.
    c. hold on to outdated personal constructs.
    d. reject invalid personal constructs.

a   *58. Kelly believed that psychologically healthy people are similar to
    a. competent scientists.
    b. skillful mechanics.
    c. creative artists.
    d. helpful therapists.
    e. writers of fiction.

b   59. For Kelly, "any personal construction that is used repeatedly in spite of consistent invalidation" defines
    a. stupidity.
    b. a psychological disorder.
    c. a learning disability.
    d. unmotivated behavior.
    e. adaptation.

d   60. Psychological disorders, Kelly said, result from
    a. early childhood traumas.
    b. genetic defects.
    c. an underdeveloped construction system.
    d. personal constructs that are either too permeable or too inflexible.
    e. too many personal constructs.

b   61. Kelly might explain client resistance and negative transference during psychotherapy as a means of reducing
    a. fear.
    b. threat.
    c. anxiety.
    d. guilt.
    e. constructs.

b   *62. The awareness of an immediate and basic change to our core structures is Kelly's definition of
    a. anxiety.
    b. threat.
    c. fear.
    d. doubt.
    e. guilt.

c   63. According to Kelly, fear is unlike threat in that fear
          a.   involves a comprehensive change in core structures.
          b.   requires a comprehensive change in peripheral structures.
          c.   involves an incidental modification of personal constructs.
          d.   is a product of fixed-role therapy.

b   64. When incompatible constructs can no longer be tolerated, a person is said
          to become
          a.   threatened.
          b.   anxious.
          c.   frightened.
          d.   frustrated.
          e.   fragmented.

a   65. According to Kelly, what results when incompatible constructs become
          intolerable and people's construction system breaks down?
          a.   pathological anxiety
          b.   learning disability
          c.   minor stress
          d.   permanent insanity
          e.   core structure strength

d   66. According to Kelly, when people act in ways inconsistent with their core roles,
          they experience
          a.   threat.
          b.   anxiety.
          c.   fear.
          d.   guilt.
          e.   shame.

e   67. With Kelly's fixed-role therapy,
          a.   the client and therapist work out a predetermined role for the client
               to play.
          b.   the construction systems of other people are anticipated.
          c.   the client tries to become another person while acting out the role.
          d.   all of the above are true.
          e.   only a and b are true.

c   68. According to Kelly, why should a therapist help clients change their
          construct systems?
          a.   to increase their number of core roles
          b.   to decrease their number of core roles
          c.   to improve their efficiency in making predictions
          d.   to enable them to understand the nature of mental illness

c   *69. The purpose of Kelly's fixed-role therapy is to
          a.   solve specific problems.
          b.   reconstruct permeable personal constructs.
          c.   allow clients to discover hidden aspects of themselves.
          d.   help clients function more productively in their jobs.
          e.   help clients function more productively in their marriages.

b   70.   Prior to developing fixed-role therapy, Kelly used an unusual procedure for modifying constructs. This procedure involved
  a.   encouraging clients to act out dreams.
  b.   offering clients "preposterous interpretations" to explain their behavior.
  c.   using himself as the model to be imitated in therapy.
  d.   refusing to see clients for six months after the initial therapy session.

b   71.   The purpose of Kelly's Rep test is to
  a.   reconstruct obsolete personal constructs.
  b.   discover ways in which clients construe significant people in their lives.
  c.   provide the therapist with a differential diagnosis of patients.
  d.   uncover previously repressed conflicts.

a   72.   A student is given a Role Title List and asked to designate people who fit the various role titles on the list. This is part of the procedure for the
  a.   Role Construct Repertory (Rep) Test.
  b.   Construct Aptitude Test.
  c.   Role Construct Orientation.
  d.   Construct Evaluation Survey.
  e.   Core Construct Checklist.

d   73.   Personal constructs on Kelly's repertory grid consist of two poles:
  a.   conscious and unconscious.
  b.   adaptive and maladaptive.
  c.   unitary and dichotomous.
  d.   emergent and implicit.
  e.   permeable and impermeable.

a   74.   Eileen Donahue (1994) investigated whether children would conceptualize themselves and others in terms of the Big Five dimensions of personality and found that
  a.   agreeableness was the most frequently used construct,
  b.   boys conceptualized themselves as extraverted and girls saw themselves as introverted.
  c.   emotional stability was the most frequently used construct.
  d.   little evidence exists for the concept of the Big Five personality dimensions

d   75.   Watson and Watts (2001) found that the Rep test was a useful instrument for identifying
  a.   extraversion.
  b.   intelligence.
  c.   adherence to a weight-loss program.
  d.   neuroticism.

c   76.   James and Large studied people with chronic pain using a special version of the Rep test and found that
  a.   people suffering chronic pain tended to be extraverted.
  b.   friends of people suffering chronic pain were usually unaware of their friend's pain.
  c.   friends of people with chronic pain saw the pain as more central to their friend's life than did the person with chronic pain.
  d.   both a and b are correct.

d   77.   As a scientific theory, Kelly's psychology of constructs is rated highest on its
           a.   ability to organize knowledge.
           b.   ability to generate research.
           c.   ability to guide action.
           d.   internal consistency.

a   78.   Kelly's view of personality was essentially
           a.   optimistic.
           b.   pessimistic.
           c.   deterministic.
           d.   causal.
           e.   biological.

CHAPTER 16
ROGERS: PERSON-CENTERED THEORY

ESSAY QUESTIONS

1. Describe Rogers's concepts of the formative and actualizing tendencies.

   A. Rogers's first basic assumption is that all matter, both organic and inorganic, tends to evolve from simpler to more complex forms. This tendency is the formative tendency.
   B. More important to humans is the actualizing tendency. Humans share this tendency with both the plant and animal kingdoms. The actualizing tendency assumes that all living things, including humans, move toward completion or fulfillment of potentials.
   C. Because humans possess an actualizing tendency, the source of psychological growth resides within the individual.
   D. Although people have a variety of needs, all their behavior is relative to the single actualizing tendency. The organism operates as a whole in moving toward actualization.
   E. Even though actualization is a natural condition of humans, people do not automatically move in that direction; that is, actualization can only be realized when people experience a relationship with a congruent or authentic partner who shows them both empathy and unconditional positive regard.
   F. The actualization tendency refers to the organismic experiences of an individual. After the self begins to evolve (during early childhood), people become motivated by self-actualization, or the tendency to actualize the self as perceived in awareness.

2. According to Rogers, what basic needs do people have? Briefly describe each.

   A. Rogers recognized two basic needs that characterize all humans: the need for maintenance and the need for enhancement.
   B. In addition to these two needs, people also have a need for positive regard and a need for positive self-regard.
   C. Maintenance needs include such basic needs as food, air, and safety. Maintenance needs tend to make personality growth difficult because they are designed to maintain the status quo.
   D. Enhancement needs break through maintenance and seek change and growth. Enhancement needs are expressed as curiosity, playfulness, self-exploration, maturation, and friendship.
   E. As the awareness of self begins to emerge, an infant develops the need to be loved and accepted by others. Rogers called this need positive regard. Humans tend to value those experiences that satisfy their needs for love, acceptance, and friendship.
   F. Along with our need for positive regard, we need to think well of our self, a need Rogers called self-regard. If we perceive that others love and accept us, then this perception tends to satisfy our need of self-regard as well as for positive regard. However, positive regard is a prerequisite for positive self-regard.

3.   Discuss the necessary and sufficient conditions for psychological growth, as
        postulated by Rogers.

   A. Rogers believed that for therapeutic growth to take place, certain conditions
       are necessary, three of which are both necessary and sufficient.
   B. For therapeutic growth to take place, an anxious or vulnerable person must
       come into contact with a congruent person who demonstrates empathy and
       unconditional positive regard for the first person. The first person must
       recognize the empathy and unconditional positive regard of the other
       person. In addition, the relationship must be of some undetermined duration.
   C. Congruence exists when a person's organismic experiences are matched by an
       awareness of them and by an ability and willingness to openly express these
       feelings. Rogers also use the terms genuine, authentic, and real to express
       this concept.
   D. Positive regard is the need to be liked, prized, loved, or accepted by another,
       and when that need is fulfilled with no strings attached, a person experiences
       unconditional positive regard. Rogers also used the terms nonpossessive
       warmth and acceptance to express unconditional positive regard.
   E. Empathy exists when one person accurately senses the feelings of another
       and is able and willing to communicate these perceptions so that the second
       person feels that the other has entered into his or her world of feelings
       without prejudice or evaluation. Rogers also used the term empathic listening
       to express this concept.

MULTIPLE CHOICE QUESTIONS

d   *4.   Carl Rogers is best known as
           a. a philosopher of science.
           b. the first president of the American Psychological Association.
           c. the originator of the first projective technique of personality assessment.
           d. the founder of client-centered therapy.

a   5.   Rogers's theory of personality has evolved out of
           a. his experiences as a client-centered therapist.
           b. his training in the physical and biological sciences.
           c. his period of education at Union Theological Seminary.
           d. the philosophical influence of John Dewey.

b   6.   As a young child, Rogers
           a. was closer to his father than to his mother.
           b. was shy and lonely.
           c. was greatly admired by family and friends.
           d. aspired to become a psychologist.

a   7.   "I lived my childhood as a middle child in a large, close-knit family, where hard
          work and a highly conservative (almost fundamentalist) Protestant Christianity
          were about equally revered. When the family moved to a farm at the time I was
          twelve, I became deeply interested and involved in scientific agriculture." The
          author of this quote is
          a.   Carl Rogers.
          b.   Gordon Allport.
          c.   Harry Stack Sullivan.
          d.   A. H. Maslow.
          e.   Rollo May.

a   8.   Before entering Columbia University to study psychology and education, Carl
          Rogers had planned to become
          a.   a minister.
          b.   a lawyer.
          c.   an actor.
          d.   a psychiatrist.
          e.   a football coach.

e   9.   During the early phase of his counseling career, Rogers was influenced by the
          practice, but not the theory, of
          a.   John Dewey.
          b.   Sigmund Freud.
          c.   Alfred Adler.
          d.   A. H. Maslow.
          e.   Otto Rank.

d   10.   As an adult, Rogers realized that his parents
          a.   were not as religious as he had earlier believed.
          b.   would have fit his concept of the persons of tomorrow.
          c.   were more understanding and less judgmental than he had believed.
          d.   had nearly disowned him when he broke from their religious beliefs.

a   11.   Rogers's early approach to therapy was most influenced by
          a.   Otto Rank.
          b.   Sigmund Freud.
          c.   E. L. Thorndike.
          d.   Alfred Adler.
          e.   Erich Fromm.

d   12.   Rogers's therapeutic approach at the University of Chicago emphasized
          a.   the advantages of a psychoanalytic approach.
          b.   a blend of psychological and psychiatric approaches.
          c.   the use of untrained laymen to treat patients.
          d.   the importance of the therapist-client relationship.
          e.   the use of extensive psychological testing to classify mental disorders.

d   *13. Rogers's approach to therapy is best termed
          a.   nondirective.
          b.   cognitive.
          c.   social learning.
          d.   client-centered.
          e.   rational-emotional.

a   *14. Rogers called the tendency for matter (organic and inorganic) to evolve from
          simpler to more complex forms
          a. the formative tendency.
          b. the actualizing tendency.
          c. self-actualization.
          d. the transcendent function.

a   15. According to Rogers,
          a. everyone possesses the actualizing tendency.
          b. fewer than 5 percent of the population possess the actualizing tendency.
          c. everyone achieves self-actualization.
          d. about half of the population possesses the actualizing tendency.

b   *16. A person's inner abilities to solve problems, alter self-concept, and become
          more self-directed reflect Rogers's concept of
          a. the formative tendency.
          b. the actualizing tendency.
          c. genuineness.
          d. the ideal self.

e   *17. For Rogers, all behavior is relative to the
          a. cognitive self.
          b. ideal self.
          c. genuine self.
          d. formative tendency.
          e. actualizing tendency.

d   18. What condition did Rogers believe must be present in a relationship that leads
          to psychological growth?
          a. genuineness
          b. unconditional acceptance
          c. empathy
          d. all of the above
          e. a and c only

b   *19. Rogers believed that infants evaluate their experiences as positive or negative
          by the criteria of
          a. the formative tendency.
          b. the actualization tendency.
          c. the self-actualization tendency.
          d. the ideal self.
          e. their parents ideals.

e   20. In Rogers's theory, self-actualization is
          a. synonymous with the actualizing tendency.
          b. synonymous with the formative tendency.
          c. a subsystem of the actualizing tendency.
          d. the tendency to actualize the perceived self.
          e. c and d.

b   21.   According to Rogers, a portion of one's experience becomes differentiated into
          a.   the ego.
          b.   a sense of self identity.
          c.   the Imperial Me.
          d.   the phenomenal field.

c   *22. Rogers believed that conflict and inner tension are a result of a discrepancy
          between the
          a.   formative and actualizing tendencies.
          b.   formative and self-actualization tendencies.
          c.   actualizing and self-actualization tendencies.
          d.   ego and ego-ideal.
          e.   ego and superego.

a   23.   According to Rogers, the _____ includes all those aspects of one's being and
          one's experience that are perceived in awareness.
          a.   self-concept
          b.   ideal-self
          c.   real self
          d.   organismic self
          e.   imaginary self

b   24.   According to Rogers, the two subsystems of the self are the
          a.   ego and the superego.
          b.   self-concept and the ideal self.
          c.   self-system and the real self.
          d.   proprium and the ego.

d   25.   Rogers said that an established self-concept
          a.   facilitates psychological growth.
          b.   is usually congruent with the organismic self.
          c.   is ordinarily more inflated than the ideal self.
          d.   makes change and growth difficult.

d   26.   According to Rogers, experiences inconsistent with one's self-concept are
          a.   readily accepted into the self-concept.
          b.   often denied.
          c.   often accepted only in distorted forms.
          d.   b and c.
          e.   none of the above.

c   27.   For Rogers, the ideal self
          a.   includes the formative tendency.
          b.   is the ultimate goal of the actualizing tendency.
          c.   is defined as one's view of self as one would like to be.
          d.   all of the above.

b   *28. Rogers claimed that incongruence exists when a person
          a.   lacks empathy.
          b.   experiences a discrepancy between self-concept and ideal self.
          c.   lacks the ability to actualize the formative tendency.
          d.   receives a minimal level of external evaluation.

a   29. According to Rogers, for a psychologically healthy person,
         a. there is a close agreement between ideal self and perceived self
         b. the organismic self learns to be consistent with the self concept.
         c. the ideal self remains on a higher level than the organismic self.
         d. there is a wide gap between the ideal self and the perceived self.

a   30. "The symbolic representation (not necessarily in verbal symbols) of some
         portion of our experience" is Rogers's definition of
         a. awareness.
         b. the actualizing tendency.
         c. the formative tendency.
         d. self-actualization.

c   31. Rogers believed that when organismic experiences are incongruent with one's
         self-concept, a person will
         a. change the self-concept.
         b. sublimate the experience.
         c. experience anxiety and guilt.
         d. actualize the self.

c   *32. Mitzi has just been complimented by Laura for her cooking. Mitzi regards
          herself as a very mediocre cook. According to Rogerian theory, Laura's
          remarks will
          a. be easily accepted into Mitzi's self-concept.
          b. alter Mitzi's organismic self.
          c. be distorted by Mitzi.
          d. allow Mitzi to experience some congruence.
          e. be repressed by Mitzi.

c   33. Rogers said that evaluations of a person by others tend to
         a. be readily incorporated into the person's self-concept.
         b. enhance change and growth.
         c. distort the person's self-concept.
         d. have a positive influence on the self-concept.

d   *34. According to Rogers, compliments and positive feedback
          a. almost always enhance a person's self-concept.
          b. seldom have a positive influence on self-concept.
          c. may be denied or distorted by the person receiving them
          d. b and c.
          e. none of the above.

e   *35. Rogers postulated two basic needs:
          a.   food and sex.
          b. security and safety.
          c. self-actualization and self-esteem.
          d. consciousness and unconsciousness.
          e. none of the above.

a 36. According to Rogers, the tendency of the person to resist change and to seek the status quo illustrates _____ needs.
 a. maintenance
 b. enhancement
 c. actualizing
 d. formative
 e. positive regard

b 37. Rogers saw curiosity, self-exploration, and playfulness as
 a. maintenance needs.
 b. enhancement needs.
 c. self-regard.
 d. positive regard.
 e. conditions of worth.

b 38. According to Rogers, _____ is a person's need to be loved, liked, or accepted by another person.
 a. enhancement
 b. positive regard
 c. social reinforcement
 d. empathy
 e. conditions of worth

a *39. Rogers believed that people's positive self-regard
 a. can exist independently of other people's attitudes toward them.
 b. depends on other people's continual positive attitude toward them.
 c. depends on other people's continual negative attitude toward them.
 d. blocks their growth toward self-actualization.

a *40. For Rogers, the source of people's positive self-regard is
 a. other people's positive regard toward them.
 b. outstanding personal achievements.
 c. the conditions of worth they receive from others.
 d. a pattern of successfully responding to other's criticisms.

b 41. Lauren perceives another person's evaluation her. Rogers believed that Lauren will
 a. deny the evaluation.
 b. experience conditions of worth.
 c. learn something of value from the experience.
 d. develop unconditional positive regard for that person.

b 42. Rogers believed that healthy individuals evaluate their experience from the viewpoint of
 a. their ideal self.
 b. their organismic self.
 c. significant others.
 d. their self-concept.
 e. society.

d   *43. According to Rogers, when the self and experience are congruent, a person
        a. experiences conditions of worth.
        b. becomes overly suspicious of others.
        c. becomes self-centered.
        d. experiences psychological adjustment.

a   44. According to Rogers, positive external evaluations
        a. do not foster psychological health.
        b. enhance the organismic self.
        c. minimize incongruence.
        d. lead to satisfaction of the actualization tendency.
        e. none of the above

b   45. To Rogers, the basic ingredient of maladjustment is
        a. repressed sexual experiences.
        b. a discrepancy between the organismic self and the perceived self.
        c. a low expectation of success.
        d. an approach-avoidance conflict.
        e. insecurity.

c   *46. According to Rogers, when people are unaware of the discrepancy between their
        self and their experience they become
        a. anxious.
        b. threatened.
        c. vulnerable.
        d. apathetic.

c   47. When a person becomes vaguely aware that the discrepancy between
        experience and self may become conscious, Rogers said that he or she
        will develop a feeling of
        a. congruence.
        b. negative self-regard.
        c. anxiety.
        d. vulnerability.

b   *48. According to Rogers, the two most frequent defensive reactions are
        a. repression and regression.
        b. denial and distortion.
        c. repression and sublimation.
        d. withdrawal and aggression.
        e. fixation and regression.

a   49. The misinterpretation of an experience in order to make it fit some aspect of
        one's self-concept matches Rogers's concept of
        a. distortion.
        b. denial.
        c. sublimating tendency.
        d. condition of worth.

d   50.   Disorganization exists, Rogers said, when
    a.   a person becomes overly defensive.
    b.   threat becomes conscious
    c.   threat becomes unconscious.
    d.   normal defenses fail to close the gap between one's experiences and one's view of self.
    e.   negative regard from others becomes conscious.

b   *51   In a state of disorganization, people's behavior may be consistent with their
    a.   actualizing tendency.
    b.   shattered self-concept.
    c.   formative tendency.
    d.   disorganizational tendency.

d   52.   In describing psychological maladjustment, Rogers preferred to speak of it in terms of
    a.   ego defense mechanisms.
    b.   traditional psychological and psychiatric classifications.
    c.   diagnostic labels applied to individuals.
    d.   defensive and disorganized behavior.

b   *53.   Which of these conditions was NOT seen by Rogers as a "necessary and sufficient" ingredient in therapeutic growth?
    a.   empathy
    b.   problem solving
    c.   unconditional positive regard
    d.   counselor congruence

c   54.   Rogers's basic assumption in therapy was that
    a.   people will move toward self-actualization when they understand the reasons for their behavior.
    b.   people become psychologically adjusted when they solve their sexual conflicts.
    c.   psychological growth is enhanced when clients receive empathy and unconditional positive regard from a congruent therapist.
    d.   anxiety and threat must be extinguished before psychological growth can take place.

c   55.   Rogers believed the most basic condition for psychological growth is
    a.   conditions of worth.
    b.   self-regard.
    c.   congruence.
    d.   unconditional positive regard.

b   56.   To Rogers, congruent people are
    a.   adjusted to their environment.
    b.   aware of their feelings and are able to express them.
    c.   not adjusted to their environment.
    d.   unmotivated.

a   57.   Rogers stated that therapists will be more effective if they communicate
          _____ to the client.
          a.   all genuine feelings
          b.   only positive genuine feelings
          c.   only negative genuine feelings
          d.   conditions of worth
          e.   b and d

b   58.   Rogers believed that the successful therapist
          a.   must be congruent in all human relationships.
          b.   must be congruent in the counseling relationship.
          c   should withhold negative feelings toward clients.
          d.   will have a Ph.D. in clinical psychology.

a   *59. According to Rogers, when therapists experience "a warm, positive and
          acceptance attitude toward what is the client" they
          a.   have unconditional positive regard for that client.
          b.   experience conditions of worth toward that client.
          c.   demonstrate feelings of empathy for that client.
          d.   possess positive self-regard for that client.

c   60.   Rogers would say that unconditional positive regard is at greatest variance with
          a.   prizing.
          b.   nonpossessive warmth.
          c.   external evaluation.
          d.   love.

d   61.   According to Rogers, which of these conditions would be MOST therapeutic?
          a.   sympathy
          b.   advice
          c.   conditions of worth
          d.   empathy
          e.   diagnosis

c   *62. For Rogers, empathy is an effective part of therapy because it
          a.   actualizes the formative tendency.
          b.   enhances conditions of worth.
          c.   enables clients to listen to their organismic self.
          d.   activates the ideal self.
          e.   facilitates adaptive incongruence.

a   63.   Rogers held that if certain therapeutic conditions are present, then people will
          a.   move toward psychological growth.
          b.   experience anxiety and fear.
          c.   be free of anxiety and fear.
          d.   experience incongruence between self and ideal self.

c   64.   What stage of Rogers's therapeutic process is characterized by avoidance of
          present feelings and a discussion limited to past or future emotions?
          a.   1st
          b.   2nd
          c.   3rd
          d.   6th
          e.   7th

b   65.   According to Rogers's view of the therapeutic process, psychological growth
          appears to be irreversible at the _____ stage.
          a. 7th
          b. 6th
          c. 5th
          d. 4th

a   66.   Rogers believed that after client-centered counseling is successful, clients
          ideally will
          a. become their own therapists.
          b. solve their interpersonal problems.
          c. experience conditions of worth.
          d. understand the reasons for their illness.
          e. extinguish fear and anxiety responses.

c   67.   Rogers referred to the tendency for the person of tomorrow to live in the
          present moment as
          a. self-actualization.
          b. positive regard.
          c. existential living.
          d. transcendence of time.

b   *68. Which of these is NOT characteristic of Rogers's "person of tomorrow?"
          a. openness to experience
          b. trust in others
          c. constant state of change
          d. harmonious relations with others

b   69.   Which term is LEAST appropriate as applied to Carl Rogers?
          a. scientist
          b. philosopher
          c. researcher
          d. therapist
          e. theorist

d   70.   In his philosophy of science, Rogers argued that methodology must be
          a. intuitive.
          b. subjective.
          c. resacralized.
          d. objective.

b   71.   The research on the effectiveness of client-centered therapy reported by
          Rogers and Dymond indicated that after therapy, clients
          a. showed greater discrepancy between self and ideal self.
          b. showed more movement toward growth than did a matched group of
              control participants.
          c. were more psychologically healthy than a matched group of
              control participants.
          d. all of the above.

a   72. In studies of the relationship between self and ideal self, Rogers found that
          a. psychologically healthy people show little discrepancy between their ideal self and real self.
          b. paranoid schizophrenic patients showed little discrepancy between self and ideal self.
          c. the real self is seldom rated higher than the ideal self.
          d. the ideal self is never rated higher than the real self.

d   73. In general, the Chicago studies demonstrated that client-centered therapy
          a. is ineffective.
          b. tends to produce a fully-functioning person.
          c. is more effective than psychoanalysis.
          d. resulted in some long-term positive growth for some clients.

a   *74. Duncan Cramer has tested Rogers's facilitative conditions in interpersonal relationships outside of therapy and has generally found that these facilitative conditions
          a. are positively related to self-esteem.
          b. are negatively related to self-esteem.
          c. are unrelated to self-esteem.
          d. are necessary in parent–child relationships, but not in husband–wife relationships.
          e. promote psychological disturbance in parent–child relationships.

b   75. The Barrett-Lennard Relationship Inventory measures these facilitative conditions: congruence, empathy,
          a. and unconditional acceptance.
          b. level or regard, and unconditionality of regard.
          c. and nonpossessive warmth.
          d. ego-centeredness, and level of esteem.

d   *76. In 1996, Alfons Vansteenwegen used Rogers's facultative conditions to investigate changes in couples who received client-centered therapy. The results suggested that
          a. men developed positive regard toward their partners whereas women developed negative regard toward their partners.
          b. partners showed initial improvement but lost all gains after one year.
          c. partners demonstrated significant early improvement but lost all gains after six years.
          d. partners demonstrated significant increases in positive regard, congruence, and empathy.

c   77. Rogers's concept of humanity is basically
          a. deterministic and pessimistic.
          b. biological.
          c. positive and optimistic.
          d. idealistic.

CHAPTER 17
MASLOW: HOLISTIC-DYNAMIC THEORY

ESSAY QUESTIONS

1. List and explain four assumptions Maslow made about motivation.

    A. Maslow's theory of personality is largely a theory about motivation. His first assumption was that the whole person—not separate parts—is motivated.
    B. Second, Maslow assumed that motivation is usually complex, stemming from several needs at the same time. In addition, some needs are at least partially unconscious so that people are not always aware of why they behave as they do.
    C. Maslow also assumed that everyone is continually motivated by one need or another. As one need is satisfied, another need gains ascendancy and replaces the first need.
    D. Fourth, people everywhere are motivated by the same basic needs. Although the manner in which people in different cultures express their needs, the fundamental needs for food, safety, friendship, esteem, and self-actualization are the same for everyone.

2. List and explain the five needs in Maslow's hierarchy.

    A. Maslow assumed that needs can be ordered on a hierarchy and that low level needs must be satisfied or at least partially satisfied before higher level needs become motivators. In order of their prepotency, these needs are (1) physiological, (2) safety, (3) love and belongingness, (4) esteem, and (5) self-actualization.
    B. Physiological needs are the most basic and occupy the bottom step on Maslow's hierarchy. These needs include the need for food, water, oxygen, maintenance of body temperature, and so on. When people do not have their physiological needs satisfied, they are motivated only by those needs. A starving person is not interested in love or esteem.
    C. After physiological needs are at least partially satisfied, people become motivated to secure safety. Safety needs include physical security, stability, protection, and freedom from danger and chaos. Young children sometimes have difficulty satisfying safety needs because they imagine danger when it is not present. People who do not adequately satisfy safety needs suffer from basic anxiety.
    D. Perhaps the needs that blocks most people from psychological growth are the love and belongingness needs. People who have love and belongingness needs only partially satisfied will strive almost continually to meet these needs. On the other hand, people who have never tasted love and belongingness, as well as people who fulfill these needs, are not strongly motivated to be loved and accepted.
    E. To the extent that people satisfy their love and belongingness needs, they are free to pursue esteem needs. Esteem needs include the need for self-respect, confidence, competence, and the esteem of others. Reputation needs include people's perception of the prestige and recognition that others bestow on them. Self-esteem needs, on the other hand, are based on feelings of competence that are independent of other people's opinions.
    F. As lower needs are met, people advance automatically to the next higher need. However, Maslow believed that it is possible to have esteem needs met

and yet nor reach the level of self-actualization. To be motivated by self-actualization needs, Maslow said, people must not only have their lower needs relatively well satisfied, but they must be free from psychopathology and be motivated by such B-values (Being-values) as truth, beauty, justice, wholeness, simplicity, and so on. People who reach self-actualization are in the process of becoming fully human.

3.   Discuss Maslow's concept of conative, aesthetic, cognitive, and neurotic needs.

A. Maslow believed that motivation is quite complex and that people are not only motivated by several needs on the hierarchy but by aesthetic, cognitive, and neurotic needs as well.
B. Needs on the hierarchy are called conative needs.
C. Aesthetic needs do not seem to be universal, and some people are motivated more by the need for beauty and aesthetically pleasing experiences than are others. Aesthetic needs, like conative needs, can lead to pathology when they are not adequately met. People living in ugly, disorderly environments feel a kind of spiritual illness, Maslow said.
D. Cognitive needs include the needs to know, to solve mysteries, to understand, and to be curious. The frustration of cognitive needs, like the thwarting of other needs, leads to a kind of pathology. When people cannot search for the truth and feel that they are constantly lied to, they become sick, resulting in paranoia and depression. The satisfaction of cognitive needs is also necessary for the pursuit of the conative needs.
E. Neurotic needs differ from the previous three dimensions of needs in that they lead to pathology regardless of whether they are satisfied. For example, a person with sadistic needs is pathological if he finds a partner to torture, and he is sick if he cannot find such a partner.

MULTIPLE CHOICE QUESTIONS

b   *4.   Maslow did more than any other psychologist to popularize the notion of
         a.   the formative tendency.
         b.   self-actualization.
         c.   holism.
         d.   transcendence.
         e.   social interest.

d   5.   If Maslow is the father of the third force in psychology, then the first two forces are
         a.   Jung and Freud.
         b.   Freud and Adler.
         c.   psychoanalysis and Freud.
         d.   behaviorism and psychoanalysis.
         e.   hierarchy of needs and self-actualization.

d   6.   Maslow criticized both psychoanalysis and behaviorism for their
         a.   overemphasis on unconscious motivation.
         b.   inability to successfully treat neurosis.
         c.   unscientific viewpoints on personality
         d.   limited view of humanity.

a   *7.   As a college student, Maslow experienced which fortuitous event that changed
           his life?
           a. He kissed his first cousin Bertha Goodman.
           b. He came close to death after being stoned by an anti-Semitic gang of men.
           c. He met Karen Horney at an APA convention.
           d. He converted to Catholicism.

a   8.   As a child, Maslow
           a. felt ugly, inferior, and depressed.
           b. felt closer to his mother than to his father.
           c. was deeply religious and aspired to become a rabbi.
           d. was both athletic and popular.

a   9.   Maslow's feelings toward his mother were marked by
           a. hatred and animosity.
           b. affection and respect.
           c. a clinging dependence.
           d. indifference.
           e. B-love.

c   10.   As a student at Wisconsin, Maslow worked closely with
           a. Carl Rogers.
           b. Raymond Cattell.
           c. Harry Harlow.
           d. Julian Rotter.
           e. Gordon Allport.

a   11.   The destruction wrought by World War II moved Maslow to devote his life to
           the study of the
           a. best in human beings.
           b. prevention of war.
           c. most effective psychological treatments for veterans.
           d. biological sources of human aggression.

e   12.   Maslow adopted the _____ approach to motivation.
           a. dualistic
           b. homeostatic
           c. philosophical
           d. deterministic
           e. holistic

d   *13. Maslow assumed that
           a. motivation is usually complex.
           b. people are continually motivated by one need or another.
           c. people in different cultures are motivated by the same basic needs or desires.
           d. all of the above.

c   *14. Which of the following is NOT an assumption underlying Maslow's theory
           of motivation?
           a. People are continually motivated by one need or another.
           b. Unconscious forces lie behind much surface motivation.
           c. People in different cultures have different basic needs.
           d. Human needs can be arranged on a hierarchy.
           e. The whole person is motivated as a unit.

a   *15. In Maslow's hierarchy of needs concept,
         a. lower level needs have prepotency over higher level needs.
         b. higher level needs have prepotency over lower level needs.
         c. esteem needs must be satisfied before love and belongingness needs become motivators.
         d. aesthetic needs must be satisfied before cognitive needs become motivators.

c   16. The most basic needs in Maslow's hierarchy are
         a. self-actualization needs.
         b. cognitive needs.
         c. physiological needs.
         d. love and belongingness needs.

d   17. Each ascending step in Maslow's hierarchy of needs represents
         a. a lower need, but one less basic to survival.
         b. a higher need, but one more basic to survival.
         c. a lower need, but one more basic to survival .
         d. a higher need, but one less basic to survival.

a   *18. According to Maslow, a woman whose physiological needs are inadequately satisfied will be motivated to
         a. satisfy physiological needs.
         b. satisfy safety needs.
         c. find companionship.
         d. satisfy esteem needs.
         e. become self-actualizing.

d   19. Maslow held that physiological needs differ from other needs in that they
         a. can be completely satisfied.
         b. can be overly satisfied.
         c. have a recurring nature.
         d. all of the above.

b   *20. Maslow claimed that safety needs are most likely to be strong motivators for
         a. hungry people.
         b. children.
         c. self-actualizing people.
         d. people who are having trouble making friends.
         e. coal miners.

b   21. Maslow classified the needs for law, order, and structure as _____ needs.
         a. physiological
         b. safety
         c. neurotic
         d. meta
         e. transcendent

c   22. Maslow claimed that safety needs differ from physiological needs in that they
         a. are the most prepotent set of needs.
         b. represent B-values.
         c. cannot be overly satiated.
         d. are metamotivated.
         e. b and d.

b   *23. According to Maslow, an individual's inability to satisfy safety needs results in
     a. metamotivation.
     b. basic anxiety.
     c. peak experiences.
     d. autonomy.
     e. expressive behavior.

b   *24. Maslow claimed that love and belongingness needs are strongest in people who have
     a. never experienced love and belongingness.
     b. partially experienced love and belongingness.
     c. their love and belongingness needs satisfied.
     d. their self-actualization needs satisfied.

e   *25. Maslow contended that people who have never received love
     a. suffer from basic anxiety.
     b. revert to satisfying more prepotent needs.
     c. seek it to the exclusion of all other needs.
     d. substitute it with aesthetic needs.
     e. may eventually devalue it.

e   26. According to Maslow, when people's esteem needs are relatively well satisfied, they will
     a. become motivated by physiological needs.
     b. automatically become motivated by self-actualization needs.
     c. become motivated by B-love.
     d. seek a D-love relationship with at least one other person.
     e. none of the above.

c   *27. Maslow included the needs for self-respect, confidence, competence, and the respect of others as
     a. safety needs.
     b. love and belongingness needs.
     c. esteem needs.
     d. neurotic needs.

e   28. Maslow claimed that when people who have satisfied their esteem needs are criticized or deprecated by others
     a. they revert to the level of love and belongingness needs.
     b. their safety needs become prepotent.
     c. their neurotic needs are activated.
     d. they cannot satisfy needs for self-actualization.
     e. they retain their sense of self-worth.

b   29. Maslow found that self-actualization needs become potent when
     a. love and belongingness needs have been met.
     b. B-values are embraced.
     c. neurotic needs are satisfied.
     d. all of the above.

b   *30. The needs in Maslow's hierarchy of needs are _____ needs.
           a. cognitive
           b. conative
           c. neurotic
           d. aesthetic

b   31. According to Maslow, a person surrounded by beauty and order would
           ordinarily satisfy
           a. cognitive needs.
           b. aesthetic needs.
           c. conative needs.
           d. esteem needs.
           e. physiological needs.

c   32. Maslow said that when cognitive needs are not satisfied, a person will become
           a. motivated by conative needs.
           b. motivated by love and belongingness needs.
           c. pathological.
           d. self-actualizing.
           e. a college professor.

c   *33. In Maslow's theory of needs, people become neurotic
           a. when they satisfy their neurotic needs.
           b. when they do not satisfy their neurotic needs.
           c. regardless of whether they satisfy their neurotic needs.
           d. after they have reached self-actualization.

b   34. According to Maslow, neurotic needs
           a. decrease as they are satisfied.
           b. cannot be fully satiated.
           c. can be self-actualizing.
           d. foster health when satisfied.
           e. both a and d.

c   35. Martyrs who sacrifice physical needs and personal safety for their beliefs, and
           heroes who risk their lives to save others illustrate Maslow's notion of
           a. B-values.
           b. metamotivation.
           c. reversed order of needs.
           d. self-actualization.
           e. neurotic needs.

a   36. Maslow hypothesized that
           a. the order of needs may be reversed in certain cases.
           b. love and belongingness needs must be satisfied more fully than
               physiological needs.
           c. the satisfaction of neurotic needs leads to psychological health.
           d. people must satisfy one need completely before any other need can
               become a motivator.
           e. cognitive needs must be satisfied before conative needs become motivators.

a   37.   Maslow believed that most behavior
           a.   has several causes.
           b.   is aimed at satisfying self-actualization needs.
           c.   is consciously motivated.
           d.   all of the above.

b   38.   Maslow classified behavior that is always motivated and that serves the purpose
           of satisfying a need as _____ behavior.
           a.   expressive
           b.   coping
           c.   neurotic
           d.   actualizing
           e.   Taoistic

b   *39. Maslow believed that all behavior
           a.   is motivated.
           b.   has a cause.
           c.   is motivated and has a cause.
           d.   is neither motivated nor has a cause.

a   40.   According to Maslow, _____ behavior is usually unlearned, spontaneous, and
           determined by forces within the person rather than by the environment.
           a.   expressive
           b.   neurotic
           c.   coping
           d.   actualizing
           e.   Taoistic

d   41.   For Maslow, coping behavior is usually
           a.   learned.
           b.   conscious.
           c.   effortful.
           d.   all of the above.

c   *42. Maslow believed that metapathology results from
           a.   modification of expressive behavior.
           b.   satiation of self-actualization needs.
           c.   deprivation of self-actualization needs.
           d.   adopting a Taoistic attitude.
           e.   transcending peak experiences.

e   *43. According to Maslow, instinctoid needs
           a.   result in pathology when frustrated.
           b.   are common among all mammals.
           c.   can be altered through learning.
           d.   all of the above.
           e.   only a and c are correct.

c   44.   If deprivation of a need leads to pathology, then Maslow would say that
          this need is
          a.   learned.
          b.   physiological.
          c.   instinctoid.
          d.   neurotic.
          e.   unrealistic.

d   45.   Instinctoid needs, Maslow said,
          a.   cannot be modified by learning.
          b.   are learned via secondary reinforcement.
          c.   are usually temporary.
          d.   are often weaker than cultural forces.
          e.   need not be satisfied in order for a person to attain psychological health.

e   46.   Maslow believed that esteem and self-actualization needs
          a.   are instinctoid.
          b.   are biological.
          c.   are later on the evolutionary scale than physiological needs.
          d.   result in pathology when frustrated.
          e.   all of the above are correct.

a   47.   For Maslow, B-values
          a.   are indicators of psychological health.
          b.   motivate people who have conquered the A-values.
          c.   motivate children more frequently than adults.
          d.   are indicators of psychopathology.

c   48.   Metamotivation, according to Maslow,
          a.   is characterized by coping behavior rather than expressive behavior.
          b.   is associated with deficiency needs
          c.   differentiates self-actualizers from non-self-actualizers.
          d.   all of the above.

d   49.   According to Maslow, metamotivation is
          a.   a characteristic of psychotic individuals.
          b.   the need for friendship and acceptance by others.
          c.   a drive to do one's best and to achieve fame.
          d.   the motivation of self-actualizing people.

d   50.   According to Maslow, the 14 B-values
          a.   distinguish self-actualizing people from those healthy people who do
               not reach self-actualization.
          b.   are so highly interrelated that they probably represent a single factor.
          c.   will probably become 20 or 25 in number as people become more
               self-actualizing.
          d.   both a and b are correct.

a   51.   According to Maslow, people who do not embrace the B-values suffer from
          a.   metapathology.
          b.   individuation.
          c.   basic anxiety.
          d.   lack of self-esteem.

d   52.   Maslow suggested that self-actualizers and some neurotic and psychotic individuals may have which of the following characteristics in common?
a.   a heightened sense of reality
b.   mystical experiences
c.   detachment from others
d.   all of the above
e.   none of the above

b   53.   Which of the following was NOT used by Maslow as a criterion for self-actualization?
a.   absence of psychopathology
b.   freedom from personal problems
c.   gratification of lower level needs
d.   acceptance of the B-values

c   54.   Maslow listed four criteria for reaching self-actualization, including
a.   having complete freedom from any type of psychopathology.
b.   achieving total satisfaction of all lower needs.
c.   being motivated by the B-values.
d.   having solved all interpersonal problems.

a   55.   According to Maslow, self-actualizing people are
a.   relatively well satisfied in their basic needs.
b.   more likely to be men than women.
c.   more likely to be young than old.
d.   motivated by deficiency needs.

e   56.   Maslow believed that self-actualizers
a.   frequently engage in wishful thinking.
b.   are relatively indifferent to external reality.
c.   are poor observers of others.
d.   have little tolerance for ambiguity.
e.   none of the above.

c   57.   Maslow believed that self-actualizers
a.   are frequently self-critical.
b.   hold extremely high standards of personal conduct for themselves and others.
c.   are not burdened by undue anxiety or shame.
d.   have a need to instruct, inform, and convert others.

b   58.   According to Maslow, self-actualizing people are characterized by
a.   a strong desire to achieve self-actualization.
b.   spontaneity, simplicity, and naturalness.
c.   a self-centered approach to life's problems.
d.   an intolerance of ambiguity.
e.   defensiveness, seriousness, and extraversion.

b   *59. In Maslow's theory, which of the following is NOT a characteristic of
           self-actualizing people?
           a. self-acceptance
           b. people-centered rather than problem-centered
           c. autonomy
           d. philosophical sense of humor
           e. resistance to enculturation

c   60. Maslow would say that the autonomy of self-actualizers is seen in their
           a. strong desire to lead others.
           b. inability to get along with others.
           c. indifference to criticism or flattery.
           d. lack of close friends.

a   *61. Maslow held that a self-actualizing person is likely to
           a: feel comfortable when alone.
           b. demand complexity and variety in life.
           c. depend on others for the satisfaction of esteem needs.
           d. value means rather than ends.

c   62. For Maslow, the peak experience
           a. is achieved by all self-actualizers.
           b. can be attained by an act of will.
           c. may occur at unexpected, ordinary moments.
           d. a and b.
           e. b and c.

c   63. Maslow found that self-actualizing people
           a. have a wider circle of friends than other people.
           b. do not enjoy food or sex as much as other people.
           c. are more likely than other people to have peak experiences.
           d. tend to be quite similar to each other.

c   64. Self-actualizers' identification with humanity and genuine interest in helping
           others reflects their
           a. basic anxiety.
           b. needs for love and belongingness.
           c. social interest.
           d. Taoistic attitude.
           e. peak experiences.

a   65. Maslow found that self-actualizers were characterized by
           a. limited but intense and close friendships.
           b. extensive but superficial friendships.
           c. a great number of deep, intimate relationships.
           d. extensive personal friendships with neurotic individuals.

b   66. Maslow believed that time and space disorientation, a decrease in self and
           ego-consciousness, and the transcendence of everyday polarities frequently
           occur during
           a. self-actualization.
           b. peak experiences.
           c. metapathology.
           d. desacralization.

e 67. Maslow believed that self-actualizers are relatively unaware of superficial differences among people of different ages, genders, or social classes. This lack of awareness reflects their
   a. efficient perception of reality.
   b. conative needs.
   c. discrimination between means and ends.
   d. peak experiences.
   e. democratic character structure.

a 68. According to Maslow, the humor of self-actualizers is
   a. intrinsic to the situation.
   b. well-planned.
   c. hostile.
   d. all of the above.
   e. only a and c are correct.

a 69. Maslow claimed that self-actualizers' ability to detach from their surroundings and to transcend any particular society is characteristic of their
   a. resistance to enculturation.
   b. metapathology.
   c. peak experiences.
   d. philosophical sense of humor.

b *70. For Maslow, B-love is
   a. a result of peak experiences.
   b. unmotivated, expressive behavior.
   c. motivated by the desire to possess another.
   d. a source of anxiety.

d 71. In Maslow's terminology, D-love is _____ love.
   a. defeated
   b. destructive
   c. determined
   d. deficiency
   e. delightful

b 72. Which of these items on the Personal Orientation Inventory is most likely to be endorsed by a self-actualizing person?
   a. "I feel uncomfortable with anything less than a perfect performance."
   b. "My moral values are self-determined."
   c. "Two people will get along best if each concentrates on pleasing the other."
   d. "I believe the Federal Government is conspiring against me."

b 73. Several studies have found that when people were instructed to "fake good" or "make a favorable impression" when filling out the Personal Orientation Inventory they scored
   a. in the high range of self-actualization.
   b. in the direction away from self-actualization.
   c. in the neurotic and psychotic range.
   d. within the normal range; the instructions had no effects on their responses.

a   *74. Maslow's Jonah complex is characterized by
        a. the fear of being one's best.
        b. self-love and narcissism.
        c. many peak experiences.
        d. an exaggerated striving for superiority.
        e. an insatiable desire for seafood.

d   75. Maslow suggested that people tend to avoid growth and self-fulfillment due to
        a. physical limitations of the body.
        b. the necessity for humility.
        c. the Jonah complex.
        d. all of the above.

b   76. According to Maslow, most people who seek therapy probably have the most
        trouble satisfying their _____ needs.
        a. safety
        b. love and belongingness
        c. esteem
        d. self-actualization
        e. aesthetic

c   77. Maslow believed that the impulse toward growth and self-actualization
        a. is characteristic of animals as well as humans.
        b. is the result of courage and determination.
        c. is a natural characteristic of humans.
        d. is usually thwarted by the satisfaction of metaneeds.

b   *78. Maslow contended that scientists should _____ science.
        a. desacralize
        b. resacralize
        c. ignore
        d. venerate

a   79. Michael Sheffield and colleagues found several scales on the Personal
        Orientation Inventory were
        a. negatively related to interpersonal problems.
        b. positively related to extraversion and anxiety.
        c. negatively related to introversion and ego strength.
        d. positively related to dominance and persistence.

d   80. Mark Runco and colleagues found that _____ was an important aspect of
        self-actualization.
        a. independence
        b. extraversion
        c. dominance
        d. creativity

b   81. Sumerlin and Bundrick studied homeless men and found that _____ was
        positively related to self-actualization.
        a. dependence
        b. self-acceptance
        c. low self-esteem
        d. a need for safety

a   82.   In general, studies using the POI and the Short Index of the POI have found
          that self-actualizing people usually
          a.   have high self-esteem.
          b.   are low in creativity.
          c.   lack close interpersonal relationships.
          d.   all of the above.

b   83.   Maslow's methods of investigation and approach to studying
          self-actualizing people
          a.   are seen as a model of scientific psychology.
          b.   are subject to severe criticism.
          c.   make replication of his original studies very easy.
          d.   a and c.
          e.   none of the above.

b   84.   In his concept of humanity, Maslow insisted that people
          a.   are inherently evil but can overcome their basic nature through productive
               interpersonal relationships.
          b.   have the basic potential for improvement and growth.
          c.   can be placed on a hierarchy, with some individuals being innately superior
               to others.
          d.   have the same needs as all other animals.

CHAPTER 18
MAY: EXISTENTIAL PSYCHOLOGY

ESSAY QUESTIONS

1. List several common assumptions found among most existentialists.
    A. The basic assumption of existentialism is that existence precedes essence; that is, existence takes precedence over essence. Existence is associated with growth and change; essence signifies stagnation and a final product.
    B. Second, existentialism assumes the unity of subject and object. A person is neither completely subjective nor completely objective. A human relationship is an I-thou relationship rather than an I-you or me-you relationship. The I-thou relationship means that both people are both subject and object.
    C. Third, people search for meaning to their lives. They ask such questions as "Who am I?" and "What does life mean?"
    D. A fourth assumption of existentialism is that each person is ultimately responsible for who he or she is. With this responsibility comes the freedom to choose and to make of ourselves whatever we can.
    E. Existentialism is basically antitheoretical. Theories tend to dehumanize people and render them as objects. Authentic experience takes precedence over artificial and theoretical explanations.

2. Define and explain being-in-the-world and nonbeing.

    A. The basic unity of person and environment is expressed by the term *Dasein*, meaning "to exist there" or, as it is usually expressed, "being- in-the-world." Modern civilization has led to people feeling isolated and alienated from both self and the world. As a result, people feel (1) separation from nature, (2) a lack of meaningful interpersonal relations, and (3) alienation from their own authentic self. Thus, three modes of the world characterize people in their being-in-the-world: *Umwelt*, *Mitwelt*, and *Eigenwelt*.
    B. *Umwelt* refers to the world around us; it is the world of objects and things, of nature and natural law. We cannot escape *Umwelt* and must learn to live in the world around us.
    C. *Mitwelt* refers to our world shared *with* another person. To become authentic, we must live in *Mitwelt*; that is, we must relate to other people as people and not as things. To live in *Mitwelt* means to accept and respect all people, not just those who are close to us.
    D. *Eigenwelt* refers to our relationship with our self. It means to be aware of our self as a human being and to accept who we are. Psychologically healthy people live in all three worlds simultaneously.
    E. Nonbeing or nothingness refers to the dread of losing our existence. Death is but one way of losing one's existence. Nonbeing is also seen in addiction to drugs, promiscuous sexual activity, and other compulsive behaviors.

3.   List and define the four forms of love, as seen by Rollo May.

    A. May identified four kinds of love in Western tradition: (1) sex, (2) eros, (3) philia, and (4) agape.
    B. Sex is a biological function that can be satisfied through release of sexual tension. May believed that sex has become cheapened in modern Western societies and is the source of much of our anxiety.
    C. Eros should not be confused with sex. Whereas sex is a physiological need that seeks gratification through the release of tension, eros is a psychological desire that seeks procreation or creation through an enduring union with a loved one.
    D. Philia provides a foundation for eros. It is an intimate nonsexual friendship between two people. Philia takes time to grow. The slowly evolving love between siblings or lifelong friends is an example of philia.
    E. Agape is the unconditional esteem or concern for another person. It is an altruistic love that demands nothing in return. It is a kind of spiritual love, as the love of God for humanity.

MULTIPLE CHOICE QUESTIONS

b 4.   Rollo May was the foremost spokesperson for the _____ approach to psychology in the United States.
    a. humanistic
    b. existential
    c. psychoanalytic
    d. transpersonal
    e. nomothetic

c *5. May's approach to understanding people is based primarily on his
    a. religious faith.
    b. scientific research.
    c. clinical experience.
    d. personal psychoanalysis.
    e. experiences in World War II.

e *6. According to May, healthy people
    a. challenge their destiny.
    b. cherish their freedom.
    c. deny the inevitability of death.
    d. all of the above.
    e. a and b only.

d 7.   May's childhood was marked by
    a. closeness to both parents.
    b. parental emphasis on educational achievements.
    c. a particularly loving relationship with his mother.
    d. parental arguments and family strife.

d   8.   As a young man, Rollo May, like Erik Erikson,
           a.   had a personal analysis with Anna Freud.
           b.   became friends with Sigmund Freud.
           c.   was strongly influenced by Alfred Adler.
           d.   traveled through Europe as a wandering artist.
           e.   had a strong desire to become a minister.

a   9.   May was influenced by Søren Kierkegaard's view of anxiety as a struggle against
           a.   nonbeing.
           b.   destiny.
           c.   fate.
           d.   intentionality.

d   10.   May was critical of
           a.   the antiscientific views of some existentialists.
           b.   attempts to dilute existential psychology into a painless method of
                psychological self-help.
           c.   Carl Rogers's views on the nature of human evil.
           d.   all of the above

a   11.   Modern existential psychology has roots in the writings of
           a.   Søren Kierkegaard.
           b.   Friedrick Nietzche.
           c.   Martin Heidegger.
           d.   Jean-Paul Sartre.

d   *12.   Kierkegaard emphasized an equilibrium between
           a.   action and nonaction.
           b.   fear and courage.
           c.   love and hate.
           d.   freedom and responsibility.

e   *13.   From an existential perspective, people acquire freedom of action
           a.   through expanding their self-awareness.
           b.   by assuming responsibility for their actions.
           c.   by minimizing the anxiety associated with their actions.
           d.   all of the above.
           e.   a and b only.

d   14.   From an existential perspective, as people realize that they are in charge of
           their own destiny, they experience the
           a.   fear of failure.
           b.   burden of freedom.
           c.   pain of responsibility.
           d.   b and c.

a   *15.   Most existentialists believe that
           a.   existence takes precedence over essence.
           b.   nonbeing takes precedence over being.
           c.   subject and object must not be divided.
           d.   life has no meaning other than pleasure.

d 16. For May, "the endeavor to understand [people] by cutting below the cleavage between subject and object" defines
    a. existence.
    b. essence.
    c. authenticity.
    d. existentialism.
    e. anxiety.

b 17. Basically, existentialists believe that theories
    a. are essential for understanding people.
    b. render individuals into objects.
    c. increase the authenticity of the individual's experience.
    d. all of the above.

a 18. Two basic concepts of existentialism are
    a. being-in-the-world and nonbeing.
    b. normal and neurotic anxiety.
    c. subject and object.
    d. reality and illusion.

c 19. Existentialists adopt a _____ approach to understanding humanity.
    a. historical
    b. scientific
    c. phenomenological
    d. religious
    e. common-sense

a *20. According to May, the essential unity of the person and environment is called
    a. *Dasein.*
    b. *Umwelt.*
    c. *Mitwelt.*
    d. *Eigenwelt.*

d 21. For existentialists, studying people from an external view
    a. is superior to studying people from an internal frame of reference.
    b. tends to decrease alienation.
    c. results in the most complete understanding of the individual's experience.
    d. violates both the people and their worlds.

c 22. Existentialists believe that most people in modern societies experience alienation due to a separation of
    a. body from soul.
    b. child from mother.
    c. self from the world.
    d. body from mind.

d 23. People's feelings of self-isolation and alienation from the world are seen in their
    a. separation from nature.
    b. lack of meaningful interpersonal relationships.
    c. alienation from authentic self.
    d. all of the above

d   *24. According to May, people's being-in-the-world is characterized by
      a. *Umwelt.*
      b. *Mitwelt.*
      c. *Eigenwelt.*
      d. all of the above.

a   25. May held that *Umwelt* includes the world of
      a. objects and things.
      b. myths.
      c. our relationships with other people
      d. other people's relationships with us.

a   26. Freud's psychoanalytic theory, with its emphasis on biological drives and
      instincts, deals most specifically with
      a. *Umwelt.*
      b. *Mitwelt.*
      c. *Eigenwelt.*
      d. *Dasein.*

b   27. According to May, respecting another's *Dasein* is a condition for living in
      a. *Umwelt.*
      b. *Mitwelt.*
      c. *Eigenwelt.*
      d. none of the above.

b   *28. Theories that emphasize interpersonal relationships deal mostly with which
      aspect of being-in-the-world?
      a. *Umwelt*
      b. *Mitwelt*
      c. *Eigenwelt*
      d. *Dasein*
      e. *Gestalt*

a   *29. According to May, *Eigenwelt* refers to our relationship to
      a. our self.
      b. others.
      c. our body.
      d. the natural world.

c   30. For May, the most obvious avenue of nonbeing is
      a. unconsciousness.
      b. sleep.
      c. death.
      d. self-consciousness.
      e. boredom.

a   *31. According to May, drug addiction, alcohol abuse, promiscuous sexual behavior,
      and other compulsive behaviors can be manifestations of
      a. nonbeing.
      b. destiny.
      c. fate.
      d. intentionality.

d   *32. May believed that we experience _____ when we become aware that our existence or some value identified with it may be destroyed.
    a. guilt
    b. shame
    c. nonbeing
    d. anxiety

d   33. May believed that neurotic anxiety
    a. is disproportionate to the threat.
    b. involves intrapsychic conflict.
    c. is managed by blocking off activity and awareness.
    d. all of the above.

e   34. _____ anxiety "is proportionate to the threat, does not involve repression, and can be confronted constructively on a conscious level," according to May.
    a. Basic
    b. Ontological
    c. Existential
    d. Neurotic
    e. Normal

c   35. May said that neurotic anxiety is experienced when
    a. our values are threatened.
    b. our existence is threatened.
    c. our values are transformed into dogma.
    d. none of the above

a   36. May claimed that, to the extent that anxiety and guilt arise from our being-in-the-world, they are
    a. ontological.
    b. neurotic.
    c. intentional.
    d. teleological.

a   37. May recognized three forms of ontological guilt, each of which corresponds to the three
    a. modes of *Dasein*.
    b. forms of anxiety.
    c. aspects of nonbeing.
    d. forms of love.

d   38. According to May, ontological guilt is experienced
    a. when essence precedes existence.
    b. only by neurotic or psychotic individuals.
    c. only in conjunction with neurotic anxiety.
    d. by most people in one form or another.

a   39. May claimed that members of technologically advanced civilizations are most likely to suffer guilt connected with
    a. *Umwelt*.
    b. *Mitwelt*.
    c. *Eigenwelt*.
    d. *Gestalt*.

b *40. For May, ontological guilt associated with *Mitwelt* arises from our
       a. separation from the natural world.
       b. inability to accurately perceive the world of others.
       c. denial of our own potentials.
       d. failure to fulfill our own potentials.

c 41. According to May, a person's refusal to accept ontological guilt
       a. leads to superior adaptation.
       b. indicates psychological health.
       c. leads to neurotic or morbid guilt.
       d. has no effect on *Dasein*.

a *42. According to May, _____ is the structure that gives meaning to our experience and allows us to make decisions about the future
       a. intentionality
       b. phenomenology
       c. ontology
       d. agape

c 43. For May, the concept of intentionality helps bridge the gap between
       a. health and illness.
       b. life and death.
       c. subject and object.
       d. guilt and shame.

d *44. For May, care is the source of
       a. love.
       b. will.
       c. purpose.
       d. both love and will.

a *45. "A delight in the presence of the other person and an affirmation of his value and development as much as one's own" is May's definition of
       a. love.
       b. care.
       c. empathy.
       d. intentionality.

d 46. May called _____ "the capacity to organize one's self so that movement in a certain direction or toward a certain goal may take place."
       a. intentionality
       b. self-control
       c. mastery
       d. will

d *47. May believed that will
       a. requires self-consciousness.
       b. implies some possibility of an either/or choice.
       c. protects "wish."
       d. all of the above.

a *48. May believed that healthy people
    a. unite love and will.
    b. separate love and will.
    c. strengthen love over will.
    d. strengthen will over love.

e 49. May identified sex, eros, philia, and agape as the
    a. primary sources of ontological guilt.
    b. modes of *Dasein*.
    c. goals of intentionality.
    d. original sources of anxiety.
    e. forms of love.

b 50. For May, the source of humanity's most intense pleasure and its most pervasive anxiety is
    a. care.
    b. sex.
    c. eros.
    d. nonbeing.

b 51. According to May, in North American society, sex is frequently confused with
    a. care.
    b. eros.
    c. pleasure.
    d. philia.

d 52. _____ is the psychological desire that seeks procreation or creation through an enduring union with a loved one, according to May.
    a. Care
    b. Agape
    c. Philia
    d. Eros

a *53. May considered eros the salvation of
    a. sex.
    b. philia.
    c. agape.
    d. care.

c 54. May said that eros
    a. is the salivation of sex.
    b. is built on the foundation of agape.
    c. is the wish to establish a lasting union.
    d. emerges during midlife.

e *55. According to May, _____ is an intimate but nonsexual friendship between two people.
    a. eros
    b. agape
    c. sublimation
    d. chumship
    e. philia

c   56. For May, _____ is an altruistic kind of love.
          a. eros
          b. philia
          c. agape
          d. sex

e   57. May believed that healthy adult relationships are based on
          a. sex.
          b. eros.
          c. philia.
          d. agape.
          e. all of the above.

a   *58. According to May, freedom comes from understanding our
          a. destiny.
          b. intentionality.
          c. ontology.
          d. essence.

c   59. For May, freedom often leads to
          a. increased neurotic anxiety.
          b. denial of neurotic anxiety.
          c. increased normal anxiety.
          d. acceptance of neurotic anxiety.

b   60. May called _____ the freedom to act on the choices one makes.
          a. essential freedom
          b. existential freedom
          c. freedom of intentionality
          d. freedom of will

b   61. For May, freedom of being is synonymous with
          a. existential freedom.
          b. essential freedom.
          c. freedom of action.
          d. freedom from destiny.
          e. intentional freedom.

c   62. May believed that _____ is our ultimate destiny.
          a. love
          b. will
          c. death
          d. despair
          e. creativity

d   63. May believed that within the boundaries of our destiny,
          a. we have no choices.
          b. all behavior is predetermined.
          c. individuals are not responsible for their actions.
          d. we have the power to choose.
          e. anything we choose can be achieved.

d   64.   May suggested that freedom and destiny are
     a.   existential illusions.
     b.   antithetical concepts.
     c.   totally incompatible with each other.
     d.   a normal paradox of life.

b   *65.   May contended that Western civilization
     a.   currently has too many nonscientific myths.
     b.   has an urgent need for myths.
     c.   is a myth.
     d.   has evolved beyond the need for a myth.

c   66.   May believed that communication
     a.   must be accurate and precise.
     b.   takes place on two levels: prototaxic and parataxic.
     c.   should transcend the immediate concrete situation and expand self-awareness.
     d.   takes place on a syntaxic level.

a   67.   May believed that the story of _____ contains the basic elements of an existential crisis: birth, exile, assertion of independence, search for identity, and death.
     a.   Oedipus
     b.   Snow White and the Seven Dwarfs
     c.   Cinderella
     d.   Three Little Pigs

d   68.   According to May, _____ are the malaise of our time.
     a.   anxiety and guilt
     b.   fear and loathing
     c.   doubt and shame
     d.   apathy and emptiness
     e.   greed and lust

d   69.   May saw psychopathology as a lack of
     a.   will.
     b.   love.
     c.   intentionality.
     d.   communicativeness.

d   70.   According to May, psychologically disturbed individuals deny their
     a.   anxiety.
     b.   guilt.
     c.   love.
     d.   destiny.
     e.   illness.

b   71.   For May, neurotic symptoms
     a.   represent a failure in adjustment.
     b.   preserve one's *Dasein*.
     c.   decrease ontological guilt.
     d.   lead to agape.

e   72. For May, the purpose of therapy is to
        a. teach the patient the existential approach to life.
        b. relieve the patient of the burden of freedom.
        c. decrease the patient's guilt and anxiety.
        d. treat specific neurotic symptoms of the patient.
        e. set patients free to make their own choices.

a   73. Existential therapists must
        a. participate fully in the human encounter with the patient.
        b. teach the patient a guiding philosophy of life.
        c. master the specialized techniques and methods of
            existential psychotherapy.
        d. maintain a dispassionate, attitude toward the patient.

d   74. Unlike Carl Rogers, Rollo May was likely to
        a. scientifically investigate psychotherapy outcomes.
        b. recognize the growth-facilitating benefits of therapy for both therapist
            and patient.
        c. emphasize the importance of an I-thou relationship.
        d. offer interpretations to a patient or client.

a   75. Research on terror management theory suggests that reminding people of their
        own death—that is, making mortality salient—tends to
        a. increase their need to preserve their worldview.
        b. increase their liking of people who have different political views.
        c. decrease their aggression against people who threaten their worldview.
        d. decrease gender-role stereotyping.

c   76. May's concept of humanity includes a belief that people are
        a. capable of large degrees of both good and evil.
        b. alienated both from themselves and from others.
        c. both a and b.
        d. neither a nor b.